THE SIGNET CLASSIC POETRY SERIES is under the general editorship of poet, lecturer, and teacher JOHN HOLLANDER.

Mr. Hollander's first volume of poetry, *A Crackling of Thorns,* won the Yale Series of Younger Poets Award for 1958. He was a recipient of a National Institute of Arts and Letters grant (1963) and has been a member of the Wesleyan University Press Poetry Board and the Bollingen Poetry Translation Prize Board. Mr. Hollander is Professor of English at Hunter College.

*Selected Poetry of Donne* is edited by Dr. Marius Bewley. An Associate Professor at Fordham University, he is the author of *The Complex Fate* and *The Eccentric Design: Form in the Classic American Novel.*

THE SIGNET CLASSIC POETRY SERIES is under
the general editorship of John Hollander and
JOHN HOLLANDER.

MILTON KLONSKY, the author of poetry ... 1925,
Institute of ... New York ... various maga-
zines, ... and the author of several ...
... has been a member of the several faculties ... the
New School ... Hunter and the Brooklyn ...
... the New School ..., Brandeis, Columbia, ...
SUNY at Stony Brook, ...

A book of poems of Dylan is edited by John Hollander
... of several volumes of poetical
criticism. He is the author of The Untuning of the Sky and
The Figure of Echo, is Professor of English at Yale.

# *John Donne*

# SELECTED POETRY

### Edited by Marius Bewley

*The Signet Classic Poetry Series*
GENERAL EDITOR: JOHN HOLLANDER

PUBLISHED BY
THE NEW AMERICAN LIBRARY, NEW YORK AND TORONTO,
THE NEW ENGLISH LIBRARY LIMITED, LONDON

Library of Congress Catalog Card Number: 66–26766

*First Printing, August, 1966*

SIGNET CLASSICS *are published* in the United States
*by The New American Library, Inc.,*
*1301 Avenue of the Americas, New York, New York 10019,*
in Canada *by The New American Library of Canada Limited,*
*295 King Street East, Toronto 2, Ontario,*
in the United Kingdom *by The New English Library Limited,*
*Barnard's Inn, Holborn, London, E.C. 1, England*

PRINTED IN THE UNITED STATES OF AMERICA

# Contents

# Introduction

## I

The reputations of few English poets have undergone such extreme fluctuations as that of John Donne. In the present century—particularly in the period between the two World Wars—Donne's poetry has been rated immeasurably higher than at any time during the preceding two hundred years. Indeed, for a brief period his new rank seemed to threaten the preeminence of Milton in the seventeenth century. Even today when the Donne fever of the twenties and thirties has considerably abated, to prefer Donne to Milton is to some extent the hallmark of the critical sensibility as contrasted with the scholarly and academic. But the point would not be pressed now with the old intensity of thirty years ago. While there may have been a shift in literary fashion, Donne's earlier popularity in this century will certainly have a lasting effect. The vast amount of Donne scholarship and criticism that was produced during the great Donne vogue—much of it sound and penetrating, some of it brilliant—has virtually guaranteed that one of the important poets of the English literary tradition will never again be submitted to this sort of thing:

> Donne is the most inharmonious of our versifiers, if he can be said to have deserved such a name by lines too rugged to seem metre. Of his earlier poems many are licentious; the later are chiefly devout. Few are good for much; the conceits have not even the merit of being intelligible; it would perhaps be difficult to select three passages that we should care to read again.

This undistinguished judgment is taken from the influential *Introduction to the Literature of Europe in the Fifteenth, Sixteenth, and Seventeenth Centuries* by Henry Hallam, the father of the gifted young man to whose memory Tennyson wrote *In Memoriam*. The third volume, in which Hallam speaks of Donne, appeared in 1839. Though more unhappily phrased, it repeats essentially the earlier judgment of Samuel Johnson in his "Life of Cowley" on the English metaphysical poets, of which "school" Donne may be counted the founding father:

> The metaphysical poets [wrote Johnson] were men of learning, and to show their learning was their whole endeavour; but unluckily resolving to show it in rhyme, instead of writing poetry they only wrote verses, and very often such verses as stood the trial of the finger better than of the ear; for the modulation was so imperfect that they were only found to be verses by counting the syllables.

Although Donne published only three or four poems in his lifetime, manuscripts of his poems passed through the hands of a select coterie of intellectuals at the universities, the Inns of Court, and some of the most brilliant and promising young men of Elizabeth's and James's reigns. Ben Jonson, the most learned poet of his time, was Donne's friend—the only professional literary man Donne accepted in that role, for like Byron, and probably for somewhat similar reasons, Donne preferred to seek his intimacies in a different sphere. But Jonson's genius, erudition, and intellectual influence in London made him an exception, as well no doubt as the admiration he felt for Donne's poetry. He told William Drummond of Hawthornden that he esteemed "John Donne the first poet in the world in some things." Donne was, in short, a leader of the *avant garde* in late Elizabethan and Jacobean London. His audience was deliberately restricted to the happy few whose education, background, and position equipped them to appreciate and esteem the most difficult poet of his day. Some snobbishness seems to have attached itself to the ability to do so. When his poems were first published as a volume in 1633, two years after his death, the printer introduced them with a note, not to the readers, but "To the Understanders." There was clearly a difference. The difficulty of Donne's poetry was the more dear to its admirers because it seemed to be so intimately associated with the genius of the English language. When Charles I, who was himself a great admirer of it, heard of a projected translation into Dutch, he expressed himself confident that no one "could acquit himself of that task with credit."

The influence of T. S. Eliot's poetry on the morale of the young literary intellectuals of the twenties and thirties must have resembled, in certain respects, the stimulus that Donne's poetry provided for an impatient generation long since surfeited with Petrarchism and the poetic conventionalities of the earlier Elizabethans. Donne's influence on the metaphysical poets who came after him, and who are commonly regarded as his heirs, seems in fact to have been in the nature of a general stimulus, an infusion of new energy, rather than the imposition of a narrowly defined manner. His principal followers are not only very different among themselves, but extremely individual in the way each has assimilated the master's influence. If we name here only the three most important and best poets in the Donne tradition, George Herbert, Richard Crashaw, and Andrew Marvell, it becomes clear that his example was no straitjacket, but that the metaphysical style permitted the widest latitude and the most individual and personal assimilation of its tenets, however those might be defined. If in the cases of a few poets the elaborately drawn conceit (which Samuel Johnson took to be the defining characteristic of metaphysical poetry) was exaggerated beyond any possible functional or organic role within the poem, and became an interest and an end in itself, that was the abuse of a style rather than an intrinsic defect.

Donne's reputation and influence continued down through the early years of the Restoration. The first edition of his poems was followed by a second in 1635, and then there were five more, this early series coming to an end with the edition of 1669. The next edition appeared only after a lapse of half a century, in 1719. Of the reasons one might adduce for this decline in Donne's reputation as a poet, perhaps the most important is related to the new taste for mathematical plainness in language fostered by the Royal Society. In his *History of the Royal Society,* 1667, Thomas Spratt commended its members for resisting extravagance of language introduced through the medium of poetry:

> They have therefore been most rigorous in putting in execution the only Remedy that can be found for this *extravagance,* and that has been a constant Resolution to reject all amplifications, digressions, and swellings of style; to return back to the primitive purity and shortness, when men deliver'd so many *things* almost in an equal number of *words.* They have extracted from all their members a close, naked, natural way of speaking, positive expressions, clear senses, a native easiness, bringing all things as near the mathematical plainness as they can, and preferring the language of artizans, countrymen, and merchants, before that of wits or scholars.

Donne's poetry could not be expected to flourish in such an intellectual climate. By 1693 he was so out of favor that Dryden, associating the term "metaphysical" with his poetry for the first time and thus inadvertently christening the school, wrote of him:

> He affects the metaphysics, not only in his satires, but in his amorous verses, where nature only should reign, and perplexes the mind of the fair sex with nice speculations of philosophy, when he should engage their hearts, and entertain them with the softnesses of love.

After that, for nearly two hundred years Donne's reputation was in shadow, to the obscurity of which Dr. Johnson contributed by rejecting the whole school of poetry in his "Life of Cowley," from which we have already quoted. Johnson's essay squarely confronts the question of what constitutes the metaphysical character of poetry in the line of Donne. He found its essence to consist in "a kind of *discordia concors;* a combination of dissimilar images, or discovery of occult resemblances in things apparently unlike. . . . The most heterogeneous ideas are yoked by violence together. . . ."

This is good enough in its way, but unfortunately it is a description which explains the failures of metaphysical poetry better than its achievements. It covers the poetry of John Cleveland or Edward Benlowes or perhaps even Cowley, but it leaves everything to be desired in the case of Donne or George Herbert or Marvell. There have been many attempts to define metaphysical poetry, or to describe its essential characteristics, in the present century. But the excellence of the best metaphysical poets cannot be captured in a formula. What is valuable in their poetry is exactly what will transcend the articles of any manifesto we may devise for them. It is probably best to begin by considering what metaphysical poetry is not.

Most of all, it is not philosophical poetry in any accurate sense of that term. It is studded with philosophical concepts and draws heavily on the technical vocabulary of metaphysics, but these are used with no design of presenting a comprehensive or coherent view of the universe and of man's place in it. This defect may appear to be supplied in some instances by the poet's reliance upon religious orthodoxy, or the appearance of it; but even here little attempt is made to expound doctrine, much less exhibit a theological system in its comprehensive consistency. The emphasis is invariably on the devotional, and the Metaphysicals end by being as remote from Dante as from Lucretius. It may be useful here to compare a passage of philosophical poetry by an Elizabethan poet with some verses from one of Donne's most famous poems which appears to be treating the same metaphysical problem, the nature of the relationship between body and soul. Despite Donne's technical proficiency in dealing with the question of how spirit, an immaterial thing, can act upon matter, his interest in the poem is centered elsewhere than in the metaphysics.

The first passage is from a long poem by Sir John Davies, *Nosce Teipsum,* published in 1599. It expounds the nature of the soul, and it undertakes this task with a

singleness of purpose and clarity of statement worthy of
the most lucid expository prose. The verses quoted here
are themselves only one step in an elaborately articulated
argument plotted with logical care and precision:

> But how shall we this union well express?
> Naught ties the Soul: her subtilty is such,
> She moves the Body, which she doth possess,
> Yet no part toucheth but by Virtue's touch.
>
> Then dwells she not therein as in a tent,
> Nor as a pilot in his ship doth sit,
> Nor as the spider in her web is pent,
> Nor as the wax retains the print in it,
>
> Nor as a vessel water doth contain,
> Nor as one liquor in another shed,
> Nor as the heat doth in the fire remain,
> Nor as a voice throughout the air is spread:
>
> But as the fair and cheerful morning light
> Doth here and there her silver beams impart,
> And in an instant doth herself unite
> To the transparent air, in all and part:
>
> Still resting whole when blows the air divide,
> Abiding pure when the air is most corrupted,
> Throughout the air, her beams dispersing wide,
> And when the air is tost, not interrupted:
>
> So doth the piercing Soul the body fill,
> Being all in all, and all in part diffused;
> Invisible, incorruptible still,
> Not forced, encountered, troubled, or confused.
>
> And as the sun above the light doth bring,
> Though we behold it in the air below,
> So from the Eternal Light the Soul doth spring,
> Though in the body she her powers do show.

It is extraordinary how Davies has managed to sustain
page after page of this kind of verse at a level which con-

sistently illuminates his argument without ever obtruding itself as nonfunctional ornament or decoration. His images are well-trained servants serving his meaning; never flatterers to seduce it from its duty, nor yet again angelic messengers bearing intimations of some higher Heaven of meaning than the one Sir John wishes to enter. There is a kind of verbal neatness and element of surprise in some of the images that may momentarily remind one of metaphysical wit, but something much simpler is involved. These images are merely illustrational, diagrammatic: they light up the meaning, but do not contribute to its substance:

> Water in conduit pipes can rise no higher
> Than the well-head from whence it first doth spring:
> Then sith to eternal God she doth aspire
> She cannot be but an eternal thing.

With this straightforward exposition of the relation between body and soul we may contrast Donne's far different treatment of the same problem. Basically, the difference arises from the fact that Donne is not interested in the problem itself, but in something else: the relation of two lovers, or the nature of love. The meaning of "The Ecstasy," one of Donne's best-known poems, has been much debated, and while it is possible to question Donne's final motive behind the poem, the argument *appears* to revolve around the proposition that love between the sexes is, or should be, a function of the total personality, not of the body alone. In scholasticism man is a composite creature made up of body and soul between which an intrinsic union exists, and man has his complete identity only in terms of this union. Soul and body together form one nature, and essentially human activity, including the emotions, proceeds from body and soul in conjunction. Sexual passion may degrade man to an animal level, but properly exercised in relation to his total personality it will be a function and fulfillment of his humanity. In contrast with some of his so-called "libertine" poems, Donne appears to be dramatizing this view in "The Ecstasy."

He presents his lovers to us in a spring landscape, implied rather than described in the opening stanza. The situation, both in setting and action, is thoroughly conventional, and had frequently been exploited by earlier Elizabethan poets. Donne's follower, Lord Herbert of Cherbury, would write a very similar poem in his "Ode upon a Question Moved, Whether Love Should Continue Forever," which should be read with "The Ecstasy" for purposes of comparison. Contemplating each other, the lovers fall into a trance, or more properly an ecstasy, for Donne is thinking of that term in mystical philosophy which describes the intimate union of the soul with God—a state in which a knowledge or sense of God, short-circuiting the senses, is intuited directly. In the poem, however, not God, but each to the other, becomes the object of this exalted way of knowing. The following excerpt makes the essential statement:

> "The Ecstasy doth unperplex"
>     (We said) "and tell us what we love;
> We see by this, it was not sex;
>     We see, we saw not what did move:
>
> "But as all several souls contain
>     Mixture of things, they know not what,
> Love, these mix'd souls doth mix again,
>     And makes both one, each this and that.
>
> "A single violet transplant,
>     The strength, the color, and the size,
> (All which before was poor, and scant,)
>     Redoubles still, and multiplies.
>
> "When love, with one another so
>     Interinanimates two souls,
> That abler soul, which thence doth flow,
>     Defects of loneliness controls.
>
> "We then, who are this new soul, know,
>     Of what we are compos'd, and made,
> For, the atomies of which we grow,
>     Are souls, whom no change can invade.

"But oh alas, so long, so far
    Our bodies why do we forbear?
They are ours, though they are not we; we are
    The intelligences, they the sphere.

\* \* \* \*

"As our blood labors to beget
    Spirits, as like souls as it can,
Because such fingers need to knit
    That subtle knot, which makes us man:

"So must pure lovers' souls descend
    To affections, and to faculties,
Which sense may reach and apprehend,
    Else a great Prince in prison lies."

In their ecstatic state it is revealed to the lovers that
their love for each other transcends sex, and is ultimately
an activity of the soul. Their souls coming together in this
love-union are strengthened, the stronger supplying the
weaknesses of the other. In this union they seem to themselves not two souls but one, and since this new soul
knows that it is compounded of two separate souls which
(according to scholasticism) are simple principles unsus-
ceptible to change or corruption, it has perfect self-knowledge of its own being. There is of course a contradiction
here since souls or spiritual principles are incapable by
their nature of being compounded into something else,
but had Donne been taking his metaphysics very seriously
this poem would hardly have been written in the first
place.

Although the lovers have discovered their love to be
spiritual in essence, it can be consummated and fulfilled
only if they resort to their bodies, for it is man's unique
distinction that in the duality of his composition heaven
and earth meet. This duality is explicitly introduced in the
lines referring to the spirits of the blood that knit the
subtle knot which makes us man. The Renaissance believed that subtle vapors or spirits were generated in the
body and communicated the functions of life to it. There
were several classes of these spirits, the most rarefied hav-

ing their seat in the brain. Although material in nature, they were the middlemen, the messengers that leaped the hiatus between material body and immaterial soul, thus maintaining the indispensable bond of communication between the two aspects of man's nature.

The widely divergent treatments that a metaphysical problem has received at the hands of Davies and Donne should make it clear that however metaphysical poetry of Donne's school may be defined, it is not philosophical poetry in any real sense, although it uses the concepts and vocabulary of philosophy. Its use of them is invariably accompanied by a complex infusion of irony, and the poet has his eye on other things than the truth of the metaphysical propositions employed. He is "metaphysical" toward nonmetaphysical ends. During the seventeenth century scholasticism continued to be taught at the two universities—greatly to the irritation and discomfort of the young Milton at Cambridge; but life had departed from it, and the intellectual temper of the time was that of Francis Bacon, not of the schoolmen. It is doubtful if metaphysical poetry like Donne's could have been written at all in a society that still commanded assent to the metaphysical system which the poet feels at liberty to treat with so free a hand. It is only because the terms and conceptions he takes over from metaphysics into his poems no longer express an activity of living thought in their proper sphere that he is able to divert them—or pervert them—to the surprising, even extraordinary, functions they perform in his poetry.

From the viewpoint of the malefactions Donne commits against the proprieties of metaphysical terminology, "The Ecstasy" is not an especially invidious example. Donne appears to be defining a kind of love to which his metaphysical images are relevant. But some years ago the French scholar Pierre Legouis persuasively argued that "The Ecstasy," like Marvell's "To His Coy Mistress," was a poem of seduction. If so, the deflection of the metaphysical vocabulary from its proper end is indeed startling. It is perhaps worth noting that the argument of "The Ecstasy," in which two lovers' souls become one over-soul as a prelude to sexual union, is paralleled (or travestied) in "The Flea," which is overtly a poem of seduction. The flea, which has sucked blood from the veins of both lovers, becomes the symbol of their transcendent union and identity:

> This flea is you and I, and this
> Our marriage bed and marriage temple is;
> Though parents grudge, and you, we're met,
> And cloister'd in these living walls of jet.

The flea, being their marriage temple by virtue of their commingled blood in its body, acquires a special sanctity so that it becomes a sacrilege to kill it. The more one reads Donne the more difficult it is to believe he was really more "metaphysically" serious in "The Ecstasy" than in the latter poem. A certain doubt about Donne's motives sooner or later crosses the minds of many of his critics. T. S. Eliot, who was one of his early modern champions, a few years after his famous essay of 1921, "The Metaphysical Poets," was led to express a revised opinion. "In making some quite commonplace investigations of the 'thought' of Donne," he wrote, "I found it quite impossible to come to the conclusion that Donne believed anything. It seemed as if, at that time, the world was filled with broken fragments of systems, and that a man like Donne merely picked up, like a magpie, various shining fragments."

Expressing a somewhat similar opinion from a different point of view, C. S. Lewis wrote in an essay on Donne's love poetry: "Paradoxical as it may seem, Donne's poetry is too simple to satisfy. Its complexity is all on the surface —an intellectual and fully conscious complexity that we soon come to the end of. Beneath this we find nothing but a limited series of 'passions'—explicit, mutually exclusive passions which can be instantly and adequately labeled as such—things which can be readily talked about, and indeed, must be talked about because, in silence they begin to lose their hard outlines and overlap, to betray themselves as partly fictitious."

But if Donne's poetry (with Eliot's help) was overacclaimed for a few years in this century, such animadversions as these are unfair despite an undoubted element of truth. Eliot is probably thinking of Donne's personal religious settlement, which was certainly a complex one, and we shall discuss it presently. But metaphysical (and theological) conviction and consistency presented peculiar difficulties in those days of religious transition that have been paralleled in ours only on the political level, and even there, only during comparatively brief intervals of intensified suspicion and witch-hunting. The sense of metaphysical insecurity that Donne's poetry finally leaves one with is, from one point of view, an added element of drama and tension. C. S. Lewis's criticism is perhaps the more damaging because it is aimed directly at the quality of the experience celebrated. The undeniable cynicism of much of Donne's love poetry is not in itself Lewis's target, but a certain emotional superficiality which appears to be related to it. Both critics seem to be condemning Donne for a lapse of sincerity, or a failure of candor. Although he does not say so, one feels that Eliot as a devout High Churchman is a little outraged by a note of latitudinarianism that no reader can fail to sense in Satyre III and some of the religious poetry, whereas Lewis is frankly desiring something that Donne was not prepared to offer: the seventeenth-century equivalent (one almost suspects) of Keats's sonnets to Fanny Brawne.

The answer to these objections must come from a fuller consideration of Donne's personality and background, but at this point we may anticipate the illumination of biography by taking a summary look at the poems. During the long period in which Donne's reputation was obscured, he found an able advocate in Coleridge. In *Biographia Literaria* Coleridge makes a highly perceptive remark about Donne. True, Coleridge is also talking about Dryden, but the application to Donne is particularly significant. "The vividness of the descriptions or declamations in Donne . . . " he writes, "is as much and as often derived from the force and fervor of the describer, as from the reflections, forms or incidents which constitute his subject and materials. The wheels take fire from the mere rapidity of their motion."

Coleridge recognized what Donne's contemporary admirers recognized: that his achievement as a poet was not in his treatment of a particular subject matter, but in the creation of a style, the revitalization of a language that was on the point of growing tired. His poetry did not illuminate ideas as such, but brought a new freshness to the language, and renewed its energy. The elegies by Donne's admirers that were included in the posthumously published edition of his poems were mostly agreed on this. The best of the elegies was by Thomas Carew, gentleman of the Privy-Chamber, royal sewer or taster to the King, and an excellent poet. Although he does not of course use the word *originality* in describing Donne's poetry, that is what his critical assessment of it amounts to. Donne, he says, has purged English poetry of "pedantic weeds"; he has replaced "servile imitation" with "fresh invention"; he has opened up new resources for the creative imagination ("pregnant phansie"), and he has done this by introducing a new austerity into his verse line. What other critics would refer to as his metrical roughness or hardness, Carew more aptly calls "masculine expression." He means by this phrase a strenuous encounter between language and meaning in which the two components, like Donne's recurrent lovers, are strengthened and renewed by merging in a common intensified identity. As Carew puts it:

> . . . to the awe of thy imperious wit
> Our stubborn language bends, made only fit
> With her tough-thick-ribb'd hoops to gird about
> Thy giant phansie, which had prov'd too stout
> For their soft melting phrases.

The antecedent of "which" in the fourth line is not Donne's "giant phansie" but "our stubborn language," which requires a masculine and imperious imagination like Donne's to dominate it and extract the meaning it is so reluctant to yield. The "soft melting phrases" of the last line belong not only to poets of antiquity, but especially to the earlier Elizabethans with their smoothly flowing, richly ornamented verses. The central ground for praise in the elegy seems to be that in Donne's writing there is a harmony and interdependence of parts, of words, emotions, and thoughts. Later in the elegy, although he is referring to the sermons rather than the poetry, he speaks of "thy brave soul, that shot such heat and light,/ As burnt our earth, and made our darkness bright." Heat stands for Donne's emotion, light for his thought. Yet these are indivisible aspects of *one* fire—in this case, Donne's sensibility expressing itself through language. Carew would appear to have anticipated in certain respects Eliot's attribution to Donne in his 1921 essay of a unified sensibility. That famous but beleaguered phrase, however its application and interpretation may have been distorted by later scholars and critics, would not have been totally unintelligible to Donne's contemporaries and immediate followers.

But as we have seen, Eliot, who had announced that Donne's thought and feeling were harmoniously one in a unified or associated sensibility, later came to question the quality and consistency of Donne's thought. Now the quality of a poet's *thinking* is certain to affect the quality of his poetry, but whether one approves or disapproves of *what* is thought—the poet's premises, his conclusions, his convictions and dogmas—is irrelevant from a literary-critical point of view. It is difficult not to suspect that it was Donne's thought rather than his thinking that troubled Eliot after his first enthusiasm had waned. It is not at all to the discredit of Donne's intelligence and erudition to say that for a man living in the twentieth century his thought may well seem negligible. The poetry neither presents original ideas (as paraphrasable entities) nor develops old ones. Nevertheless, it is among the most intelligent, nervously alert poetry in English. What it does do supremely well is to develop a complexly poised attitude toward experience. Donne was not only a man of unusual intelligence and learning, but, despite the fact that his motives have often been suspected, he was morally and spiritually sensitive beyond most of his contemporaries.

Being at the same time ambitious and worldly, his greatest problem was to reconcile these two contradictory aspects of his character. Deeper than the intellectual and moral inconsistency sensed by Eliot, or the emotional superficiality that repelled Lewis, his poetry possesses a strong pragmatic purpose, which is to bring himself and his talents into line with the demands made by his political society on an Elizabethan who seeks to make his way in the world, without at the same time betraying his conscience and integrity more than absolutely necessary. The world being what it was in those days, this was a tall order. The astonishing thing is not that Donne sometimes appears to have failed, but that on the whole he succeeded so well.

## II

Donne was ordained a priest of the Church of England on January 23, 1615. He was already forty-three—late in the day to begin such a career. It is certain that Donne, whose prospects of secular advancement had once appeared so bright, would have welcomed an alternative course, but he was virtually pushed to the altar. In view of the distinction and dedicated devotion of Donne's subsequent career, the Anglican faithful might well see a directing Providence in the pattern of events that brought about his ordination, but from a more secular point of view it was that royal source of bounty, King James I, who did the pushing.

King James was familiar with Donne's intellectual gifts through a polemical book Donne had written, and which appeared in 1610, defending the Oath of Allegiance which attested the King's supremacy as temporal head of the Anglican Church. The general argument of the book is revealed in its full title: *Pseudo-Martyr, wherein out of certain Propositions and Gradations, This Conclusion is evicted. That Those which are of the Romane Religion in this Kingdome, may and ought to take the Oath of Allegeance.* After that, James would hear of no advancement for

Donne outside the Church. Although it was certainly to the King's advantage to have such a man working for him *inside* the Anglican fabric, it is no small tribute to his perspicacity and intelligence that he saw Donne so clearly in the role of churchman almost from the first. When pressured by his favorite, Robert Ker, Earl of Somerset, to confer political advancement on Donne, according to Donne's friend and first biographer, Izaak Walton: ". . . the King gave a positive denial to all requests and, having a discerning spirit, replied, 'I know Mr. Donne is a learned man, has the abilities of a learned divine, and will prove a powerful preacher. And my desire is to prefer him in that way, and in that way I will deny you nothing for him.' " With these words in his ears, Donne submitted to the inevitable, but he did so with good grace. After a young manhood that may have been blemished, but was probably only fashionably unedifying, Donne became the most popular preacher, and one of the greatest, of his Church in a century renowned for its pulpit eloquence. So Donne, who had been described by an early friend as "a great visitor of ladies, a great frequenter of plays," in the words of Walton, "became *crucified to the world,* and all those vanities, those imaginary pleasures that are daily enacted on that restless stage; and they were as perfectly crucified to him."

Undoubtedly Walton exaggerates: it is difficult for us to think of Donne as a saint, even though many of his contemporaries did so. However that may be, enough advancement was accorded Donne in the Church to satisfy at least in part the desire for influence, place, and fortune he had always felt while still in the world. He was made a chaplain to the King, and he held the important appointment of Reader in Divinity to the Benchers of Lincoln's Inn, where he had studied much earlier. In 1621 he was elected Dean of St. Paul's, the cathedral church of the Bishop of London, and had he lived a little longer he would have died a bishop himself, for Charles I admired Dr. Donne no less than his father had.

By the time Donne ascended the altar steps the poems that make up *Songs and Sonnets* had almost certainly all been written. On the eve of his ordination Donne, who had been content for his poems to be circulated in manuscript, suddenly had a desire to publish them. But his friends dissuaded him. The Anglican Church in those days could point to many men of wit and secular sophistication in its priesthood who wrote verses and even published them. But many of the love poems of Donne's youth were hardly the sort to appear with propriety under the name of a clergyman of forty-three, especially one who was not averse to getting ahead in the Church. While the dates of the Divine Poems are very uncertain, some of them at least were still to be written, but they do not raise the same kind of problems or excite speculation in the way the earlier poems do. The Donne whose poetry and enigmatic personality have attracted the twentieth century so strongly is the cynical young poet of the last decade of Elizabeth's reign, and the financially distressed young husband and father of the early years of James's. It is here rather than in the priestly years that one must look for suggestions and clews that may help us toward a better understanding of Donne. Eliot, the erstwhile champion turned Devil's advocate, in the act of sacrificing Donne to Lancelot Andrewes, wrote: "About Donne there hangs the shadow of the impure motive." But it is not difficult to be severe about impure motives when an invitation to martyrdom is not lying on the hall table, and when one does not have a large and growing family of children who are vulgarly susceptible to hunger and cold. Critics in general would probably agree that Donne's motives (like most men's) were not perfectly undevious. Therefore, let us consider here as briefly as possible what those motives may have been, and how his poetry was affected by them.

Donne was born and educated a Catholic at a time when adherence to the ancient faith was attended by the heaviest liabilities and penalties. If we are to understand the complexity of his personality, it would be difficult to exaggerate the importance of this fact. His great-grandmother had been the sister of St. Thomas More, Chancellor of England, who had been beheaded in 1535 for refusing the Oath of Allegiance—that same oath which

Donne was to defend in *Pseudo-Martyr*. But St. Thomas More had been only the first of a long line of heroic Catholics in Donne's family who were willing to suffer exile and death for their faith. Donne's own brother Henry, his younger by a year, died in prison to which he had been sent for concealing a Roman priest. Donne's father, a wealthy ironmonger of London, was apparently a more aggressive businessman than Catholic, but his mother was devout, and her brothers Elias and Jasper Heywood were among the first English members of the Society of Jesus. Jasper indeed was Superior of the Jesuit Mission to England. Donne knew his learned (and by all reports) arrogant uncle Jasper in his childhood, and one suspects from the violent animus of Donne's later references to the Jesuits that Jasper may have impressed his nephew not only powerfully but unfavorably. His prose satire, *Ignatius His Conclave,* published in 1611, in which the founder of the Society of Jesus outplays Machiavelli on his own ground and even overawes Lucifer, was, to say the least, an unusual performance to come from the nephew of the Jesuit Prefect.

Even Philip II was shocked by the incredible ineptitude of the Papal Bull, *Regnans in Excelsis,* which in 1570 declared Elizabeth deposed and released her subjects from their allegiance. From that moment the Queen's government had little alternative but to regard Catholics as traitors, whether it wanted to or not. It was St. Pope Pius V far more than the excellent Queen who was responsible for the English martyrs. Magnificent they may have been, but Donne was determined not to join them. A far more serious question for the brilliant, ambitious young worldling was the question of a career. In Elizabethan England virtually all public careers were closed to Catholics. They were not even welcomed at the two universities. As degrees were conferred by Oxford and Cambridge only after the candidate had taken the Oath of Allegiance, Catholics were excluded from academic honors though they might study at one of the colleges. In 1584 at the age of twelve Donne was matriculated at Oxford where he remained for three years, after which, according to Walton, he studied at Cambridge for a similar period, but not taking the required loyalty oath, he left both universities without a degree. Later, after his conversion to Anglicanism, he received an honorary Master of Arts degree from Oxford for having written *Pseudo-Martyr,* and after his ordination he received a Doctor of Divinity degree from Cambridge by King James's royal mandate.

From the universities Donne proceeded to study law in London, first at Thavies Inn and then at Lincoln's Inn, where many years later he was to become Reader in Divinity. At some uncertain period during this decade—probably between 1594 and 1596—he traveled abroad in Spain and Italy, where he mastered the languages. In 1596 he joined the famous expedition against Cadiz under the joint command of the Earl of Essex and the now elderly Lord Admiral Howard, who had defeated the Armada eight years earlier. Donne described the fierce sea fight that preceded the raid on Cadiz in his most graphic epigram:

> Out of a fired ship which, by no way
> But drowning, could be rescued from the flame,
> Some men leap'd forth, and ever as they came
> Near the foe's ships, did by their shot decay;
> So all were lost, which in the ship were found,
>     They in the sea being burnt, they in the burnt
>         ship drown'd.

The following year Donne joined the Islands Voyage, also under the command of Essex, which planned to intercept the Spanish treasure ships off the Azores. Out of his experience on this expedition he wrote "The Storm" and "The Calm," the second poem being a favorite with Ben Jonson.

It is to the 1590's that most, if not all, the cynical and libertine love poems belong. It is also during this period that Donne was converted to Anglicanism. As we have already seen, Donne's motives have been questioned; but he was no hypocrite who found it easy or even possible to take the most profitable and expedient line devoid of personal conviction. He was not the kind of man who could have smothered conscience, but it was pragmatically essential for him to become intellectually persuaded against the Roman claims, and he steered a course that, for less than spiritual reasons, was directly headed toward a break with Rome. Izaak Walton assigns the conversion to Anglicanism to the period during which Donne was at Lincoln's Inn:

> About the nineteenth year of his age, he, being then unresolv'd what Religion to adhere to, and, considering how much it concern'd his soul to choose the most Orthodox, did therefore (though his youth and health promised him a long life) to rectifie all scruples that might concern that, presently lay aside all study of the Law: and, of all other Sciences that might give him a denomination; and begun seriously to survey, and consider the Body of Divinity, as it was then controverted betwixt the *Reformed* and the *Roman Church.*

Satyre III, one of Donne's finest poems, perhaps belongs to these years, although it may be as late as 1597. The poem is an examination not so much of the respective claims of the Roman, Anglican, and Genevan churches, as a statement of the necessity for conducting such an examination. Characteristically, Donne arrives at no conclusion except that man must search unceasingly for the truth. But in the course of the poem he gives us some unforgettable pictures of types of Elizabethan Christians. The energetic quality of Donne's thinking is strikingly reflected in the strenuous rhythm of these often-quoted lines which dramatize the labor and effort exerted by the poet in his search. It is easy enough to falsify the motives of conversion to oneself and others, but it is impossible to fake conviction in poetry like this:

> On a huge hill,
> Cragged, and steep, Truth stands, and he that will
> Reach her, about must, and about must go;
> And what the hill's suddenness resists, win so;
> Yet strive so, that before age, death's twilight,
> Thy soul rest, for none can work in that night.

Whatever the date of Satyre III we know that Donne had been ordained several years when he wrote Holy Sonnet XVIII. The theological argument of this sonnet is much the same as that of the earlier satire:

> Show me dear Christ, Thy spouse, so bright and clear.
> What! is it She, which on the other shore
> Goes richly painted? or which robb'd and tore
> Laments and mourns in Germany and here?
> Sleeps she a thousand, then peeps up one year?
> Is she self-truth and errs? now new, now outwore?
> Doth she, and did she, and shall she evermore
> On one, on seven, or on no hill appear?
> Dwells she with us, or like adventuring knights
> First travel we to seek and then make love?
> Betray kind husband Thy spouse to our sights,
> And let mine amorous soul court Thy mild dove,
> Who is most true, and pleasing to Thee, then
> When she is embrac'd and open to most men.

The scarcely submerged comparison of the Church, the Bride of Christ, with a prostitute is surely one of the most startling images in English poetry, and the devout reverence with which Donne brings it off may be taken as a measure of his genius. The profound sincerity of such poetry is unquestioned, but it reflects the sincerity of Donne's love of God, not necessarily of his theology.

It seems to me that Grierson was undoubtedly correct in his reading of this sonnet when he wrote that "it revealed Donne, already three years in orders, as still conscious of all the difficulties involved in a choice between the three divisions of Christianity." Another interpretation of the sonnet is possible, and it has been most recently defended by Helen Gardner in her edition of *The Divine Poems* (Appendix C). She believes that the contrast is "between the Church promised in Scripture and the Church as it appears in the world and throughout history." The two interpretations are not perhaps as mutually exclusive as Miss Gardner's argument implies. To a priest in Donne's uneasy position an ecumenical escape hatch might prove a godsend, and, in any case, there was a strong element of ecumenism latent in seventeenth-century Anglican theology, which saw itself as the "Via Media" between churches which, if fallen into degenerate practices, were still branches (albeit somewhat withered) of the Universal Church. But the power and distinction of this sonnet (and it is very powerful and distinguished indeed) is centered in its note of anguished uncertainty and doubt, which has become even intensified since Satyre III. It is difficult to disagree with the temperate conclusion Grierson draws about Donne on the basis of this poem: "That Donne entirely convinced himself of the validity of the Anglican position may perhaps be doubted."

Donne appears not so much to have been converted *to* the Church of England as he was converted *away from* the Church of Rome. The result is that his later theological convictions are broadly tolerant. In leaving Rome he appears not so much to have acquired new beliefs as to have discarded old ones. But in 1601 Donne wrote an extremely curious poem that makes one wonder if, even in his twenty-ninth year, his sympathies were not still deeply, if secretly, with the ancient Church. This poem, like *The Second Anniversary* of 1612, is titled *The Progress of the Soul*. It is a mere fragment, for although we possess fifty-two ten-line stanzas, the argument has barely got under way when Donne breaks off. That argument is an extraordinary one based on the Pythagorean doctrine of metempsychosis, or reincarnation. It sets out to show us the progress of the soul of heresy from its vegetable form in the apple which Eve ate in Eden, through successive reincarnations in all the great heretics of history—Mahomet, Luther, Calvin—to its final abode in the reigning Queen of England, the supreme authority in the Anglican Church.

By 1601 Donne was almost certainly a professed Anglican. Walton, as we have seen, implies that his conversion was much earlier. He had been secretary to Sir Thomas Egerton since 1598, and Egerton was Elizabeth's Attorney-General, Lord Keeper of the Great Seal, and a member of the Privy Council. His official position opposed him to Catholics, and probably his temperament as well. He had prosecuted the Jesuit martyr Edmund

Campion, who had been hanged, drawn, and quartered in 1581, and his zeal in the interests of the State Church continued well into the next reign. He would certainly not have taken Donne into his household had his religious position been suspect. Sir Herbert Grierson and others have suggested that the hostility to Elizabeth reflected in this poem is to be associated with the Queen's unpopularity that followed upon the execution of the Earl of Essex in 1601. Donne certainly admired Essex, had served under him in the Cadiz and Azores expeditions, and had seen him at closer quarters when Elizabeth committed him as a state prisoner into Egerton's keeping in 1599 after he had fled from Ireland without her permission. But however Donne may have sympathized with Essex, the hostility to Elizabeth in this poem is specifically theological in character. She is to be presented as the great heresiarch of history, in direct line of descent through Calvin and Luther back to the Edenic apple that brought evil into the world.

*The Progress of the Soul* has never been popular or widely admired. It is in some respects an ugly poem—repellent is the term the critics usually favor in speaking of it. But it is also a brilliant poem in parts, and it gives us a vivid insight into Donne's deeply disturbed state of mind at the time. It makes one thing quite clear: his transition to Anglicanism was not an easy one. The poem breaks off as the soul, having passed through various lower forms of life, enters its first human being, Themech, sister and wife to Cain. The last three lines indicate in what a spirit of skepticism Donne must have written the poem:

> There's nothing simply good, nor ill alone,
> Of every quality comparison
> The only measure is, and judge, opinion.

The year in which Donne wrote *The Progress of the Soul* was also the year of his marriage. Anne More was Lady Egerton's niece, and during most of the period Donne was employed as the Lord Keeper's secretary, Anne was living at Sir Thomas's house in London, where she must have been frequently in Donne's company. The two fell in love, Anne being then only sixteen, Donne twenty-eight. They were secretly married in London in December, 1601. Anne's father, Sir George More, did not see Donne as a suitable son-in-law, and on being informed of the match he was sufficiently outraged to persuade Sir Thomas Egerton (who was reluctant) to dismiss his secretary. For a brief period Donne was even committed to the Fleet prison while Sir George vainly endeavored to secure an annulment. Donne's once-brilliant prospects vanished overnight. The patrimony he had inherited some years before had long since been dissipated on his travels abroad; he was in debt, had lost his position with Sir Thomas for good, and although his father-in-law came to accept the marriage, he was not yet willing to give the couple financial assistance. The next years were impoverished and difficult, and matters were not helped by the rapid succession of children who were born to them. Among the expedients to which Donne resorted was to become what would now be called a research assistant to Dr. Thomas Morton, who later became Bishop of Durham. Morton was considered a highly successful controversialist with the Catholics, and Donne was employed in collecting material from the writings of the Church Fathers and from canon law for his use. Inexorably, circumstances drove Donne, as we have seen, in the direction of the Anglican ministry; but he resisted as long as he could, and continued to seek advancement through the customary channel of patronage.

It was in pursuit of patronage that Donne wrote and published two strange poems, *The First Anniversary*, 1611, and *The Second Anniversary*, 1612. These two poems were written to commemorate the death of Elizabeth Drury, the young daughter of Sir Robert Drury, who had died in 1610 just short of her fifteenth birthday. Sir Robert was a courtier of large fortune and ambition. It is not clear if Donne had known him before he sent him the first commemoration of his daughter's death, but it is certain he had never seen the girl. At any rate, Donne's extravagant praises of the daughter won the father's heart. Donne and his wife were given quarters in the great mansion in Drury Lane, and late in 1611 Donne accompanied

Sir Robert and Lady Drury to the continent on a trip
extending over ten months.

The Elizabethans and the seventeenth century were able
to take hyperbolic praise and fulsome flattery in stride, but
even Donne's contemporaries were shocked by the Anniversaries. Ben Jonson declared, "That Donne's Anni-
versarie was profane and full of blasphemies; that he told
Mr. Donne, if it had been written of the Virgin Marie it
had been something; to which he answered that he described the Idea of a Woman, and not as she was." Apparently Donne came to regret having published the two
poems, but modern criticism has responded to them more
warmly. Their apparent extravagance seems to conceal a
deeper and more elaborate meaning behind the ostensible
subject. They irresistibly invite exegesis and interpretation.

Repeatedly critics have asked what the girl-symbol
stands for in the Anniversaries, and they have come up
with a variety of answers. It is difficult to derive much illumination from Donne's reported remark that "he described the Idea of a Woman, and not as she was"; but as
one becomes familiar with the poems, Elizabeth Drury
seems to grow into a macrocosmic symbol capable of existing on several levels simultaneously. On the simplest
level she is Sir Robert's dead daughter. There are other
passages in which the dead girl clearly seems to signify
the Roman Church; others again in which the Anglican
Church seems to be meant. On the political level, Elizabeth Drury merges with Queen Elizabeth. There are perhaps other faces as well to this multiple symbol, but the
figure of the apotheosized girl controls the different levels
of meaning, and allows Donne to weave one of the most
subtle webs of theological and political innuendo in seventeenth-century poetry.

It is impossible in a brief introduction of this nature
to analyze or even adequately describe the tangled and
complex argument which seems to be hidden away in the
Anniversaries, but in *The Second Anniversary* Donne appears to commit himself in favor of the State Church
headed by Elizabeth. His commitment still appears, however, to carry certain ironical overtones. These lines if di-

rected to the dead child (as they pretend to be) are
merely embarrassing, but applied to the dead Queen, they
are not only filled with important meaning, but are
deliciously double-edged.

> She, who being to herself a State, enjoy'd
> All royalties which any State employ'd;
> For she made wars, and triumph'd; reason still
> Did not o'erthrow, but rectify her will:
> And she made peace, for no peace is like this,
> That beauty, and chastity together kiss:
> She did high justice, for she crucified
> Every first motion of rebellious pride:
> And she gave pardons, and was liberal,
> For, only her self except, she pardon'd all:
> She coin'd, in this, that her impressions gave
> To all our actions all the worth they have:
> She gave protections; the thoughts of her breast
> Satan's rude officers could ne'er arrest.
> As these prerogatives being met in one,
> Made her a sovereign State; religion
> Made her a Church; and these two made her all.

If Donne's words mean anything, there can be no doubt
that he is talking about the old Queen here, and his compliments are, to say the least, ambiguous. The reference to
Elizabeth's crucifying "Every first motion of rebellious
pride" may refer to the severity with which Catholic recu-
sants were treated in the reign as much, or more, than to
royal self-discipline. "High" could mean overbearing in
Donne's day as in ours, and we can't be sure who the
object of her "high justice" is—herself or others; and one
remembers that impolite reference Donne had made in
*The Progress of the Soul:* that Christ's cross was made
from the Forbidden Tree on which the fatal apple grew
whose soul finally ended up in Queen Elizabeth. The profit
motive looms significantly large in the latter half of the
quotation. However we may interpret the details, it is difficult to evade the recognition that Elizabeth Drury symbolizes something much more pointed than (in the words
of one critic) "a symbol of pure spirit, of immortal beauty,

harmony, and innocence." This passage in which the dead girl is metamorphosed into the dead Queen should be compared with the comparable but more complex passage in *The First Anniversary,* lines 25–54.

The earlier seventeenth century was notoriously afflicted with a peculiar melancholy or despondency of which Hamlet may be taken as an exemplar. The late Theodore Spencer indeed once found strong resemblances between Donne and the Prince. The causes of this prevalent frame of mind, which asserts itself so widely in late Elizabethan and Jacobean literature, had been much discussed. It was certainly related to a widely shared conviction that the world had decayed from an Edenic beginning, through several cycles of decline and recovery, to a thoroughly degenerate present in which both nature and man shared. The astronomical discoveries of the sixteenth century which dislodged the earth from the center of the universe had greatly contributed to the general sense of unfocusing and break-up, at least among the intellectuals. The subject of universal dissolution is one of the themes of *The First Anniversary,* and the death of the girl Elizabeth is used to symbolize it. On this level, however, the girl Elizabeth is not the Queen, but she appears to represent the Catholic Church as in the following passage, where her identification with the Blessed Virgin is too absolutely made to be accidental:

> She, of whom the Ancients seem'd to prophesy,
> When they call'd virtues by the name of *she;*
> She in whom virtue was so much refin'd,
> That for alloy unto so pure a mind
> She took the weaker sex; she that could drive
> The poisonous tincture, and the stain of Eve,
> Out of her thoughts, and deeds; and purify
> All, by a true religious alchemy;
> She, she is dead; she's dead: when thou know'st this,
> Thou know'st how poor a trifling thing man is.

It seems highly probable that the "true religious alchemy" that purifies all of Original Sin is a concealed reference to the Catholic sacramental system; and although the Angli-

can Church had copied that system to some extent, Donne
is referring to the original and not the copy, for he insists
upon the fact that she is dead. The following passage from
*The First Anniversary* supports this interpretation:

> For there's a kind of world remaining still,
> Though she which did inanimate and fill
> The world, be gone, yet in this last long night,
> Her ghost doth walk; that is, a glimmering light,
> A faint weak love of virtue, and of good,
> Reflects from her, on them which understood
> Her worth; and though she have shut in all day,
> The twilight of her memory doth stay;
> Which, from the carcass of the old world, free,
> Creates a new world, and new creatures be
> Produc'd: the matter and the stuff of this,
> Her virtue, and the form our practice is.

In this passage there appears to be (but again in a
secret and concealed way) a comparison between the
Catholic and the Anglican churches, almost in the manner
of Dryden's *The Hind and the Panther*. Donne is here in
process of making a qualified acceptance of the new
Church, but his prejudice still seems markedly in favor of
Rome. The meaning of the above lines, once the theological significance of the girl-symbol is accepted, is that the
True Church is the life and the soul of the world, but the
True Church has entered its "last long night." In view of
the persecution of the Catholic Church in England and the
nature of the Elizabethan compromise, such a meaning is
clear enough. Elizabeth Drury alive, Donne is saying, sym-
bolized the Catholic Church; but she is dead and he turns
to contemplate the consequences of her death for the
world. All is not entirely hopeless, for her ghost still walks
abroad, and in her ghost—or the image of Elizabeth Drury
dead—Donne may well be giving us his image of Anglicanism. There is, he seems to be saying, a real relation
between the Roman and the Anglican churches, just as
there is a real relation between Elizabeth Drury and her
ghost. The theological content and liturgy of Anglicanism,
his argument goes, are actually newly created from the

doctrine and the liturgy of Rome. But this new world created by the ghost is not quite the brave new world that Shakespeare saw: there is something spurious about the life it shows, and Donne's picture of the life that remains is not a very reassuring one although he tries to make the best of it. The figure of Elizabeth Drury, then, is a symbol of both the Roman and the Anglican churches, and the tension between Elizabeth Drury alive and Elizabeth Drury dead is a way of differentiating between the two. It is the ambivalence in Donne's attitude to the two churches that simultaneously gives depth to his irony and serves to conceal it from a common recognition that would have proved dangerous.[1]

Such an interpretation as the one offered here of the Anniversaries must necessarily remain conjectural, although passage by passage the poems support it with unusual consistency. But if this reading is, in the main, correct, then Donne certainly intended it should be concealed, or at least camouflaged. It would have been madness for a man of that day to have said such things openly unless he courted martyrdom, and Donne did not. How little he did so is perhaps indicated by the almost sinister cleverness with which he hid his real meaning. The ambiguously multiple images and landscapes of some of Dali's paintings seem utterly primitive and simple-minded by comparison. Nor does it seem particularly strange, when one has studied Donne's personality in his life and works, that he might have felt an overpowering compulsion to make such a concealed confession of his views about the world he lived in, and his relations with it. There are elements of the tortured, the theatrical, and the perversely sincere in such a performance that correspond closely to the conception of Donne's character that has been presented here.

[1] The substance of these remarks on the Anniversaries has been abridged from an article of mine, "Religious Cynicism in Donne's Poetry," *Kenyon Review*, Autumn, 1952. The identification with Queen Elizabeth has also been very persuasively argued by Marjorie Hope Nicolson in *The Breaking of the Circle*, 1950. A valuable study which sees the Anniversaries as carefully plotted religious meditations in the Ignatian tradition is "John Donne in Meditation: The Anniversaries," by Louis L. Martz, from *The Poetry of Meditation: A Study in English Religious Literature of the Seventeenth Century*, 1954.

And Donne would have been capable of taking ironical pleasure in the fact that these poems which carry such concealed criticisms and judgments on his world were, on the surface and to all intents and purposes, the time-serving flattery of a courtier seeking advancement and place.

Donne died in 1631 in the odor of sanctity and theater, which is as it should have been. Walton gives us this vividly memorable picture of Donne's last performance:

A Monument being resolved upon, Dr. Donne sent for a Carver to make for him in wood the figure of an Urn, giving him directions for the compass and height of it; and to bring with it a board of the just height of his body. These being got: then without delay a choice Painter was got to be in a readiness to draw his Picture, which was taken as followeth:—Several Charcole-fires being first made in his large Study, he brought with him into that place his winding-sheet in his hand, and, having put off all his cloathes, had this sheet put on him, and so tyed with knots at his head and feet, and his hands so placed, as dead bodies are usually fitted to be shrowded and put into their Coffin, or grave. Upon this Urn he thus stood with his eyes shut, and with so much of the sheet turned aside as might shew his lean, pale, death-like face, which was purposely turned towards the East, from whence he expected the second coming of his and our Saviour Jesus. In this posture he was drawn at his just height; and when the Picture was fully finished, he caused it to be set by his bed-side, where it continued, and became his hourly object till his death.

Donne had been an enthusiastic playgoer in his youth in the most brilliant days of the English drama. One of the greatest figures of the theater was his lifelong friend, and although the pulpit was Donne's stage, perhaps the single most characteristic quality of his poetry is its dramatic impact. An English critic has spoken of the Shakespearian affinities of his verse. Over and over again there is an immediate dramatic projection in his poems, coming as soon as the poet speaks. The language seems to grow directly from the dramatic situation or tension that underprops each poem. It is perhaps this dramatization of feelings very like our own that helps us to experience his poetry with an intimacy offered us by none of his contemporaries among the nondramatic poets. Donne has been called both a medieval and a modern, but he deserves the second epithet far more richly than the first, which he may not deserve at all. The ability to use a scholastic terminology, even more seriously than Donne, is by no means unknown in the twentieth century, and it does not necessarily imply that the user belongs in the Middle Ages. The conflicts in Donne's personality, reflected so perfectly in his art, his perplexities of faith and doubt, the tortured ambiguity one senses so strongly in his motives, his cynicism and his capacity for affection, the ironical quality of his self-knowledge and his psychological curiosity—all these have a familiar look in our day. And yet in a curious way we have remained a little uncertain about the exact place Donne ought to occupy in the roster of great English poets. Commenting on this fact on the tercentenary of Donne's death, Allen Tate pointed to a quality in him that most readers must continue to feel: "The uncertainty of these critics about Donne's place," he said, "is remarkable in the case of a poet three hundred years dead. The uncertainty comes of Donne's being still alive."

MARIUS BEWLEY
*Fordham University*

# A General Note on the Text

The overall textual policy for the Signet Classic Poetry series attempts to strike a balance between the convenience and dependability of total modernization, on the one hand, and the authenticity of an established text on the other. Starting with the Restoration and Augustan poets, the General Editor has set up the following guidelines for the individual editors:

Modern American spelling will be used, although punctuation may be adjusted by the editor of each volume when he finds it advisable. In any case, syllabic final "ed" will be rendered with grave accent to distinguish it from the silent one, which is written out without apostrophe (e.g., "to gild refinèd gold," but "asked" rather than "ask'd"). Archaic words and forms are to be kept, naturally, whenever the meter or the sense may require it.

In the case of poets from earlier periods, the text is more clearly a matter of the individual editor's choice, and the type and degree of modernization has been left to his decision. But in any event, archaic typographical conventions ("i," "j," "u," "v," etc.) have all been normalized in the modern way.

JOHN HOLLANDER

# A Note on This Edition

This selection from Donne's poems in modernized spelling is based substantially on the text established by Sir Herbert Grierson, although occasional variants have been adopted from more recent editors. On questions of capitalization and punctuation Donne's text involves problems of peculiar difficulty for anyone attempting to present it in contemporary English. No attempt has been made to reach uniform consistency in these matters. The object has been rather to leave Donne's sensibility unviolated so far as possible by modern English usage, while at the same time minimizing the aura of unfamiliarity that may hover over early seventeenth-century poetry for the undergraduate.

MARIUS BEWLEY

# Chronology

1572    John Donne born in London. Some uncertainty exists concerning the exact year, but 1572 is now generally accepted in preference to 1571 or 1573.

1574    John Donne's father made Warden of the Ironmongers' Company.

1576    John Donne the elder dies, leaving a fortune of some £4,000 to his widow and children. Within six months Elizabeth Donne marries her second husband, Dr. John Syminges, president of the Royal College of Physicians.

1581    Donne's uncle, Jasper Heywood, returns to England as superior of the Jesuit Mission.

1584    Donne and his younger brother Henry are matriculated at Hart Hall, Oxford.

1587    Taking no degree at Oxford, Donne apparently transfers to Cambridge, where he remains three years.

1588    Donne's stepfather, Dr. Syminges, dies.

1591    Donne's mother marries her third husband, Richard Rainsford. Donne is admitted as a law student to Thavies Inn, London.

1592    Transfers to Lincoln's Inn on May 6. According to Izaak Walton's somewhat untrustworthy chronology, it would have been at this time that Donne began an investigation of the theological claims of the Roman and Anglican churches, reading and annotating for that purpose Cardinal Bellarmine's _Disputations concerning the Controversies of the Faith against the Heretics of this Present Time._

1594–96    It is known that Donne spent two or more years abroad in Italy and Spain, where he mastered the languages. The date of these travels is disputed, but the best evidence seems to indicate 1594–96. When Donne came of age, probably in 1593, he received his patrimony of some £700, which Walton says was largely expended in these travels.

1596    Takes service under Essex in the Cadiz expedition.

1597    Joins Essex in the Islands Voyage to the Azores. Writes "The Storm" and "The Calm" as a result of his experiences on this expedition.

1598    Becomes secretary to Sir Thomas Egerton, the Lord Keeper of the Great Seal.

The group of poems comprising _Songs and Sonnets_ are sometimes assigned to the years 1590–1601, but many of the best ones were written later, some much later. "The Sun Rising" and "The Canonization" were probably written after the accession of James in 1603. As Twickenham Park did not become Lady Bedford's home until 1608, "Twickenham Garden" was probably written no earlier than that date. "A Valediction: Forbidding Mourning" was written, according to Walton, in 1611. If "A nocturnal upon St. Lucy's Day" commemorates the death of his wife, as some critics believe, it was written as late as 1617.

Satyres I, II, III, and IV probably belong to the years 1593–97. Satyre V was written in 1598 or 1599 while Donne was secretary to Sir Thomas Egerton.

The Verse Letters begin with "The Storm" and "The Calm" in 1597 and continue down to 1614.

1601    Donne writes *The Progress of the Soul*.

It is probable that Donne sat in Queen Elizabeth's last Parliament, October 27 to December 19. If so, he owed his seat to the influence of Sir Thomas Egerton.

In December Donne secretly marries Anne More, the niece of Sir Thomas Egerton's second wife.

1602    Donne is discharged from the service of Sir Thomas Egerton at the insistence of Sir George More, his father-in-law. Is briefly imprisoned on the charge of marrying a girl without her father's consent.

1602–04  Donne and his wife accept the hospitality of Anne's relative, Sir Francis Wooley, at Pyrford Park in Surrey.

1603    Constance, Donne's eldest daughter, is born. Queen Elizabeth dies. King James visits Pyrford where he probably meets Donne for the first time.

1604    Donne's eldest son, John (the future editor of his father's writings), is born.

1605    Donne and his wife leave Pyrford Park for a small house in Mitcham, where they remain five years. Donne maintains rooms in London, and is employed by Dr. Thomas Morton, later Bishop of Durham, to assist him with his controversial writings against the Catholics.

1608    Donne writes, but not for publication, *Biathana-*

*tos,* a treatise justifying suicide under carefully defined conditions.

1609    Writes *Pseudo-Martyr* in defense of the royal supremacy. It is published the following year.

1610    Writes *Ignatius His Conclave,* which is published in 1611.
        Granted an Honorary Master's Degree by Oxford for *Pseudo-Martyr.*

1611    Meets Sir Robert Drury. Writes *The First Anniversary.* Takes up residence at Drury House in London. Travels on the continent with Sir Robert from November, 1611, to September, 1612.

1612    Writes *The Second Anniversary* while in France.

1614    Donne is again in Parliament as a member for Taunton, but it is dissolved after two months.

1614–15 Composes *Essays in Divinity,* a series of private meditations, while pondering whether or not to take Orders.

1615    Ordained a priest in the Anglican Church, January 23.
        Cambridge confers a Doctor of Divinity Degree on Donne by the King's mandate.

1616–22 Reader in Divinity to the Benchers of Lincoln's Inn.

1617    Anne Donne dies.

1619–20 Accompanies Viscount Doncaster on his embassy to Germany.

1621    Appointed Dean of St. Paul's.

1624    Appointed to "St. Dunstan's in the West."

1630    On the first Friday in Lent he preaches his last

sermon before Charles I, published under the title *Death's Duel,* with the addition: "Being His Last Sermon, and Called by His Majesty's Household The Doctor's Own Funeral Sermon."

1631     Dies in London, March 31, apparently of cancer.

# Selected Bibliography

## Editions of the Works

*The Poems of John Donne*. Herbert J. C. Grierson (ed.).
2 vols. New York and London: Oxford University
Press, 1912. The second volume contains introductions
and notes. This was reissued in 1929 in a one-volume
edition without the notes but with a new introduction.

*Donne's Sermons: Selected Passages*. Logan Pearsall Smith
(ed.). New York and London: Oxford University Press,
1919. An excellent introduction and brief selections.

*Complete Poetry and Selected Prose*. John Hayward (ed.).
New York: Random House, Inc., 1929.

*Donne: The Divine Poems*. Helen Gardner (ed.). London
and Toronto: Oxford University Press, 1952; New
York: Oxford University Press, 1953. A good introduction and commentary.

*John Donne: The Anniversaries*. Frank Manley (ed.).
Baltimore: Johns Hopkins Press, 1963.

## Biographies

Gosse, Edmund. *Life and Letters*. 2 vols. London: 1899.
Although a highly readable work, this has been largely
superseded by later work that has corrected many fac-
tual errors.

Hardy, Evelyn. *Donne: A Spirit in Conflict*. London: Con-
stable & Co., Ltd.; Toronto: The Macmillan Co. of

Canada, Ltd., 1943. A full and detailed biography, but weak in its treatment of the poetry, and showing a tendency to lapse into purple prose.

Le Comte, Edward. *Grace to a Witty Sinner: A Life of Donne*. New York: Walker & Company, 1965. The best of the full-scale biographies.

Walton, Izaak. *Lives*. First published in 1640. This collection of five short biographies by Donne's friend and admirer contains lives of two of Donne's friends, Sir Henry Wotton and George Herbert, as well as of Donne. It is available in *Oxford World's Classics* (New York and London: Oxford University Press, 1927). Although Walton is a hagiolater where Donne is concerned, this brief life is the foundation of later biographies, and gives a vivid, if perhaps somewhat misleading, impression of the man.

*Criticism*

Alvarez, Alfred. *The School of Donne*. London: Chatto & Windus, 1961; Toronto: Clarke, Irwin & Company, Ltd., 1961; New York: Pantheon Books, Inc., 1962. A brief but excellent critical introduction to Donne and his followers. Perhaps the best place to start from.

Coffin, C. M. *John Donne and the New Philosophy*. New York: Columbia University Press; London: Oxford University Press, 1937. A study of the seventeenth-century intellectual climate, and the effect of the new science on Donne's poetry.

Eliot, T. S. "The Metaphysical Poets," *Selected Essays, 1917–1932*. New York: Harcourt, Brace & Company, Inc.; London: Faber & Faber, Ltd., 1932. The single most influential critical essay in the Donne "revival" of the twenties. For Eliot's revised opinion of Donne, consult his essay included in *A Garland for John Donne* (see below).

Grierson, Sir Herbert. *Criticism and Creation*. New York:

The Macmillan Company, 1949; London: Chatto & Windus, 1949; Toronto: Clarke, Irwin & Company, Ltd., 1951. Among other essays this includes a good treatment of Donne and Anglicanism, "Donne and the 'Via Media.' " Grierson's introduction to his anthology *Metaphysical Lyrics and Poems of the Seventeenth Century,* (New York and London: Oxford University Press, 1921) is a critical milestone in the field. It is reprinted in the volume edited by William R. Keast, listed below.

Keast, William R. *Seventeenth-Century English Poetry.* New York: Oxford University Press, 1962. A very good collection of critical essays by various authors, at least ten of which are pertinent to Donne.

Leavis, F. R. "The Line of Wit," *Revaluation: Tradition and Development in English Poetry.* London: Chatto & Windus; Toronto: The Macmillan Co. of Canada, Ltd., 1936. This pioneering critical essay in the analysis and evaluation of early seventeenth-century poetry, emphasizing Donne, remains indispensable. It is reprinted in the volume edited by William R. Keast, listed above.

Legouis, Pierre. *Donne the Craftsman.* New York and London: Oxford University Press, 1928.

Leishman, J. B. *The Monarch of Wit.* London: Hutchinson & Co. (Publishers), Ltd., 1951. A detailed examination of all the poems.

Nicolson, Marjorie Hope. *The Breaking of the Circle.* Evanston, Ill.: Northwestern University Press, 1950. Contains some excellent chapters on the Anniversary poems.

Simpson, Evelyn M. *A Study of the Prose Works of John Donne.* New York and London: Oxford University Press, 1924. Reissued in 1948. One of the most lucid treatments of Donne's thought. There is an excellent biographical chapter.

Spencer, Theodore (ed.). *A Garland for John Donne, 1631–1931.* Cambridge, Mass.: Harvard University Press; London: Oxford University Press, 1932. Published to mark Donne's tercentenary, the volume includes essays by T. S. Eliot, Mario Praz, Evelyn Simpson, John Sparrow, and others.

Tuve, Rosemond. *Elizabethan and Metaphysical Imagery.* Chicago: University of Chicago Press; London: Cambridge University Press, 1947. An influential book, written in partial reaction against the critical approach of the preceding decades. It attempts to minimize the "modernity" of the Elizabethans and Metaphysicals by relating their poetry to the rhetorical and critical conventions of the sixteenth and seventeenth centuries.

Williamson, George. *The Donne Tradition: A Study in English Poetry from Donne to the Death of Cowley.* Cambridge, Mass.: Harvard University Press; London: Oxford University Press, 1930.

# SONGS
### AND
# SONNETS

### The Good-Morrow

I wonder, by my troth, what thou and I
Did, till we lov'd? Were we not wean'd till then?
But suck'd on country pleasures, childishly?
Or snorted° we in the seven sleepers' den?°
'Twas so; but this, all pleasure's fancies be.      5
If ever any beauty I did see,
Which I desir'd, and got, 'twas but a dream of thee.

And now good morrow to our waking souls,
Which watch not one another out of fear;
For love, all love of other sights controls,      10

4 snorted snored, i.e., slept.   4 the seven sleepers' den According
to the legend related by Gregory of Tours, seven Christian youths
from Ephesus were imprisoned in a mountain cave and left to
starve during the Decian persecution in A.D. 250. They fell into a
miraculous sleep of nearly two hundred years, awakening again in
the reign of the Christian emperor Theodosius II.

And makes one little room an everywhere.
Let sea-discoverers to new worlds have gone,
Let maps to other, worlds on worlds have shown,°
Let us possess one world, each hath one, and is one.

15 My face in thine eye, thine in mine appears,
And true plain hearts do in the faces rest,
Where can we find two better hemispheres
Without sharp North, without declining West?
What ever dies was not mix'd equally;
20 If our two loves be one, or, thou and I
Love so alike, that none do slacken, none can die.°


*Song*


Go and catch a falling star,
    Get with child a mandrake root,°
Tell me where all past years are,
    Or who cleft the Devil's foot,
5 Teach me to hear mermaids singing,
    Or to keep off envy's stinging,
            And find
            What wind
Serves to advance an honest mind.


10 If thou be'st born to strange sights,
    Things invisible to see,
Ride ten thousand days and nights,
    Till age snow white hairs on thee,
Thou, when thou return'st, wilt tell me

13 **Let . . . shown** This line may be rearranged to read: Let maps
have shown many worlds to others. In the seventeenth century
"other" could be used as the plural form.   19–21 **What . . . die**
That which was uncompounded or simple was not subject to decay.
Grierson quotes St. Thomas Aquinas: "For there is no corruption
save where there is contrariety."   2 **mandrake root** the mandragora
plant. It had a forked root and was thought to resemble the human
body. There was a notion current that it shrieked when pulled from
the ground. It was used in love philters, and was believed to facili-
tate pregnancy.

All strange wonders that befell thee,                    15
        And swear
        Nowhere
Lives a woman true, and fair.

If thou find'st one, let me know,
  Such a pilgrimage were sweet;                    20
Yet do not, I would not go,
  Though at next door we might meet,
Though she were true, when you met her,
And last, till you write your letter,
        Yet she                    25
        Will be
False, ere I come, to two, or three.


## Woman's Constancy

Now thou hast lov'd me one whole day,
Tomorrow when thou leav'st, what wilt thou say?
Wilt thou then antedate some new made vow?
        Or say that now
We are not just those persons which we were?                    5
Or, that oaths made in reverential fear
Of Love, and his wrath, any may forswear?
Or, as true deaths true marriages untie,
So lovers' contracts, images of those,
Bind but till sleep, death's image, them unloose?                    10
        Or, your own end to justify,
For having purpos'd change, and falsehood; you
Can have no way but falsehood to be true?
Vain lunatic, against these scapes° I could
        Dispute, and conquer, if I would,                    15
        Which I abstain to do,
For by tomorrow, I may think so too.


14 scapes evasions, subterfuges.

### The Undertaking

I have done one braver° thing
    Than all the Worthies° did,
And yet a braver thence doth spring,
    Which is, to keep that hid.

5  It were but madness now to impart
    The skill of specular stone,°
When he which can have learn'd the art
    To cut it, can find none.

So, if I now should utter this,
10    Others (because no more
Such stuff to work upon there is)
    Would love but as before.

But he who loveliness within
    Hath found, all outward loathes,
15  For he who color loves, and skin,
    Loves but their oldest clothes.

If, as I have, you also do
    Virtue attir'd in woman see,
And dare love that, and say so too,
20    And forget the He and She;°

And if this love, though placèd so,
    From profane men you hide,

---

**1 braver** finer, more splendid.    **2 Worthies** The nine Worthies are usually listed as Joshua, David, and Judas Maccabeus; Hector, Alexander, and Julius Caesar; Arthur, Charlemagne, and Godfrey of Bouillon: three Jews, three Gentiles, three Christians.    **6 specular stone** It is thought Donne is referring to selenite, a crystalline stone which in antiquity had been used for glazing and glass. For these purposes it was cut into very thin strips. In Donne's day it was believed that none had been found since ancient times. Therefore, Donne takes it as an example of futility to learn the art or skill of working in a stone which no longer exists.    **20 forget the He and She** i.e., forget sex.

Which will no faith on this bestow,
　　Or, if they do, deride:

Then you have done a braver thing                    *25*
　　Than all the Worthies did;
And a braver thence will spring,
　　Which is, to keep that hid.


### The Sun Rising

　　　Busy old fool, unruly Sun,
　　　　Why dost thou thus,
Through windows, and through curtains call on us?
Must to thy motions lovers' seasons run?
　　　　Saucy pedantic wretch, go chide                    *5*
　　　　Late school boys, and sour prentices,
　　Go tell court-huntsmen that the King will ride,°
　　Call country ants to harvest offices;
Love, all alike, no season knows, nor clime,
Nor hours, days, months, which are the rags of time.    *10*

　　　Thy beams, so reverend and strong
　　　　Why shouldst thou think?
I could eclipse and cloud them with a wink,
But that I would not lose her sight so long:
　　　　If her eyes have not blinded thine,                    *15*
　　　　Look, and tomorrow late, tell me
　　Whether both the Indias of spice and mine°
　　Be where thou left'st them, or lie here with me.
Ask for those Kings whom thou saw'st yesterday,
And thou shalt hear, All here in one bed lay.                    *20*


7 **Go tell . . . ride** J. B. Leishman writes in *The Monarch of Wit*:
"This line I think we can say with certainty, was written . . . after
James I had been on the throne long enough for his passion for
hunting to have become, as it did, a topic both of private conversation and public satire."    17 **both the Indias of spice and mine**
The East Indies were the Spice Islands; the West Indies were famous
for their mines of precious metals.

> She is all States, and all Princes, I,
>       Nothing else is.
> Princes do but play us; compar'd to this,
> All honor's mimic; all wealth alchemy.

25          Thou, sun, art half as happy as we,
>       In that the world's contracted thus;
>    Thine age asks ease, and since thy duties be
>    To warm the world, that's done in warming us.
> Shine here to us, and thou art everywhere;

30  This bed thy center is, these walls, thy sphere.


### The Indifferent

> I can love both fair and brown,°
> Her whom abundance melts, and her whom want
>       betrays,
> Her who loves loneness best, and her who masks and
>       plays,
> Her whom the country form'd, and whom the town,

5   Her who believes, and her who tries,°
> Her who still° weeps with spongy eyes,
> And her who is dry cork, and never cries;
> I can love her, and her, and you and you,
> I can love any, so she be not true.

10  Will no other vice content you?
> Will it not serve your turn to do as did your mothers?
> Or have you all old vices spent, and now would find
>       out others?
> Or doth a fear, that men are true, torment you?
> Oh we are not, be not you so,

15  Let me, and do you, twenty know.
> Rob me, but bind me not, and let me go.
> Must I, who came to travel thorough° you,
> Grow your fix'd subject, because you are true?

1 **brown** The Elizabethan conventional ideal of beauty was blond
rather than brunette.   5 **tries** tests her lover.   6 **still** perpetually.
17 **thorough** through.

Venus heard me sigh this song,
And by Love's sweetest part, variety, she swore          20
She heard not this till now; and that it should be so no
    more.
She went, examin'd, and return'd ere long,
And said, "Alas, some two or three
Poor heretics in love there be,
Which think to 'stablish dangerous constancy.          25
But I have told them, 'Since you will be true,
You shall be true to them, who are false to you.' "


### Love's Usury

For every hour that thou wilt spare me now,
       I will allow,
Usurious God of Love, twenty to thee,
When with my brown, my gray hairs equal be;
Till then, Love, let my body reign, and let          5
Me travel, sojourn, snatch, plot, have, forget,
Resume my last year's relict:° think that yet
       We'd never met.

Let me think any rival's letter mine,
       And at next nine          10
Keep midnight's promise; mistake by the way
The maid, and tell the lady of that delay;°
Only let me love none, no, not the sport;
From country grass, to comfitures° of Court,
Or city's *quelque choses,* let report          15
       My mind transport.

This bargain's good; if when I'm old, I be
       Inflam'd by thee,

7 **relict** widow, i.e., last year's discarded mistress. 10–12 **And at next . . . delay** to be casual enough to keep midnight's assignation at nine the following morning, having spent the interval with the maid instead of the lady, and to be impudent enough to tell the lady the truth. 14 **comfitures** sweetmeats.

If thine own honor, or my shame, or pain,
20 Thou covet most, at that age thou shalt gain.
Do thy will then, then subject and degree,
And fruit of love, Love I submit to thee,
Spare me till then, I'll bear it, though she be
        One that loves me.


*The Canonization*


For God's sake hold your tongue, and let me love,
    Or° chide my palsy, or my gout,
My five gray hairs or ruin'd fortune flout,
      With wealth your state, your mind with arts improve,
5       Take you a course, get you a place,
      Observe his honor, or his grace,°
Or the King's real, or his stampèd face°
    Contemplate, what you will, approve,
    So you will let me love.

10 Alas, alas, who's injur'd by my love?
    What merchant's ships have my sighs drown'd?
Who says my tears have overflow'd his ground?
      When did my colds a forward spring remove?
      When did the heats which my veins fill
15       Add one more to the plaguy bill?°
Soldiers find wars, and lawyers find out still
    Litigious men, which quarrels move,
    Though she and I do love.°

2 **Or** either. 6 **Observe . . . grace** pay court to an important person
with an eye to advancement. Two important spheres of influence
are suggested in the two titles of a judge and a duke. 7 **stamped
face** the King's face stamped on coins. 15 **plaguy bill** the weekly
notice of deaths issued during epidemics of the plague. 10–18 **Alas,
alas . . . do love** Cleanth Brooks comments in *The Well Wrought
Urn* on the ironical references in the second stanza to the outworn
Petrarchan conventions of Elizabethan love poetry—the exaggerated sighs, tears, chills, and fevers. "The implication is that the
poet himself recognizes the absurdity of the Petrarchan love metaphors."

Call us what you will, we are made such by love;
   Call her one, me another fly,                    20
We are tapers too, and at our own cost die,
   And we in us find the Eagle and the Dove.°
      The Phœnix° riddle hath more wit
      By us,° we two being one, are it.
So to one neutral thing both sexes fit,                    25
   We die and rise the same, and prove
   Mysterious by this love.°

We can die by it, if not live by love,
   And if unfit for tombs and hearse
Our legend be, it will be fit for verse;                    30
   And if no piece of chronicle° we prove,
      We'll build in sonnets pretty rooms;
      As well a well-wrought urn becomes
The greatest ashes, as half-acre tombs,
   And by these hymns, all shall approve                    35
   Us *canoniz'd* for Love:

22 **the Eagle and the Dove** symbols of strength and gentleness.
23 **Phoenix** the bird of Egyptian and Arabian legend, only one of
which existed at a time. It therefore embodied both sexes in itself.
After living five or six centuries, it cremated itself in its nest of
spices and arose from its own ashes in renewed youth and strength.
It is therefore a symbol of immortality.    24 **By us** Because the
Phoenix also symbolizes our immortal love, its enigma takes on
added and richer meaning.    19–27 **Call us . . . love** In Elizabethan
slang "to die" referred to the death of physical desire following
sexual consummation. It was also a belief of the time that sexual
activity shortened life. These ideas implicitly contribute to the
complexity of the stanza. Like the taper that consumes itself in
burning, the lovers shorten their own lives by resorting to sex.
But "die" carries also a submerged allusion to martyrdom, which
is developed in the two following stanzas. Death is followed by
resurrection in the image of the Phoenix, and the rebirth of physical
desire is the meaning of l. 26. Donne speaks of this renewal of
physical passion in a manner that (not ironically but wittily) suggests religious mystery.    31 **piece of Chronicle** history or an in-
scription on a monument.

And thus invoke us: You whom reverend love
   Made one another's hermitage;
You, to whom love was peace, that now is rage;
40    Who did the whole world's soul contract, and drove
      Into the glasses of your eyes
       So made such mirrors, and such spies,
   That they did all to you epitomize,
    Countries, towns, courts: beg from above
45  A pattern of your love!°


### The Triple Fool

I am two fools, I know,
For loving, and for saying so
   In whining poetry;
But where's that wiseman, that would not be I,
5   If she would not deny!
Then as the earth's inward narrow crooked lanes
Do purge sea water's fretful salt away,
   I thought, if I could draw my pains
Through rhyme's vexation, I should them allay,
10 Grief brought to numbers cannot be so fierce,
For he tames it, that fetters it in verse.

   But when I have done so,
Some man, his art and voice to show,
   Doth set° and sing my pain,
15 And, by delighting many, frees again
   Grief, which verse did restrain.
To love and grief tribute of verse belongs,
But not of such as pleases when 'tis read,
   Both are increasèd by such songs:
20 For both their triumphs so are publishèd,
And I, which was two fools, do so grow three;
Who are a little wise, the best fools be.

37–45 **And thus . . . love** The world petitions the lovers, now
canonized and declared saints of Love, to intercede with Heaven
to provide a pattern of love for others to follow.  14 **set** set to
music.

## Lover's Infiniteness

If yet I have not all thy love,
Dear, I shall never have it all,
I cannot breathe one other sigh, to move;
Nor can entreat one other tear to fall.
And all my treasure, which should purchase thee,          5
Sighs, tears, and oaths, and letters I have spent,
Yet no more can be due to me,
Than at the bargain made was meant,
If then thy gift of love were partial,
That some to me, some should to others fall,          10
   Dear, I shall never have thee all.

Or if then thou gavest me all,
All was but all which thou hadst then,
But if in thy heart, since, there be or shall,
New love created be, by other men,          15
Which have their stocks entire, and can in tears,
In sighs, in oaths, and letters outbid me,
This new love may beget new fears,
For this love was not vowed by thee.
And yet it was, thy gift being general,          20
The ground, thy heart is mine, whatever shall
   Grow there, dear, I should have it all.

Yet I would not have all yet,
He that hath all can have no more,
And since my love doth every day admit          25
New growth, thou shouldst have new rewards in store;
Thou canst not every day give me thy heart,
If thou canst give it, then thou never gavest it:
Love's riddles are, that though thy heart depart,
It stays at home, and thou with losing savest it:          30
But we will have a way more liberal,
Than changing hearts, to join them, so we shall
   Be one, and one another's All.

## Song

Sweetest love, I do not go
    For weariness of thee,
Nor in hope the world can show
    A fitter love for me;
5      But since that I
Must die at last, 'tis best
To use myself in jest,
    Thus by feign'd deaths° to die.

Yesternight the Sun went hence,
10    And yet is here today;
He hath no desire nor sense,
    Nor half so short a way:
      Then fear not me,
But believe that I shall make
15 Speedier journeys, since I take
    More wings and spurs than he.

O how feeble is man's power,
    That if good fortune fall,
Cannot add another hour,
20    Nor a lost hour recall!
      But come bad chance,
And we join to it our strength,
And we teach it art and length,
    Itself o'er us to advance.°

25 When thou sigh'st, thou sigh'st not wind,
    But sigh'st my soul away;
When thou weep'st, unkindly kind,
    My life's blood doth decay.
      It cannot be
30 That thou lov'st me, as thou say'st,

---

8 **feign'd deaths** rehearsals of death by leaving his mistress, which
is a form of death to him.   21–24 **But come . . . to advance** Our
imaginations often make bad luck appear worse and last longer.

If in thine my life thou waste,
   Thou art the best of me.

Let not thy divining° heart
   Forethink me any ill;
Destiny may take thy part,                                    35
   And may thy fears fulfill;
     But think that we
Are but turn'd aside to sleep;
They who one another keep
   Alive, ne'er parted be.                            40


## The Legacy

When I died last, and, dear, I die
   As often as from thee I go,
   Though it be but an hour ago,
And lovers' hours be full eternity,
   I can remember yet, that I                          5
     Something did say, and something did bestow;
Though I be dead, which sent me, I should be
Mine own executor and legacy.°

I heard me say, "Tell her anon,
   That my self," (that is you, not I)°                10
"Did kill me;" and when I felt me die,
I bid me send my heart, when I was gone,
But I alas could there find none,
   When I had ripp'd me, and search'd where hearts
     did lie;
It kill'd me again, that I who still was true,               15
In life, in my last will should cozen° you.

---

33 **divining** prophetic.    7–8 **Though I . . . legacy** These somewhat
tortured lines can be paraphrased: Though I, who am responsible
to myself for my going, have died because I left you, I am myself
the legacy I bequeath, and I am my own lawyer to see the will
executed.    9–10 **I heard . . . not I** Conventionally in Donne the
lovers by an exchange or fusion of identities become one, a paradoxical duality in unity.    16 **cozen** cheat. He is unable to send his
mistress his heart (his legacy to her) because she has it already.
He finds instead his mistress' heart in his own breast.

Yet I found something like a heart,
  But colors° it, and corners had;
  It was not good, it was not bad,
20 It was entire to none, and few had part.
  As good as could be made by art
  It seem'd; and therefore for our losses sad,
I meant to send this heart instead of mine,
But oh, no man could hold it, for 'twas thine.


*A Fever*°


Oh do not die, for I shall hate
  All women so, when thou art gone,
That thee I shall not celebrate,
  When I remember, thou wast one.


5 But yet thou canst not die, I know;
  To leave this world behind, is death;
But when thou from this world wilt go,
  The whole world vapors with thy breath.


Or if, when thou, the world's soul, goest,
10 It stay, 'tis but thy carcass then,
The fairest woman, but thy ghost,
  But corrupt worms, the worthiest men.


O wrangling schools, that search what fire°
  Shall burn this world, had none the wit
15 Unto this knowledge to aspire,
  That this her fever might be it?


18 **colors** His mistress' heart is colored, i.e., deceitful, not true.
10 **A Fever** The conceit developed in this poem that the world's
health or very existence is dependent on a woman or girl antici-
pates the imagery and argument of *The First Anniversary*.  13 **fire**
The Stoic philosophers taught that successive cosmic cycles of creation would be destroyed by fire, or reabsorbed into the Primal Fire
of God. There was much division of opinion on the nature of this
fire.

And yet she cannot waste by this,
  Nor long bear this torturing wrong,
For much corruption needful is
  To fuel such a fever long.          20

These burning fits but meteors be,
  Whose matter in thee is soon spent.
Thy beauty, and all parts, which are thee,
  Are unchangeable firmament.°

Yet 'twas of my mind, seizing thee,       25
  Though it in thee cannot persévere.
For I had rather owner be
  Of thee one hour, than all else ever.


## Air and Angels

Twice or thrice had I loved thee,
Before I knew thy face or name,
So in a voice, so in a shapeless flame,
*Angels* affect us oft, and worship'd be;°
  Still when, to where thou wert, I came,     5
Some lovely glorious nothing I did see.
  But since my soul, whose child love is,
Takes limbs of flesh, and else could nothing do,
  More subtle than the parent is,
Love must not be, but take a body too,°     10
  And therefore what thou wert, and who,
     I bid Love ask, and now
That it assume thy body, I allow,
And fix itself in thy lip, eye, and brow.

---

24 **unchangeable firmament** The sphere of the fixed stars was believed to be incorruptible.  3–4 **So in . . . be** Being immaterial spirits, it is necessary for angels to assume some material vesture when they communicate with men.  7–10 **But since . . . body too** These lines may be paraphrased: Since my soul has put on a body, my love (the child of my soul), ought not to be of a rarer essence than its parent or cause.

15 Whilst thus to ballast love, I thought,
   And so more steadily to have gone,
   With wares which would sink admiration,
   I saw I had Love's pinnace overfraught,
       Every thy hair° for love to work upon
20 Is much too much, some fitter must be sought;
       For, nor in nothing, nor in things
   Extreme, and scatt'ring° bright, can love inhere;
       Then as an Angel, face, and wings
   Of air, not pure as it, yet pure doth wear,
25     So thy love may be my love's sphere;
           Just such disparity
   As is 'twixt Air and Angels' purity,
   'Twixt women's love, and men's will ever be.°


### Break of Day°

'Tis true, 'tis day; what though it be?
O wilt thou therefore rise from me?
Why should we rise, because 'tis light?
Did we lie down, because 'twas night?
5 Love which in spite of darkness brought us hither,
Should in despite of light keep us together.

Light hath no tongue, but is all eye;
If it could speak as well as spy,
This were the worst that it could say,
10 That being well, I fain would stay,

19 **Every thy hair** each hair of yours.  22 **scatt'ring** dazzling.
23–27 **Then as . . . ever be** Angels materialize themselves by assum-
ing bodies of air which, though pure, cannot be so pure as the
angelic essence, which is spiritual. The love of the speaker abides
or inheres in his mistress as an angelic essence in his sphere of
corporeal air. The cynical turn or reversal given the poem in the
last two lines has distressed some critics. Helen Gardner in *The
Business of Criticism* finds these lines "the intellectual equivalent
of pulling away a chair from under a person about to sit down."
However, attempts to interpret these lines away from their obvious
meaning—woman's inferiority—are not convincing.  0 **Break of
Day** The speaker of this poem is a woman.

And that I lov'd my heart and honor so,
That I would not from him, that had them, go.

Must business thee from hence remove?
Oh, that's the worst disease of love;
The poor, the foul, the false, love can                    15
Admit, but not the busied man.
He which hath business, and makes love, doth do
Such wrong, as when a married man doth woo.

## The Anniversary

All Kings, and all their favorites,
   All glory of honors, beauties, wits,
The Sun itself, which makes times, as they pass,
Is elder by a year, now, than it was
When thou and I first one another saw:                     5
All other things, to their destruction draw,
   Only our love hath no decay;
This, no tomorrow hath, nor yesterday;
Running, it never runs from us away,
But truly keeps his first, last, everlasting day.          10

Two graves must hide thine and my corse,
   If one might, death were no divorce;
Alas, as well as other Princes, we,
(Who Prince enough in one another be,)
Must leave at last in death, these eyes, and ears,         15
Oft fed with true oaths, and with sweet salt tears;
   But souls where nothing dwells but love
(All other thoughts being inmates°) then shall prove
This, or a love increasèd there above,
When bodies to their graves, souls from their graves
      remove.                                              20

And then we shall be throughly° blest,
   But we no more, than all the rest;
18 **inmates** transient lodgers only.   21 **throughly** thoroughly.

Here upon earth, we are Kings, and none but we
Can be such Kings, nor of such subjects be;
25  Who is so safe as we? where none can do
Treason to us, except one of us two.
    True and false fears let us refrain,
Let us love nobly, and live, and add again
Years and years unto years, till we attain
30  To write threescore: this is the second of our reign.


### A Valediction: Of My Name, in the Window

#### I.

My name engrav'd herein
Doth contribute my firmness to this glass,
    Which, ever since that charm, hath been
    As hard, as that which grav'd it° was;
5  Thine eye will give it price enough to mock
    The diamonds of either rock.°

#### II.

'Tis much that glass should be
As all confessing, and through-shine° as I;
    'Tis more, that it shows thee to thee,
10    And clear reflects thee to thine eye.
But all such rules, Love's magic can undo,
    Here you see me, and I am you.

#### III.

As no one point, nor dash,
Which are but accessories to this name,

4 **that which grav'd it** a diamond.    6 **The diamonds . . . rock.**
According to Chambers, two famous sources of diamonds are indicated here, the East and the West Indies.    8 **through-shine** transparent.

The showers and tempests can outwash,    15
  So shall all times find me the same;
You this entireness better may fulfill,
    Who have the pattern with you still.°


## IV.

  Or if too hard and deep
This learning be, for a scratch'd name to teach,    20
  It, as a given death's head° keep,
  Lovers' mortality to preach,
Or think this ragged bony name to be
    My ruinous anatomy.


## V.

  Then, as all my souls be,    25
Emparadis'd in you, (in whom alone
  I understand, and grow and see,)°
  The rafters of my body, bone
Being still with you, the muscle, sinew, and vein,
    Which tile this house, will come again.    30


## VI.

  Till my return, repair
And recompact my scattered body so.
  As all the virtuous powers which are
  Fix'd in the stars, are said to flow
Into such characters,° as gravèd be    35
    When these stars have supremacy:


17–18 **You this ... still** These may be paraphrased: The constancy
of my love, reflected in the durability of my signature on glass,
should prove a pattern for you to emulate.    21 **death's head** a
*memento mori.*    25–27 **Then as ... and see** The vegetable, sentient,
and rational souls of scholastic philosophy, each governing its ap-
propriate activity: growth, sense perception, reason.    34 **stars ...
characters** The influences of the stars were believed to enter into
magic characters drawn when those stars were in the ascendant.

### VII.

So since this name was cut
When love and grief their exaltation had,
   No door 'gainst this name's influence shut;
40     As much more loving, as more sad,
'Twill make thee; and thou shouldst, till I return,
     Since I die daily, daily mourn.

### VIII.

When thy inconsiderate hand
Flings ope this casement, with my trembling name,
45     To look on one,° whose wit or land,
   New battery to thy heart may frame,
Then think this name alive, and that thou thus
     In it offend'st my Genius.°

### IX.

And when thy melted maid,°
50 Corrupted by thy lover's gold, and page,
   His letter at thy pillow hath laid,
   Disputed it, and tam'd thy rage,
And thou begin'st to thaw towards him, for this,
     May my name step in, and hide his.

### X.

55     And if this treason go
To an overt act, and that thou write again,
   In superscribing, this name flow
   Into thy fancy, from the pane.
So, in forgetting thou rememb'rest right,
60     And unaware to me shalt write.

---

45 **one** a rival.  48 **Genius** my guardian spirit.  49 **melted maid** persuaded by the new rival to be his accomplice.

## XI.

But glass and lines must be
No means our firm substantial love to keep;°
   Near death inflicts this lethargy,
   And this I murmur in my sleep;
Impute this idle talk, to that I go,        65
      For dying men talk often so.


### *Twicknam Garden°*

Blasted with sighs, and surrounded with tears,
   Hither I come to seek the spring,
   And at mine eyes, and at mine ears,
Receive such balms as else cure everything;
   But oh, self-traitor, I do bring      5
The spider love, which transubstantiates all,
   And can convert manna to gall,
And that this place may thoroughly be thought
   True Paradise, I have the serpent brought.


'Twere wholesomer for me, that winter did      10
   Benight the glory of this place,
   And that a grave frost did forbid
These trees to laugh, and mock me to my face;
   But that I may not this disgrace
Endure, nor yet leave loving, Love let me      15
   Some senseless piece of this place be;
Make me a mandrake,° so I may groan here,
   Or a stone fountain weeping out my year.

---

61–62 **But glass . . . to keep** may be paraphrased: But the constancy
of our love must not be allowed to rest on such a device as this.
0 **Twicknam Garden** Twickenham Park was the residence of
Donne's friend, Lucy Russell, Countess of Bedford. Seven of his
verse letters are addressed to the Countess of Bedford in addition
to this poem.  17 **mandrake** See note to "Go, and catch a falling
star," page 52.

Hither with crystal vials, lovers come,
20    And take my tears, which are love's wine,
    And try your mistress' tears at home,
For all are false, that taste not just like mine;
    Alas, hearts do not in eyes shine,
Nor can you more judge woman's thoughts by tears,
25    Than by her shadow, what she wears.
O perverse sex, where none is true but she,
    Who's therefore true, because her truth kills me.


### A Valediction: Of the Book°

I'll tell thee now (dear love) what thou shalt do
    To anger destiny, as she doth us;
    How I shall stay, though she eloign° me thus,
And how posterity shall know it too;
5        How thine may out-endure
        Sybil's glory,° and obscure
        Her° who from Pindar could allure,
And her,° through whose help Lucan is not lame,
And her,° whose book (they say) Homer did find, and
    name.

10 Study our manuscripts, those myriades
    Of letters, which have passed twixt thee and me,
    Thence write our Annals, and in them will be

0 **A Valediction: Of the Book** Mr. J. B. Leishman writes of this
poem: ". . . I think we may assume that, like the other valedictions,
it was addressed to his wife, that it accompanied a manuscript
volume of love-poems, and that the statements (hyperbolical as
some of them are) which Donne makes about the nature of these
poems apply to some, though not all, of the *Songs and Sonets*. . . ."
3 **eloign** remove. 6 **Sybil's glory** One of several women (usually
numbered at ten) of antiquity who were said to possess powers
of prophecy and divination. 7 **Her** Corinna of Thebes defeated
Pindar in poetical contests on five occasions. 8 **her** Lucan's wife
was said to have assisted him in correcting several books of his
*Pharsalia*. 9 **her** A tradition exists that Homer took the subject
of the Trojan War from a book by Phantasia of Memphis. Another
version says that he found it in the writing of Helena, daughter of
Musaeus.

To all whom love's subliming° fire invades,
    Rule and example found;
      There, the faith of any ground        15
    No schismatic will dare to wound,
    That sees, how Love this grace to us affords,
To make, to keep, to use, to be these his Recórds.

This book, as long-liv'd as the elements,
    Or as the world's form, this all-grav'd tome        20
    In cypher writ, or new made idiom,°
We for Love's clergy only are instruments:
      When this book is made thus,
      Should again the ravenous
      Vandals and Goths inundate us,        25
    Learning were safe; in this our Universe
Schools might learn sciences, spheres music, angels
      verse.

Here Love's divines (since all divinity
    Is love or wonder) may find all they seek,
    Whether abstract spiritual love they like,        30
Their souls exhal'd° with what they do not see,
      Or, loath so to amuse
      Faith's infirmity, they choose
      Something which they may see and use;
    For, though mind be the heaven, where love doth
      sit,        35
Beauty a convenient type may be to figure it.

Here more than in their books may lawyers find
    Both by what titles mistresses are ours,
    And how prerogative° these states devours,
Transferr'd from Love himself, to womankind,        40
      Who, though from heart, and eyes,

13 **subliming** purifying.    19–21 **This book . . . idiom** Donne's suggestion is that Love's votaries form a select coterie, and the uninitiated—those who do not truly love—cannot understand their feelings or language.    31 **exhal'd** drawn out by.    39 **prerogative** an official right or privilege. Women, usurping the prerogatives that belong to Love, exact tribute of admiration and praise from men, but refuse to acknowledge that they have obligations in return.

They exact great subsidies,
        Forsake him who on them relies,
    And for the cause, honor, or conscience give,
45  Chimeras, vain as they, or their prerogative.

Here statesmen (or of them, they which can read)
        May of their occupation find the grounds:
        Love and their art alike it deadly wounds,
    If to consider what 'tis, one proceed,
50          In both they do excel
            Who the present govern well,
            Whose weakness none doth, or dares tell;
    In this thy book, such will their nothing see,
As in the Bible some can find out alchemy.°

55  Thus vent° thy thoughts; abroad I'll study thee,
        As he removes far off, that great heights takes;
        How great love is, presence best trial makes,
    But absence tries how long this love will be;
60          To take a latitude,
            Sun, or stars, are fitliest view'd
            At their brightest, but to conclude
    Of longitudes, what other way have we,
But to mark when, and where, the dark eclipses be?°

46–54 **Here statesmen . . . alchemy** Love and politics resemble each
other in this: neither can bear close investigation. Cynics and the
unscrupulous, who either deceive or frighten others into silence,
thrive best in both activities. This book in which true love is revealed
will nevertheless show up the fraudulent pretensions of false lovers,
just as one may study fraudulent science in the Bible.  55 **vent** give
expression to.  59–63 **To take . . . be** In explanation of these lines,
Grierson writes: "The latitude of a spot may always be found by
measuring the distance from the zenith of a star whose altitude, i.e.
distance from the equator, is known. . . . This method of estimating
longitude was, it is said, first discovered by noting that an eclipse
which took place during the battle of Arbela was observed at Alex-
andria an hour later. If the time at which an instantaneous phe-
nomenon such as an eclipse of the moon begins at Greenwich (or
whatever be the first meridian) is known, and the time of its beginning
at whatever place a ship is be then noted, the difference gives the
longitude."

## Community

Good we must love, and must hate ill,
For ill is ill, and good good still,
    But there are things indifferent,
Which we may neither hate, nor love,
But one, and then another prove,                                    5
    As we shall find our fancy bent.

If then at first wise Nature had
Made women either good or bad,
    Then some we might hate, and some choose,
But since she did them so create,                                   10
That we may neither love, nor hate,
    Only this rests: All, all may use.

If they were good it would be seen,
Good is as visible as green,
    And to all eyes itself betrays:                                 15
If they were bad, they could not last,
Bad doth itself, and others waste,
    So, they deserve nor blame, nor praise.

But they are ours as fruits are ours,
He that but tastes, he that devours,                                20
    And he that leaves all, doth as well:
Chang'd loves are but chang'd sorts of meat,
And when he hath the kernel eat,
    Who doth not fling away the shell?

## Love's Growth

I scarce believe my love to be so pure
        As I had thought it was,
        Because it doth endure
Vicissitude, and season, as the grass;

5    Methinks I lied all winter, when I swore
     My love was infinite, if spring make it more.
     But if this medicine, love, which cures all sorrow
     With more, not only be no quintessence,°
     But mix'd of all stuffs, paining soul, or sense,
10   And of the Sun his working vigor borrow,
     Love's not so pure, and abstract, as they use
     To say, which have no mistress but their muse,
     But as all else, being elemented too,
     Love sometimes would contemplate, sometimes do.


15   And yet no greater, but more eminent,°
            Love by the spring is grown;
            As, in the firmament,
     Stars by the Sun are not enlarg'd, but shown.°
     Gentle love deeds, as blossoms on a bough,
20   From love's awakened root do bud out now.
     If, as in water stirr'd more circles be
     Produc'd by one, love such additions take,
     Those, like so many spheres, but one heaven make,
     For they are all concentric° unto thee;
25   And though each spring do add to love new heat,
     As princes do in times of action get
     New taxes, and remit them not in peace,
     No winter shall abate the spring's increase.


8 **quintessence** The fifth essence of a thing, extracted in its absolutely
purest distillation. It was apart from and above the four elements,
and had medicinal virtues because of its perfect purity. It was sometimes said to be a mixture of all substances painful to man.    15 **eminent** conspicuous.    18 **Stars . . . shown** Stars appear to be larger
at sunrise.    24 **concentric** In Ptolemaic astronomy, the earth was at
the center of the universe, surrounded by ten concentric spheres. The
first seven carry the planets. The eighth sphere, the Firmament,
carries the fixed stars. The sense of these two lines also depends
upon the observation that stars appear to be larger at sunrise.

*Love's Exchange*

Love, any devil else but you
Would for a given soul give something too.
At Court your fellows every day,
Give the art of rhyming, huntsmanship, or play,
For them which were their own before;°                    5
Only I have nothing which gave more,
But am, alas, by being lowly, lower.

I ask no dispensation now
To falsify a tear, or sigh, or vow,
I do not sue from thee to draw                    10
A *non obstante*° on nature's law,
These are prerogatives, they inhere
In thee and thine; none should forswear
Except that he *Love's* minion were.

Give me thy weakness, make me blind,                    15
Both ways, as thou and thine, in eyes and mind;
Love, let me never know that this
Is love, or, that love childish is;
Let me not know that others know
That she knows my pains, lest that so                    20
A tender shame make me mine own new woe.

If thou give nothing, yet thou art just,
Because I would not thy first motions trust;
Small towns which stand stiff, till great shot
Enforce them, by war's law condition not.°                    25
Such in love's warfare is my case,

---

3–5 **At Court . . . before** The patron devils of rhyming, hunting, and
gambling impart skill in their respective arts to their followers at
Court who are already enslaved.   11 **non obstante** a legal dispensation or release from the observance of an existing law.   24–25 **Small
towns . . . not** According to military custom, towns that resist until
reduced by heavy artillery must surrender unconditionally.

I may not article for grace,
Having put Love at last to show this face:°

This face, by which he could command
30  And change the idolatry of any land,
This face, which wheresoe'r it comes,
Can call vow'd men from cloisters, dead from tombs,
And melt both poles at once, and store
Deserts with cities, and make more
35  Mines in the earth, than quarries were before.

For this, Love is enrag'd with me,
Yet kills not. If I must example be
To future rebels; if the unborn
Must learn, by my being cut up, and torn:
40  Kill, and dissect me, Love; for this
Torture against thine own end is,
Rack'd carcasses make ill anatomies.

## Confined Love

Some man unworthy to be possessor
Of old or new love, himself being false or weak,
Thought his pain and shame would be lesser,
If on womankind he might his anger wreak,
45          And thence a law did grow,
            One might but one man know;
            But are other creatures so?

Are sun, moon, or stars by law forbidden
To smile where they list, or lend away their light?
50  Are birds divorc'd, or are they chidden
If they leave their mate, or lie abroad a night?
            Beasts do no jointures lose
            Though they new lovers choose,
            But we are made worse than those.

28 **this face** his mistress' face.

Whoe'er rigg'd fair ship to lie in harbors,                    15
And not to seek new lands, or not to deal withal?
  Or built fair houses, set trees, and arbors,
Only to lock up, or else to let them fall?
      Good is not good, unless
      A thousand it possess,                    20
      But doth waste with greediness.


## The Dream

Dear love, for nothing less then thee
Would I have broke this happy dream,
    It was a theme
For reason, much too strong for phantasy,
Therefore thou wak'dst me wisely; yet                    5
My dream thou brok'st not, but continued'st it,
Thou art so truth, that thoughts of thee suffice,
To make dreams truths; and fables histories;
Enter these arms, for since thou thought'st it best,
Not to dream all my dream, let's act the rest.                    10

As lightning, or a taper's light,
Thine eyes, and not thy noise wak'd me;
    Yet I thought thee
(For thou lovest truth) an Angel, at first sight,
But when I saw thou sawest my heart,                    15
And knew'st my thoughts, beyond an Angel's art,
When thou knew'st what I dreamt, when thou knew'st
    when
Excess of joy would wake me, and cam'st then,
I must confess, it could not choose but be
Profane, to think thee anything but thee.                    20

Coming and staying show'd thee, thee,
But rising makes me doubt, that now,
    Thou art not thou.
That love is weak, where fear's as strong as he;
'Tis not all spirit, pure, and brave,                    25

If mixture it of *fear, shame, honor,* have.
Perchance as torches which must ready be,
Men light and put out, so thou deal'st with me,
Thou cam'st to kindle, goest to come; then I
30  Will dream that hope again, but else would die.


### A Valediction: Of Weeping°

Let me pour forth
My tears before thy face, whilst I stay here,
For thy face coins them, and thy stamp they bear,
And by this mintage they are something worth,
5          For thus they be
Pregnant of thee;
Fruits of much grief they are, emblems of more,
When a tear falls, that thou falls° which it bore,
So thou and I are nothing then, when on a divers shore.

10          On a round ball°
A workman that hath copies by, can lay
An Europe, Afric, and an Asia,
And quickly make that, which was nothing, *All;*
So doth each tear,
15          Which thee doth wear,
A globe, yea world, by that impression grow,
Till thy tears mix'd with mine do overflow
This world, by waters sent from thee, my heaven
dissolvèd so.

O more than Moon,
20  Draw not up seas to drown me in thy sphere,
Weep me not dead, in thine arms, but forbear
To teach the sea, what it may do too soon;

0 **A Valediction: Of Weeping** Donne probably addressed this poem
to his wife.  8 **that thou falls** "Thou" is a noun referring to the
reflection of his mistress mirrored in his falling tear.  10 **ball** A
globe map of the world is referred to in this and the following lines.

      Let not the wind
      Example find,
To do me more harm, than it purposeth;          *25*
Since thou and I sigh one another's breath,
Whoe'er sighs most, is cruellest, and hastes the other's
    death.


## Love's Alchemy

Some that have deeper digg'd love's mine than I,
Say, where his centric happiness doth lie:
      I have lov'd, and got, and told,
But should I love, get, tell, till I were old,
I should not find that hidden mystery;          *5*
      Oh, 'tis imposture all:
And as no chemic yet the Elixir got,°
      But glorifies his pregnant pot,
      If by the way to him befall
Some odoriferous thing, or med'cinal,          *10*
  So, lovers dream a rich and long delight,
  But get a winter-seeming summer's night.

Our ease, our thrift, our honor, and our day,
Shall we, for this vain bubble's shadow pay?
      Ends love in this, that my man,°          *15*
Can be as happy as I can; if he can
Endure the short scorn of a bridegroom's play?°
      That loving wretch that swears,
'Tis not the bodies marry, but the minds,
      Which he in her angelic finds,          *20*
      Would swear as justly, that he hears,
In that day's rude hoarse minstrelsy,° the spheres.
  Hope not for mind in women; at their best
  Sweetness and wit, they are but Mummy° possess'd.

7 **no chemic yet the Elixir got** No alchemist has yet discovered the
elixir of life.  15 **man** servant.  17 **bridegroom's play** the wedding
ceremony.  22 **minstrelsy** the wedding music.  24 **Mummy** Medieval physicians used powdered mummy as a medicine.

## The Flea°

Mark but this flea, and mark in this,
How little that which thou deny'st me is;
It suck'd me first, and now sucks thee,
And in this flea, our two bloods mingled be;
5  Thou know'st that this cannot be said
A sin, nor shame, nor loss of maidenhead,
   Yet this enjoys before it woo,
   And pamper'd swells with one blood made of two,
   And this, alas, is more than we would do.

10  Oh stay, three lives in one flea spare,
Where we almost, yea more than married are.
This flea is you and I, and this
Our marriage bed, and marriage temple is;
Though parents grudge, and you, we're met,
15  And cloister'd in these living walls of jet.
   Though use make you apt to kill me,
   Let not to that, self-murder added be,
   And sacrilege, three sins in killing three.

Cruel and sudden, hast thou since
20  Purpled thy nail, in blood of innocence?
Wherein could this flea guilty be,
Except in that drop which it suck'd from thee?
Yet thou triumph'st, and say'st that thou
Find'st not thyself, nor me, the weaker now;
25  'Tis true, then learn how false, fears be;
   Just so much honor, when thou yield'st to me,
   Will waste, as this flea's death took life from thee.

0 **The Flea** This poem is discussed in the Introduction.

## The Curse

Whoever guesses, thinks, or dreams he knows
Who is my mistress, wither by this curse;
    His only, and only his purse
    May some dull heart to love dispose,
And she yield then to all that are his foes;        *5*
  May he be scorn'd by one, whom all else scorn,
  Forswear to others, what to her he hath sworn,
  With fear of missing, shame of getting, torn:

Madness his sorrow, gout his cramp, may he
Make, by but thinking who hath made him such:    *10*
    And may he feel no touch
    Of conscience, but of fame, and be
Anguish'd, not that 'twas sin, but that 'twas she:
  In early and long scarceness may he rot,
  For land which had been his, if he had not    *15*
  Himself incestuously an heir begot:°

May he dream treason, and believe, that he
Meant to perform it, and confess, and die,
    And no record tell why:
    His sons, which none of his may be,    *20*
Inherit nothing but his infamy:
  Or may he so long parasites have fed,
  That he would fain be theirs, whom he hath bred,
  And at the last be circumcis'd for bread:°

The venom of all stepdames, gamesters' gall,    *25*
What tyrants, and their subjects interwish,
    What plants, mines, beasts, fowl, fish,
    Can contribute, all ill which all

14–16 **In early . . . begot** May he beget a child incestuously within his own family, thereby interposing an heir between himself and lands he would have inherited otherwise.   23–24 **That he . . . bread** May he be so impoverished by parasites that he in turn must live off the people who formerly lived off him. May he become a Jew in the desperation of his search for a livelihood.

Prophets, or poets spake; And all which shall
30  Be annex'd in schedules unto this by me,
    Fall on that man; for if it be a she,
    Nature beforehand hath out-cursèd me.


### The Message


Send home my long-stray'd eyes to me,
Which (Oh) too long have dwelt on thee;
Yet since there they have learn'd such ill,
        Such forc'd fashions,
5       And false passions,
            That they be
            Made by thee
Fit for no good sight, keep them still.


Send home my harmless heart again,
10 Which no unworthy thought could stain;
But if it be taught by thine
        To make jestings
        Of protestings,
            And cross both
15          Word and oath,
Keep it, for then 'tis none of mine.


Yet send me back my heart and eyes,
That I may know, and see thy lies,
And may laugh and joy, when thou
20      Art in anguish
        And dost languish
            For someone
            That will none,°
Or prove as false as thou art now.


23 **That will none** Perhaps this means: For someone who will have
nothing to do with you.

### A Nocturnal upon St. Lucy's Day, Being the Shortest Day°

'Tis the year's midnight, and it is the day's,
Lucy's,° who scarce seven hours herself unmasks;
  The sun is spent, and now his flasks°
  Send forth light squibs,° no constant rays;
    The world's whole sap is sunk:                    5
The general balm the hydroptic° earth hath drunk,
Whither, as to the bed's feet, life is shrunk,
Dead and interr'd; yet all these seem to laugh,
Compar'd with me, who am their epitaph.

Study me then, you who shall lovers be              10
At the next world, that is, at the next Spring:
  For I am every dead thing,
  In whom love wrought new alchemy.
    For his art did express
A quintessence even from nothingness,              15
From dull privations, and lean emptiness:
He ruin'd me, and I am re-begot
Of absence, darkness, death; things which are not.°

All others, from all things, draw all that's good,
Life, soul, form, spirit, whence they being have;  20

0 **A Nocturnal . . . Day** This poem may have been written for the
Countess of Bedford, as Grierson suggests; or for Donne's wife, as
Leishman thinks. In either case it would have been occasioned by
a serious illness or a parting, not by a death, unless it was indeed
written as late as 1617, the year of his wife's death.  2 **Lucy's**
December 13, believed by Donne to be the shortest day in the year
while the Julian calendar was in effect.  3 **flasks** powder horns.
4 **squibs** small explosive charges.  6 **hydroptic** dropsical, therefore
inordinately thirsty.   12–18 **For I . . . which are not** Alchemy sought
to distill the quintessence of things, the "fifth element." Donne's
grief leads him to regard himself as composed of privations and of
nothingness. He has been ruined by his love for a woman who has
died (the death in all probability being only an imagined one).
Destroyed, he has been re-begot of absence, darkness, death.

I, by Love's limbeck, am the grave
  Of all that's nothing. Oft a flood
    Have we two wept, and so
Drown'd the whole world, us two; oft did we grow
25 To be two Chaoses, when we did show
  Care to aught else; and often absences
Withdrew our souls, and made us carcasses.

But I am by her death (which word wrongs her),
  Of the first nothing, the Elixir° grown;
30   Were I a man, that I were one,
    I needs must know; I should prefer,
      If I were any beast,
Some ends, some means; yea plants, yea stones detest,
And love;° all, all some properties invest;
35 If I an ordinary nothing were,
  As shadow, a light, and body must be here.

But I am none; nor will my Sun renew.
  You lovers, for whose sake, the lesser sun
    At this time to the Goat° is run
40   To fetch new lust, and give it you,
      Enjoy your summer all;
Since she enjoys her long night's festival,
Let me prepare towards her, and let me call
This hour her Vigil, and her Eve, since this
45 Both the year's and the day's deep midnight is.

### Witchcraft by a Picture

I fix mine eye on thine, and there
  Pity my picture burning in thine eye;
My picture drown'd in a transparent tear,
  When I look lower I espy;

---

29 **Elixir** the distilled quintessence.   34 **And love** Attractions and
repulsions (love and hate) exist even in the world of plants and
inanimate things.   39 **Goat** Capricorn, a sign of the zodiac through
which the sun passes in spring.

Hadst thou the wicked skill                              5
By pictures made and marr'd, to kill,
How many ways might'st thou perform thy will?

But now I have drunk thy sweet salt tears,
    And though thou pour more I'll depart;
My picture vanish'd, vanish fears                       10
    That I can be endamag'd by that art;
        Though thou retain of me
One picture more, yet that will be,
Being in thine own heart, from all malice free.

### The Bait

Come live with me, and be my love,°
And we will some new pleasures prove
Of golden sands, and crystal brooks,
With silken lines, and silver hooks.

There will the river whispering run                      5
Warm'd by thy eyes, more than the Sun;
And there the enamour'd fish will stay,
Begging° themselves they may betray.

When thou wilt swim in that live bath,
Each fish, which every channel hath,                    10
Will amorously to thee swim,
Gladder to catch thee, than thou him.

If thou, to be so seen, be'st loath,
By Sun, or Moon, thou dark'nest both,
And if myself have leave to see,                        15
I need not their light, having thee.

Let others freeze with angling reeds,
And cut their legs, with shells and weeds,

1 **Come . . . love** This poem is a response to one of Christopher
Marlowe's that begins with the same line.   8 **Begging** begging that.

Or treacherously poor fish beset,
20  With strangling snare, or windowy net:

Let coarse bold hands, from slimy nest
The bedded fish in banks out-wrest,
Or curious traitors, sleavesilk° flies,
Bewitch poor fishes' wand'ring eyes.

25  For thee, thou need'st no such deceit,
For thou thyself art thine own bait;
That fish, that is not catch'd thereby,
Alas, is wiser far than I.


## The Apparition

When by thy scorn, O murd'ress, I am dead,
And that thou think'st thee free
From all solicitation from me,
Then shall my ghost come to thy bed,
5   And thee, feign'd vestal, in worse arms shall see;
Then thy sick taper will begin to wink,
And he, whose thou art then, being tir'd before,
Will, if thou stir, or pinch to wake him, think
          Thou call'st for more,
10  And in false sleep will from thee shrink,
And then, poor aspen wretch, neglected thou
Bath'd in a cold quicksilver sweat wilt lie
          A verier ghost than I;
What I will say, I will not tell thee now,
15  Lest that preserve thee; and since my love is spent,
I had rather thou shouldst painfully repent,
Than by my threat'nings rest still innocent.


23 **sleavesilk** fine silk thread.

## The Broken Heart

He is stark mad, whoever says
  That he hath been in love an hour;
Yet not that love so soon decays,
  But that it can ten in less space devour;
Who will believe me, if I swear                              5
That I have had the plague a year?
    Who would not laugh at me, if I should say,
    I saw a flask° of powder burn a day?

Ah, what a trifle is a heart,
  If once into love's hands it come!                         10
All other griefs allow a part
  To other griefs, and ask themselves but some;
They come to us, but us Love draws,
He swallows us, and never chaws:
    By him, as by chain'd shot,° whole ranks do die,        15
    He is the tyrant pike, our hearts the fry.

If 'twere not so, what did become
  Of my heart, when I first saw thee?
I brought a heart into the room,
  But from the room, I carried none with me:                 20
If it had gone to thee, I know
Mine would have taught thine heart to show
    More pity unto me: but Love, alas,
    At one first blow did shiver it as glass.

Yet nothing can to nothing fall,                             25
  Nor any place be empty quite,
Therefore I think my breast hath all
  Those pieces still, though they be not unite;
And now, as broken glasses show
A hundred lesser faces, so                                   30

8 **flask** powder horn. 15 **chain'd shot** cannon balls chained together
which separated at chain length when shot.

My rags of heart can like, wish, and adore,
But after one such love, can love no more.


### A Valediction: Forbidding Mourning°

As virtuous men pass mildly away,
  And whisper to their souls, to go,
Whilst some of their sad friends do say;
  "The breath goes now," and some say, "No,"

5  So let us melt, and make no noise,
  No tear-floods, nor sigh-tempests move;
'Twere profanation of our joys
  To tell the laity our love.

Moving of the earth° brings harms and fears,
10  Men reckon what it did and meant,
But trepidation of the spheres,°
  Though greater far, is innocent.

Dull sublunary lovers' love
  (Whose soul is sense) cannot admit
15 Absence, because it doth remove
  Those things which elemented it.

But we by a love, so much refin'd,
  That ourselves know not what it is,
Inter-assured of the mind,
20  Care less, eyes, lips, and hands to miss.

Our two souls therefore, which are one,
  Though I must go, endure not yet

0 A Valediction: Forbidding Mourning This poem was written by
Donne for his wife in 1611 on the eve of his departure for France
with Sir Robert Drury.  9 Moving of the earth earthquakes.
11 trepidation of the spheres heavenly movements or disturbances
thought to explain the precession of the equinoxes.

A breach, but an expansion,
   Like gold to airy thinness beat.

If they be two, they are two so                                25
   As stiff twin compasses are two:
Thy soul the fix'd foot, makes no show
   To move, but doth, if the other do.

And though it in the center sit,
   Yet when the other far doth roam,               30
It leans, and hearkens after it,
   And grows erect, as that comes home.

Such wilt thou be to me, who must
   Like the other foot, obliquely run;
Thy firmness makes my circle° just,                            35
   And makes me end, where I begun.


### The Ecstasy°

Where, like a pillow on a bed,
   A pregnant bank swell'd up, to rest
The violet's reclining head,
   Sat we two, one another's best.

Our hands were firmly cemented                                  5
   With a fast balm, which thence did spring,
Our eye-beams twisted, and did thread
   Our eyes, upon one double string;

So to intergraft our hands, as yet
   Was all the means to make us one,                10
And pictures in our eyes to get
   Was all our propagation.

35 **Circle** The circle or sphere was the popular symbol of perfection
in the seventeenth century.   0 **The Ectasy** This poem is discussed in
the Introduction.

As 'twixt two equal armies, Fate
    Suspends uncertain victory,
15 Our souls, (which to advance their state
    Were gone out) hung 'twixt her, and me.

And whilst our souls negotiate there,
    We like sepulchral statues lay;
All day, the same our postures were,
20     And we said nothing, all the day.

If any, so by love refin'd,
    That he soul's language understood,
And by good love were grown all mind,
    Within convenient distance stood,

25 He (though he knew not which soul spake,
    Because both meant, both spake the same)
Might thence a new concoction take,
    And part far purer than he came.

"This Ecstasy doth unperplex"
30     (We said) "and tell us what we love;
We see by this, it was not sex;
    We see, we saw not what did move:

"But as all several souls contain
    Mixture of things, they know not what,
35 Love, these mix'd souls doth mix again,
    And makes both one, each this and that.

"A single violet transplant,
    The strength, the color, and the size,
(All which before was poor, and scant,)
40     Redoubles still, and multiplies.

"When love, with one another so
    Interinanimates two souls,
That abler soul, which thence doth flow,
    Defects of loneliness controls.

"We then, who are this new soul, know                    45
   Of what we are compos'd, and made,
For, the atomies of which we grow,
   Are souls, whom no change can invade.

"But oh alas, so long, so far
   Our bodies why do we forbear?                    50
They are ours, though they are not we; we are
   The intelligences, they the sphere.

"We owe them thanks, because they thus,
   Did us, to us, at first convey,
Yielded their forces, sense, to us,                    55
   Nor are dross to us, but allay.

"On man heaven's influence works not so,
   But that it first imprints the air,
So soul into the soul may flow,
   Though it to body first repair.                    60

"As our blood labors to beget
   Spirits, as like souls as it can,
Because such fingers need to knit
   That subtle knot, which makes us man:

"So must pure lovers' souls descend                    65
   To affections, and to faculties,
Which sense may reach and apprehend,
   Else a great Prince in prison lies.

"To our bodies turn we then, that so
   Weak men on love reveal'd may look;                    70
Love's mysteries in souls do grow,
   But yet the body is his book.

"And if some lover, such as we,
   Have heard this dialogue of one,
Let him still mark us, he shall see                    75
   Small change, when we are to bodies gone."

*Love's Deity*

I long to talk with some old lover's ghost,
  Who died before the God of Love was born:
I cannot think that he, who then lov'd most,
  Sunk so low as to love one which did scorn.
5     But since this god produc'd a destiny,
And that vice-nature,° custom, lets it be:
  I must love her, that loves not me.

Sure, they which made him god, meant not so much,
  Nor he, in his young godhead practic'd it;
10    But when an even flame two hearts did touch,
  His office was indulgently to fit
Actives to passives. Correspondency
Only his subject was; it cannot be
  Love, till I love her that loves me.

15 But every modern god will now extend
  His vast prerogative, as far as Jove.
To rage, to lust, to write to, to commend,
  All is the purlieu of the God of Love.°
Oh were we wak'ned by this tyranny
20    To ungod this child again, it could not be
  I should love her, who loves not me.

Rebel and atheist too, why murmur I,
  As though I felt the worst that love could do?
Love might make me leave loving, or might try
25    A deep plague, to make her love me too,
Which, since she loves before,° I am loath to see;
Falsehood is worse than hate; and that must be,
  If she whom I love, should love me.

---

6 **vice-nature** second nature.  17–18 **To rage . . . of Love** These various actions now fall within the dominion of the god of love. 26 **loves before** has a lover antedating me.

## Love's Diet

To what a cumbersome unwieldiness
And burdenous corpulence my love had grown,
   But that I did, to make it less,
   And keep it in proportion,
Give it a diet, made it feed upon                    5
That which love worst endures, *discretion.*

Above one sigh a day I allow'd him not,
Of which my fortune, and my faults had part;
   And if sometimes by stealth he got
   A she-sigh from my mistress' heart,                    10
And thought to feast on that, I let him see
'Twas neither very sound, nor meant to me.

If he wrung from me a tear, I brin'd it so
With scorn or shame, that him it nourish'd not;
   If he suck'd hers, I let him know
   'Twas not a tear, which he had got,                    15
His drink was counterfeit, as was his meat;
For eyes which roll towards all, weep not, but sweat.

Whatever he would dictate, I writ that,
But burnt my letters; when she writ to me,                    20
   And that that favor made him fat,
   I said, if any title be
Convey'd by this, ah! what doth it avail,
To be the fortieth name in an entail?

Thus I reclaim'd my buzzard love, to fly                    25
At what, and when, and how, and where I choose;
   Now negligent of sport I lie,
   And now as other falconers use,
I spring° a mistress, swear, write, sigh and weep:
And the game kill'd, or lost, go talk, and sleep.                    30

29 **spring** to start or flush game from cover in hunting.

### The Will

Before I sigh my last gasp, let me breathe,
Great love, some legacies: here I bequeath
Mine eyes to Argus,° if mine eyes can see;
If they be blind, then, Love, I give them thee;
My tongue to Fame; to ambassadors mine ears;
    To women or the sea, my tears.
  Thou, Love, hast taught me heretofore
By making me serve her who had twenty more,
That I should give to none, but such as had too much
    before.

    My constancy I to the planets give;
My truth to them, who at the Court do live;
    Mine ingenuity and openness,
To Jesuits; to buffoons my pensiveness;
My silence to any who abroad hath been;
    My money to a Capuchin.°
  Thou, Love, taught'st me, by appointing me
To love there, where no love receiv'd can be,
Only to give to such as have an incapacity.

    My faith I give to Roman Catholics;
All my good works unto the Schismatics°
    Of Amsterdam; my best civility
And courtship, to an University;°
My modesty I give to soldiers bare;
    My patience let gamesters share.

3 **Argus** in Greek mythology the guardian appointed by Hera to watch Io after she had been transformed into a cow. He possessed a hundred eyes, from which he was called Panoptes, or all-seeing. 15 **Capuchin** Although the Capuchins, an order of begging friars, were vowed to poverty, there was widespread laxity of observance. Donne's reference to them is ironical.  20 **Schismatics** The Puritan sect referred to here believed that salvation came through faith alone, and that good works were useless.  21–22 **civility . . . University** The manners of scholarship in the seventeenth century were notoriously bad.

Thou, Love, taught'st me, by making me          25
Love her that holds my love disparity,°
Only to give to those that count my gifts indignity.

I give my reputation to those
Which were my friends; mine industry to foes;
To Schoolmen I bequeath my doubtfulness;          30
My sickness to physicians, or excess;
To Nature, all that I in rhyme have writ;
    And to my company my wit.
Thou, Love, by making me adore
Her, who begot this love in me before,          35
Taught'st me to make, as though I gave, when I did
        but restore.

To him for whom the passing bell next tolls,
I give my physic books; my written rolls
Of moral counsels, I to Bedlam give;
My brazen medals, unto them which live          40
In want of bread; to them which pass among
    All foreigners, mine English tongue.
Thou, Love, by making me love one
Who thinks her friendship a fit portion
For younger lovers, dost my gifts thus disproportion.  45

Therefore I'll give no more; but I'll undo
The world by dying; because love dies too.
Then all your beauties will be no more worth
Than gold in mines, where none doth draw it
        forth;
And all your graces no more use shall have          50
    Then a sundial in a grave.
Thou, Love, taught'st me, by making me
Love her, who doth neglect both me and thee,
To invent, and practice, this one way to annihilate all
        three.

26 **that holds my love disparity** who holds my love unworthy of her.

### The Funeral

Whoever comes to shroud me, do not harm
      Nor question much
That subtle wreath of hair, which crowns my arm;
The mystery, the sign, you must not touch,
5      For 'tis my outward Soul,
Viceroy to that, which then to heaven being gone,
      Will leave this to control,
And keep these limbs, her provinces, from dissolution.

For if the sinewy thread my brain lets fall
10      Through every part,
Can tie those parts, and make me one of all;
These hairs which upward grew, and strength and art
      Have from a better brain,
Can better do it; except she meant that I
15      By this should know my pain,
As prisoners then are manacled, when they're con-
      demn'd to die.

Whate'er she meant by it, bury it with me,
      For since I am
Love's martyr, it might breed idolatry,
20    If into others' hands these relics came;
      As 'twas humility
To afford to it all that a soul can do,
      So, 'tis some bravery,
That since you would save none of me, I bury some of
      you.

## The Blossom

Little think'st thou, poor flower,
  Whom I have watch'd six or seven days,
And seen thy birth, and seen what every hour
Gave to thy growth, thee to this height to raise,
And now dost laugh and triumph on this bough,          5
        Little think'st thou
That it will freeze anon, and that I shall
Tomorrow find thee fall'n, or not at all.

Little think'st thou, poor heart,
  That labor'st yet to nestle thee,          10
And think'st by hovering here to get a part
In a forbidden or forbidding tree,
And hop'st her stiffness by long siege to bow:
        Little think'st thou,
That thou tomorrow, ere that sun doth wake,          15
Must with this sun, and me a journey take.

But thou, which lov'st to be
  Subtle to plague thyself, wilt say,
"Alas, if you must go, what's that to me?
Here lies my business, and here I will stay:          20
You go to friends, whose love and means present
        Various content
To your eyes, ears, and tongue, and every part.
If then your body go, what need you a heart?"

Well then, stay here; but know,          25
  When thou hast stay'd and done thy most,
A naked thinking heart, that makes no show,
Is, to a woman, but a kind of ghost;
How shall she know my heart; or having none,
        Know thee for one?          30
Practice may make her know some other part,
But take my word, she doth not know a heart.

Meet me at London, then,
Twenty days hence, and thou shalt see
35  Me fresher, and more fat, by being with men,
Than if I had stayed still with her and thee.
For God's sake, if you can, be you so too:
        I would give you
There, to another friend, whom we shall find
40  As glad to have my body, as my mind.


*The Primrose, Being at Montgomery Castle,°* upon
*the Hill, on Which it is Situate*

        Upon this primrose hill,
        Where, if Heav'n would distill
A shower of rain, each several drop might go
To his own primrose, and grow manna so;°
5   And where their form, and their infinity
        Make a terrestrial galaxy,
        As the small stars do in the sky:
I walk to find a true love;° and I see
That 'tis not a mere woman, that is she,
10  But must, or more, or less than woman be.

        Yet know I not, which flower
        I wish; a six, or four;
For should my true-love less than woman be,
She were scarce anything; and then, should she
15  Be more than woman, she would get above
        All thought of sex, and think to move
        My heart to study her, and not to love;
Both these were monsters; since there must reside

0 **Montgomery Castle** It had been the home of Magdalene Herbert,
Donne's friend and mother of George Herbert.  1–4 **Upon . . . so**
Primroses grow so densely on the hill that no drop of rain can
reach the earth, but is cupped in some particular flower which it
provides with nourishment.  8 **true love** Primroses regularly have
five petals. Those with more or less were regarded as symbols of true
love.

Falsehood in woman, I could more abide,
She were by art, than Nature falsified.                    20

          Live, Primrose, then, and thrive
              With thy true number five;
And women, whom this flower doth represent,
With this mysterious number be content;
Ten is the farthest number; if half ten                    25
          Belong unto each woman, then
          Each woman may take half us men;
Or, if this will not serve their turn, since all
Numbers are odd, or even, and they fall
First into this five, women may take us all.                    30


## The Relic

          When my grave is broke up again
              Some second guest to entertain,
          (For graves have learn'd that woman-head°
          To be to more than one a bed°)
              And he that digs it spies                    5
A bracelet of bright hair about the bone,
              Will he not let us alone,
And think that there a loving couple lies,
Who thought that this device might be some way
To make their souls, at the last busy day,°                    10
Meet at this grave, and make a little stay?

          If this fall in a time, or land,
              Where mis-devotion° doth command,
          Then, he that digs us up will bring
          Us to the Bishop, and the King,                    15
              To make us relics; then
Thou shalt be a Mary Magdalen, and I
              A something else thereby;

3 **woman-head** feminine trait.   4 **to more than one a bed** The
newly dead were often buried in old graves.   10 **last busy day** the
Resurrection.   13 **mis-devotion** Catholicism.

All women shall adore us, and some men;
20 And, since at such time miracles are sought,
I would have that age by this paper° taught
What miracles we harmless lovers wrought.

First, we lov'd well and faithfully,
Yet knew not what we lov'd, nor why;
25 Difference of sex no more we knew,
Than our guardian angels do;
    Coming and going,° we
Perchance might kiss, but not between those meals°
    Our hands ne'er touch'd the seals,
30 Which nature, injur'd by late law, sets free:°
These miracles we did; but now, alas,
All measure, and all language, I should pass,
Should I tell what a miracle she was.

### The Damp°

When I am dead, and doctors know not why,
    And my friends' curiosity
Will have me cut up to survey each part,
When they shall find your picture in my heart,
5    You think a sudden damp of love
    Will through all their senses move,
And work on them as me, and so prefer°
Your murder, to the name of massacre.

Poor victories! But if you dare be brave,
10    And pleasure in your conquest have,
First kill the enormous giant, your *Disdain,*
And let the enchantress *Honor* next be slain,
    And like a Goth and Vandal rise,

21 **this paper** this poem.   27 **Coming and going** at greeting and
at parting.   28 **meals** because the kiss was nourishment to the soul.
29–30 **Our hands . . . sets free** Nature allows sexual freedom to all
life except men, who are injured by these restraints. Nevertheless,
we never attempted to violate them.   0 **The Damp** a chill, melancholy state.   7 **prefer** advance, promote.

Deface records, and histories
Of your own arts and triumphs over men,                    15
And without such advantage kill me then.

For I could muster up as well as you
   My giants, and my witches too,
Which are vast *Constancy,* and *Secretness,*
But these I neither look for, nor profess;                    20
   Kill me as woman, let me die°
   As a mere man; do you but try
Your passive valor, and you shall find then,
In that you've odds enough of any man.


## The Dissolution

She's dead; and all which die
 To their first elements resolve;
 And we were mutual elements to us,
  And made of one another.
My body then doth hers involve,                    5
And those things whereof I consist, hereby
In me abundant grow, and burdenous,
  And nourish not, but smother.
My fire of passion, sighs of air,
Water of tears, and earthly sad despair,                    10
  Which my materials be,
But near worn out by love's security,
She, to my loss, doth by her death repair,
 And I might live long wretched so
But that my fire doth with my fuel grow.                    15
  Now as those active kings
 Whose foreign conquest treasure brings,
Receive more, and spend more, and soonest break:
This (which I am amaz'd that I can speak)
  This death, hath with my store                    20
  My use increas'd.

21 **let me die** See note to "The Canonization" on "die" (p. 59).

And so my soul, more earnestly releas'd,
Will outstrip hers; as bullets flown before
A latter bullet may o'ertake, the powder being more.

### A Jet Ring Sent

Thou art not so black as my heart,
Nor half so brittle as her heart, thou art;
What wouldst thou say? shall both our properties by
thee be spoke,
Nothing more endless, nothing sooner broke?

5      Marriage rings are not of this stuff;
Oh, why should aught less precious or less tough°
Figure our loves? Except in thy name thou have bid it
say,
"I am cheap, and naught but fashion, fling me
away."

Yet stay with me since thou art come,
10     Circle this finger's top, which didst her thumb.
Be justly proud, and gladly safe, that thou dost dwell
with me,
She that, oh, broke her faith, would soon break thee.

### Negative Love

I never stoop'd so low, as they
Which on an eye, cheek, lip, can prey,
Seldom to them, which soar no higher
Than virtue or the mind to admire,
5   For sense, and understanding may
Know what gives fuel to their fire:
My love, though silly, is more brave,

6 less **tough** less precious or tough than gold of which wedding
rings were made.

For may I miss, whene'er I crave,
If I know yet, what I would have.

If that be simply perfectest                           10
Which can by no way be express'd
  But *negatives,* my love is so.
  To All, which all love, I say no.
If any who deciphers best,
  What we know not, our selves, can know,   15
Let him teach me that nothing; this
As yet my ease and comfort is,
Though I speed not, I cannot miss.

## The Prohibition

  Take heed of loving me;
At least remember, I forbade it thee:
Not that I shall repair my unthrifty waste
Of breath and blood, upon thy sighs, and tears.
By being to thee then what to me thou wast;         5
But, so great joy, our life at once outwears:
Then, lest thy love, by my death, frustrate be,
If thou love me, take heed of loving me.

  Take heed of hating me,
Or too much triumph in the victory.                   10
Not that I shall be mine own officer,°
And hate with hate again retaliate;
But thou wilt lose the style of conqueror,
If I, thy conquest, perish by thy hate.
Then, lest my being nothing lessen thee,             15
If thou hate me, take heed of hating me.

  Yet, love and hate me too,
So, these extremes shall neither's office do;
Love me, that I may die the gentler way;

11 **be mine own officer** I shall not retaliate in person.

20  Hate me, because thy love's too great for me;
    Or let these two, themselves, not me decay;
    So shall I, live,° thy stage, not triumph be;
    Lest thou thy love and hate and me undo,
    *To let me live, O love and hate me too.*°


### The Expiration

So, so, break off this last lamenting kiss,
    Which sucks two souls, and vapors both away;
Turn thou, ghost, that way, and let me turn this,
    And let ourselves benight our happiest day:
5  We ask'd none leave to love; nor will we owe
    Any so cheap a death, as saying, "Go";

Go; and if that word have not quite kill'd thee,
    Ease me with death, by bidding me go too.
Or, if it have, let my word work on me,
10    And a just office on a murderer do.
Except it be too late, to kill me so,
    Being double dead, going, and bidding go.


### The Computation

For the first twenty years, since yesterday,
    I scarce believ'd thou couldst be gone away,
For forty more, I fed on favors past,
    And forty on hopes, that thou wouldst they might
        last.
5  Tears drown'd one hundred, and sighs blew out two;
    A thousand, I did neither think, nor do,
Or not divide, all being one thought of you;
Or, in a thousand more, forgot that too.

22 **live** alive.   24 **To let . . . me too** because each cancels out the
fatal effect of the other.

Yet call not this long life; but think that I
Am, by being dead, immortal; can ghosts die?  10


### The Paradox

No lover saith, "I love," nor any other
    Can judge a perfect lover;
He thinks that else none can, nor will agree
    That any loves but he:
I cannot say I lov'd, for who can say  5
    He was kill'd yesterday?
Love with excess of heat, more young, than old,
    Death kills with too much cold;
We die but once, and who lov'd last did die,
    He that saith twice, doth lie:  10
For though he seem to move, and stir a while,
    It doth the sense beguile.
Such life is like the light which bideth yet
    When the light's life is set,
Or like the heat, which fire in solid matter  15
    Leaves behind, two hours after.
Once I lov'd and died; and am now become
    Mine epitaph and tomb.
Here dead men speak their last, and so do I;
    Love-slain, lo! here I lie.  20


### Farewell to Love

    Whilst yet to prove,°
I thought there was some deity in love,°
    So did I reverence, and gave
Worship, as atheists at their dying hour
Call, what they cannot name, an unknown power,  5
    As ignorantly did I crave:

1 **Whilst yet to prove** before I knew anything about love.  2 **some deity in love** something divine in love.

Thus when
Things not yet known are coveted by men,
    Our desires give them fashion, and so
10 As they wax lesser, fall, as they size,° grow.


But, from late fair
His Highness sitting in a golden chair,°
    Is not less cared for after three days
By children, than the thing which lovers so
15 Blindly admire, and with such worship woo;
    Being had, enjoying it decays:
        And thence,
What before pleas'd them all,° takes but one sense,
    And that so lamely, as it leaves behind
20 A kind of sorrowing dullness to the mind.


Ah, cannot we,
As well as cocks and lions° jocund be
    After such pleasures? Unless wise
Nature decreed (since each such act, they say,
25 Diminisheth the length of life a day)
    This, as she would man should despise
        The sport;
Because that other curse of being short,
    And only for a minute made to be
30 Eager, desires to raise posterity.°


Since so, my mind
Shall not desire what no man else can find;
    I'll no more dote and run
To pursue things which had endamag'd me.


10 **size** i.e., increase.   12 **Highness . . . chair** refers to a doll or toy
bought by children at a fair, and which amuses them only for a few
days.   18 **them all** all the senses.   22 **cocks and lions** According to
Galen, these were not depleted by sexual activity.   23–30 **Unless
wise . . . posterity** Different readings have been advanced for these
lines, but they probably mean that since sexual activity is believed
to shorten man's life, wise nature has arranged that the act of
procreation should be followed by melancholy and physical deple-
tion to discourage man from self-destructive indulgence, to which he
would otherwise be impelled by "that other curse of being short."

And when I come where moving beauties be,                    35
  As men do when the summer's sun
      Grows great,
Though I admire their greatness, shun their heat;
  Each place can afford shadows. If all fail,
'Tis but applying worm-seed° to the tail.                    40


## A Lecture upon the Shadow

Stand still, and I will read to thee
A lecture, Love, in love's philosophy.
    These three hours that we have spent,
    Walking here, two shadows went
Along with us, which we ourselves produc'd;                   5
But, now the Sun is just above our head,
    We do those shadows tread;
    And to brave clearness all things are reduc'd.
  So whilst our infant loves did grow,
  Disguises did, and shadows, flow                         10
From us, and our cares; but now 'tis not so.

That love hath not attain'd the high'st degree,
Which is still diligent lest others see.

Except our loves at this noon stay,
We shall new shadows make the other way.                      15
    As the first were made to blind
    Others, these which come behind
Will work upon ourselves, and blind our eyes.
If our loves faint, and westwardly decline;
    To me thou, falsely, thine,                         20
    And I to thee mine actions shall disguise.
  The morning shadows wear away,
  But these grow longer all the day,
But oh, love's day is short, if love decay.

---

40 **worm-seed** an anaphrodisiac, which impairs sexual desire.

25  Love is a growing, or full constant light;
    And his first minute, after noon, is night.


### Sonnet: The Token

Send me some token, that my hope may live,
    Or that my easeless thoughts may sleep and rest;
Send me some honey to make sweet my hive,
    That in my passion I may hope the best.
5   I beg no riband wrought with thine own hands,
    To knit our loves in the fantastic strain
Of new-touch'd youth; nor ring to show the stands
    Of our affection, that as that's round and plain,
So should our loves meet in simplicity;
10      No, nor the corals which thy wrist enfold,
Lac'd up together in congruity,
    To show our thoughts should rest in the same hold;
No, nor thy picture, though most gracious,
    And most desir'd, because best like the best;
15  Nor witty lines, which are most copious
    Within the writings which thou hast address'd.

    Send me nor this, nor that, to increase my store,
    But swear thou think'st I love thee, and no more.


### Self-Love°

He that cannot choose but love,
    And strives against it still,
Never shall my fancy move,
    For he loves 'gainst his will;
5   Nor he which is all his own,
    And can at pleasure choose,—

0 **Self Love** Originally unnamed, this poem was given its present
title by Sir Edmund Chambers in his edition of Donne's poems in
1896.

When I am caught he can be gone,
And when he list, refuse.
Nor he that loves none but fair,
For such by all are sought; 10
Nor he that can for foul ones care,
For his judgment then is nought:
Nor he that hath wit, for he
Will make me his jest or slave;
Nor a fool, for when others . . . , 15
He can neither . . . . . . ;
Nor he that still his mistress pays,
For she is thrall'd therefore:
Nor he that pays not, for he says
Within, she's worth no more. 20
Is there then no kind of men
Whom I may freely prove?
I will vent that humor then
In mine own self-love.

# ELEGIES

## ELEGIE I°

### *Jealousy*

Fond woman, which wouldst have thy husband die,
And yet complain'st of his great jealousy;
If swoll'n with poison, he lay in his last bed,
His body with a sere-bark° covered,
Drawing his breath, as thick and short, as can
The nimblest crotcheting musician,
Ready with loathsome vomiting to spew
His soul out of one hell into a new,

5

---

0 **Elegie I** Edmund Gosse in his biography of Donne published in 1899 believed that Elegie I was autobiographical, and that Donne was having an affair with a woman married to a cripple when he wrote it. But the dramatic vividness in Donne's poems is deceptive. He would perhaps have agreed with T. S. Eliot that "the more perfect the artist, the more completely separate in him will be the man who suffers and the mind which creates." At any rate, in later life he once remarked that his poems were better the less truth there had been in them. In 1912 Grierson noted certain significantly suggestive resemblances and parallels between this poem and Elergy XIX from Book II of Ovid's *Amores* (which has been translated by Dryden). It is doubtless in such a direction one should look for the origin of this poem and others like it.   4 **sere-bark** Noting that Donne has substituted "sere-bark" for "sere-cloth," Grierson writes: "The 'sere-cloth' with which the sick man is covered is his own eruptive skin."

Made deaf with his poor kindred's howling cries,
Begging with few feign'd tears, great legacies,                    10
Thou wouldst not weep, but jolly and frolicky be,
As a slave which tomorrow should be free;
Yet weep'st thou, when thou seest him hungerly
Swallow his own death, heart's-bane jealousy.
O give him many thanks, he's courteous,                            15
That in suspecting kindly warneth us.
We must not, as we us'd, flout openly,
In scoffing riddles, his deformity;
Nor at his board together being sat,
With words, nor touch, scarce looks adulterate.                    20
Nor when he swoll'n, and pamper'd with great fare,
Sits down, and snorts, cag'd in his basket chair,
Must we usurp his own bed any more,
Nor kiss and play in his house, as before.
Now I see many dangers; for that is                                25
His realm, his castle, and his diocese.
But if, as envious men, which would revile
Their Prince, or coin his gold, themselves exile
Into another country, and do it there,
We play in another house, what should we fear?                     30
There we will scorn his household policies,
His seely° plots, and pensionary spies,
As the inhabitants of Thames' right side
Do London's mayor; or Germans, the Pope's pride.

32 **seely** pitiable, because of weak condition.

# ELEGIE II°

## *The Anagram*

 Marry, and love thy Flavia, for she
 Hath all things, whereby others beauteous be,
 For, though her eyes be small, her mouth is great,
 Though they be ivory, yet her teeth be jet,
5 Though they be dim, yet she is light enough,
 And though her harsh hair fall, her skin is rough;
 What though her cheeks be yellow, her hair's red,
 Give her thine, and she hath a maidenhead.
 These things are beauty's elements, where these
10 Meet in one, that one must, as perfect, please.
 If red and white and each good quality
 Be in thy wench, ne'er ask where it doth lie.
 In buying things perfum'd, we ask if there
 Be musk and amber in it, but not where.
15 Though all her parts be not in the usual place,
 She hath yet an anagram of a good face.
 If we might put the letters but one way,
 In the lean dearth of words, what could we say?
 When by the gamut some musicians make
20 A perfect song, others will undertake,
 By the same gamut chang'd, to equal it.

0 **Elegie II** Verse of this kind in which an absurd or grotesque proposition is defended had a long history behind it before Donne took it up. The Italians in particular favored it. "The Anagram" is related in spirit to some capricious exercises in prose from Donne's youth which were published after his death under the title, *Juvenilia: or certaine Paradoxes, and Problems.* The book, which contains eleven paradoxes and ten problems, is not likely to please a modern reader. Donne defended such propositions and explored such problems as: "A Defense of Women's Inconstancy," "That Women ought to Paint," "That it is possible to find some virtue in some Women," "That Nature is our worst guide," "That only Cowards dare die," "Why are the Fairest falsest?" These or similar subjects occur frequently enough in his poetry, but in *Paradoxes and Problems* we have only a tedious ingenuity and nothing more.

Things simply good can never be unfit.
She's fair as any, if all be like her,
And if none be, then she is singular.
All love is wonder; if we justly do                          25
Account her wonderful, why not lovely too?
Love built on beauty, soon as beauty, dies,
Choose this face, chang'd by no deformities.
Women are all like Angels; the fair be
Like those which fell to worse; but such as she,             30
Like to good Angels, nothing can impair:
'Tis less grief to be foul, than to have been fair.
For one night's revels, silk and gold we choose,
But, in long journeys, cloth, and leather use.
Beauty is barren oft; best husbands° say,                    35
There is best land where there is foulest way.
Oh what a sovereign plaster will she be,
If thy past sins have taught thee jealousy!
Here needs no spies, nor eunuchs; her commit
Safe to thy foes; yea, to a marmoset.                        40
When Belgia's cities the round countries drown,
That dirty foulness guards and arms the town:
So doth her face guard her; and so, for thee,
Which, forc'd by business, absent oft must be,
She, whose face, like clouds, turns the day to night,        45
Who, mightier than the sea, makes Moors seem white,
Who, though seven years she in the stews had laid,
A Nunnery durst receive, and think a maid,
And though in childbed's labor she did lie,
Midwives would swear, 'twere but a tympany,°                 50
Whom, if she accuse herself, I credit less
Than witches, which impossibles confess,
Whom dildoes, bedstaves, and her velvet glass
Would be as loath to touch as Joseph was:
One like none, and lik'd of none, fittest were,             55
For things in fashion every man will wear.

---

35 **husbands** husbandmen, farmers    50 **tympany** swollen condition

# ELEGIE III

### *Change*

Although thy hand and faith, and good works too,
Have seal'd thy love, which nothing should undo,
Yea, though thou fall back, that apostasy
Confirm thy love; yet much, much I fear thee.
5  Women are like the Arts, forc'd unto none,
Open to all searchers, unpriz'd, if unknown.
If I have caught a bird, and let him fly,
Another fowler using these means, as I,
May catch the same bird; and, as these things be,
10  Women are made for men, not him, nor me.
Foxes and goats, all beasts change when they please,
Shall women, more hot, wily, wild than these,
Be bound to one man, and did Nature then
Idly make them apter to endure than men?
15  They are our clogs, not their own; if a man be
Chain'd to a galley, yet the galley's free;
Who hath a plow-land, casts all his seed corn there,
And yet allows his ground more corn should bear;
Though Danube into the sea must flow,
20  The sea receives the Rhine, Volga, and Po.
By nature, which gave it, this liberty
Thou lov'st, but oh! canst thou love it and me?
Likeness glues love: and if that thou so do,
To make us like and love, must I change too?
25  More than thy hate, I hate it, rather let me
Allow her change, than change as oft as she,
And so not teach, but force my opinion
To love not anyone, nor everyone.
To live in one land, is captivity,
30  To run all countries, a wild roguery;
Waters stink soon if in one place they bide,
And in the vast sea are more putrifi'd:
But when they kiss one bank, and leaving this

Never look back, but the next bank do kiss,
Then are they purest; Change is the nursery     *35*
Of music, joy, life, and eternity.


# ELEGIE IV

## *The Perfume*

Once, and but once found in thy company,
All thy suppos'd escapes° are laid on me;
And as a thief at bar is question'd there
By all the men that have been robb'd that year,
So am I (by this traitorous means surpris'd)     *5*
By thy hydroptic father catechiz'd.
Though he had wont to search with glazèd eyes,
As though he came to kill a cockatrice,°
Though he hath oft sworn that he would remove
Thy beauty's beauty, and food of our love,     *10*
Hope of his goods, if I with thee were seen,
Yet close and secret, as our souls, we have been.
Though thy immortal mother which doth lie
Still buried in her bed, yet will not die,
Takes this advantage to sleep out daylight,     *15*
And watch thy entries, and returns all night,
And, when she takes thy hand, and would seem kind,
Doth search what rings, and armlets she can find,
And kissing notes the color of thy face,
And fearing lest thou art swoll'n, doth thee embrace;     *20*
To try if thou long, doth name strange meats,
And notes thy paleness, blushing, sighs, and sweats;
And politicly° will to thee confess
The sins of her own youth's rank lustiness;
Yet love these sorceries did remove, and move     *25*
Thee to gull thine own mother for my love.

---

**2 escapes** transgressions.   **8 cockatrice** a legendary monster, part cock, part serpent, capable of killing with its glance.   **23 politicly** cunningly.

Thy little brethren, which like fairy sprites
Oft skipp'd into our chamber those sweet nights,
And kiss'd, and ingled° on thy father's knee,
30  Were brib'd next day to tell what they did see:
The grim eight-foot-high iron-bound servingman,
That oft names God in oaths, and only then,
He that to bar the first gate doth as wide
As the great Rhodian Colossus stride,
35  Which, if in hell no other pains there were,
Makes me fear hell, because he must be there:
Though by thy father he were hir'd to this,
Could never witness any touch or kiss.
But oh, too common ill, I brought with me
40  That which betray'd me to my enemy:
A loud perfume, which at my entrance cried
Even at thy father's nose, so were we spied.
When, like a tyrant king, that in his bed
Smelt gunpowder, the pale wretch shivered.
45  Had it been some bad smell, he would have thought
That his own feet, or breath, that smell had wrought.
But as we in our Isle° imprisoned,
Where cattle only, and diverse dogs are bred,
The precious unicorns, strange monsters call,
50  So thought he good strange, that had none at all.
I taught my silks, their whistling to forbear,
Even my oppress'd shoes, dumb and speechless were,
Only, thou bitter-sweet,° whom I had laid
Next me, me traitorously hast betray'd,
55  And unsuspected hast invisibly
At once fled unto him, and stay'd with me.
Base excrement of earth, which dost confound
Sense from distinguishing the sick from sound;
By thee the silly amorous sucks his death
60  By drawing in a leprous harlot's breath;
By thee, the greatest stain to man's estate
Falls on us, to be call'd effeminate;
Though you be much lov'd in the Prince's hall,
There, things that seem, exceed substantial;

29 **ingled** caressed.    47 **Isle** England    53 **thou bitter-sweet** the perfume.

Gods, when ye fum'd on altars, were pleas'd well        65
Because you were burnt, not that they lik'd your smell;
You are loathsome all, being taken simply alone,
Shall we love ill things join'd, and hate each one?
If you were good, your good doth soon decay;
And you are rare, that takes the good away.        70
All my perfumes I give most willingly
To embalm thy father's corse. What? will he die?


# ELEGIE V

### His Picture

Here take my picture; though I bid farewell,
Thine, in my heart, where my soul dwells, shall dwell.
'Tis like me now, but I dead, 'twill be more
When we are shadows both, than 'twas before.
When weather-beaten I come back, my hand,        5
Perhaps with rude oars torn, or sunbeams tann'd,
My face and breast of haircloth, and my head
With care's rash sudden storms being o'erspread,
My body a sack of bones, broken within,
And powder's blue stains scatter'd on my skin:        10
If rival fools tax thee to have lov'd a man
So foul, and coarse, as, oh, I may seem then,
This shall say what I was: and thou shalt say,
Do his hurts reach me? doth my worth decay?
Or do they reach his judging mind, that he        15
Should now love less, what he did love to see?
That which in him was fair and delicate,
Was but the milk, which in love's childish state
Did nurse it: who now is grown strong enough
To feed on that which to disused tastes seems tough.        20

# ELEGIE VI

## *Oh, Let Me Not Serve So*

Oh, let me not serve so, as those men serve
Whom honor's smokes at once fatten and starve,
Poorly enrich'd with great men's words or looks;
Nor so write my name in thy loving books
5　As those idolatrous flatterers, which still
Their Princes' styles, with many realms fulfill
Whence they no tribute have, and where no sway.
Such services I offer as shall pay
Themselves, I hate dead names: oh then let me
10　Favorite in ordinary, or no favorite be.
When my soul was in her own body sheath'd,
Nor yet by oaths betroth'd, nor kisses breath'd
Into my purgatory, faithless thee,
Thy heart seem'd wax, and steel thy constancy:
15　So careless flowers strew'd on the water's face,
The curlèd whirlpools suck, smack, and embrace,
Yet drown them; so, the taper's beamy eye
Amorously twinkling, beckons the giddy fly,
Yet burns his wings; and such the devil is,
20　Scarce visiting them, who are entirely his.
When I behold a stream, which, from the spring,
Doth with doubtful melodious murmuring,
Or in a speechless slumber, calmly ride
Her wedded channel's bosom, and then chide
25　And bend her brows, and swell if any bough
Do but stoop down, or kiss her upmost brow;
Yet, if her often gnawing kisses win
The traitorous bank to gape, and let her in,
She rusheth violently, and doth divorce
30　Her from her native, and her long-kept course,
And roars, and braves it, and in gallant scorn,
In flattering eddies promising return,
She flouts the channel, who thenceforth is dry;
Then say I, that is she, and this am I.

Yet let not thy deep bitterness beget                           35
Careless despair in me, for that will whet
My mind to scorn; and oh, love dull'd with pain
Was ne'er so wise, nor well arm'd as disdain.
Then with new eyes I shall survey thee, and spy
Death in thy cheeks, and darkness in thine eye.                 40
Though hope bred faith and love, thus taught, I shall
As nations do from Rome, from thy love fall.
My hate shall outgrow thine, and utterly
I will renounce thy dalliance: and when I
Am the recusant, in that resolute state,                        45
What hurts it me to be excommunicate?


# ELEGIE VII

### *Nature's Lay Idiot*

Nature's lay idiot, I taught thee to love,
And in that sophistry, oh, thou dost prove
Too subtle: Fool, thou didst not understand
The mystic language of the eye nor hand:
Nor couldst thou judge the difference of the air             5
Of sighs, and say, this lies, this sounds despair:
Nor by the eyes' water call a malady
Desperately hot, or changing feverously.
I had not taught thee then the alphabet
Of flowers, how they devicefully being set                  10
And bound up, might with speechless secrecy
Deliver errands mutely, and mutually.
Remember since° all thy words us'd to be
To every suitor: *Aye, if my friends agree;*
Since, household charms, thy husband's name to teach,        15
Were all the love tricks that thy wit could reach;
And since, an hour's discourse could scarce have made
One answer in thee, and that ill array'd
In broken proverbs, and torn sentences.

13 **since** when

20   Thou art not by so many duties his,
     That from the world's common having sever'd thee,
     Inlaid thee, neither to be seen, nor see,
     As mine: who have with amorous delicacies
     Refin'd thee into a blissful paradise.
25   Thy graces and good words my creatures be;
     I planted knowledge and life's tree in thee,
     Which, oh, shall strangers taste? Must I, alas,
     Frame and enamel plate, and drink in glass?
     Chafe wax for others' seals? break a colt's force
30   And leave him then, being made a ready horse?

# ELEGIE VIII

## *The Comparison*

     As the sweet sweat of roses in a still,
     As that which from chaf'd musk-cat's pores doth trill,
     As the almighty balm of the early East,
     Such are the sweat drops of my mistress' breast,
5   And on her brow her skin such lustre sets,
     They seem no sweat drops, but pearl coronets.
     Rank sweaty froth thy mistress' brow defiles,
     Like spermatic issue of ripe menstruous boils,
     Or like the scum, which, by need's lawless law
10   Enforc'd, Sanserra's starved men° did draw
     From parboil'd shoes, and boots, and all the rest
     Which were with any sovereign fatness bless'd,
     And like vile lying stones in saffron'd tin,°
     Or warts, or weals, they hang upon her skin.
15   Round as the world's her head, on every side,
     Like to the fatal ball which fell on Ide,

10 **Sanserra's starved men** In 1573 the French Protestants in Sancerra
were subjected to a long and terrible siege by the Catholics.
13 **lying stones . . . tin** false jewels set in tin colored to resemble gold.

Or that whereof God had such jealousy,
As, for the ravishing thereof we die.°
Thy *head* is like a rough-hewn statue of jet,
Where marks for eyes, nose, mouth, are yet scarce set;    20
Like the first Chaos, or flat seeming face
Of Cynthia, when the earth's shadows her embrace.
Like Proserpine's white beauty-keeping chest,
Or Jove's best fortune's urn, is her fair breast.
Thine's like worm-eaten trunks, cloth'd in seal's skin,    25
Or grave, that's dust without, and stink within.
And like that slender stalk, at whose end stands
The woodbine quivering, are her arms and hands.
Like rough bark'd elm boughs, or the russet skin
Of men late scourg'd for madness, or for sin,    30
Like sun-parch'd quarters on the city gate,°
Such is thy tann'd skin's lamentable state.
And like a bunch of ragged carrots stand
The short swoll'n fingers of thy gouty hand.
Then like the chemic's° masculine equal fire,    35
Which in the limbeck's warm womb doth inspire
Into the earth's worthless dirt a soul of gold,
Such cherishing heat her best lov'd part doth hold.
Thine's like the dread mouth of a fired gun,
Or like hot liquid metals newly run    40
Into clay molds, or like to that Etna
Where round about the grass is burnt away.
Are not your kisses then as filthy, and more,
As a worm sucking an envenom'd sore?
Doth not thy fearful hand in feeling quake,    45
As one which gath'ring flowers, still fears a snake?
Is not your last act harsh, and violent,
As when a plow a stony ground doth rent?
So kiss good turtles, so devoutly nice
Are priests in handling reverent sacrifice,    50
And such in searching wounds the surgeon is
As we, when we embrace, or touch, or kiss.

16–18 **Like to . . . we die** round like the apple of discord thrown by
Eris among the feasting gods on Ida, or the forbidden apple of Eden.
31 **gate** The limbs of executed criminals were exhibited over the
city gates.    35 **chemic's** alchemists.

> Leave her, and I will leave comparing thus,
> She, and comparisons are odious.

# ELEGIE IX°

## *The Autumnal*

No *Spring* nor *Summer* Beauty hath such grace,
    As I have seen in one *Autumnal* face.
Young *beauties* force our love, and that's a *rape,*
    This doth but *counsel,* yet you cannot 'scape.
5  If 'twere a *shame* to love, here 'twere no *shame,*
    *Affection* here takes *Reverence's* name.
Were her first years the *Golden Age?* That's true,
    But now she's *gold* oft tried, and ever new.
That was her torrid and inflaming time,
10    This is her tolerable *tropic clime.*
Fair eyes, who asks more heat than comes from hence,
    He in a fever wishes pestilence.
Call not these wrinkles, *graves;* If *graves* they were,
    They were *Love's graves;* for else he is nowhere.
15  Yet lies not Love *dead* here, but here doth sit
    Vow'd to this trench, like an *anchorite.*
And here, till hers, which must be his *death,* come,
    He doth not dig a *grave,* but build a *tomb.*
Here dwells he, though he sojourn ev'rywhere,
20    In *Progress,* yet his standing house is here.
Here, where still *Evening* is; not *noon,* nor *night;*
    Where no *voluptuousness,* yet all *delight.*
In all her words, unto all hearers fit,
    You may at *Revels,* you at *Council,* sit.
25  This is love's timber, youth his under-wood;
    There he, as wine in *June,* enrages blood,

---

0 **Elegie IX** The first part of the elegy, especially the opening couplet,
is so fine that the last part seems disappointing. It is adddressed to
Magdalene Herbert, mother of George Herbert and Lord Herbert
of Cherbury. It is somewhat surprising to reflect that Mrs. Herbert
was only in her early forties when the poem was written.

Which then comes seasonabliest, when our taste
   And appetite to other things is past.
*Xerxes'* strange *Lydian* love,° the *platane* tree,
   Was lov'd for age, none being so large as she,    *30*
Or else because, being young, nature did bless
   Her youth with age's glory, *Barrenness.*
If we love things long sought, *Age* is a thing
   Which we are fifty years in compassing;
If transitory things, which soon decay,    *35*
   *Age* must be loveliest at the latest day.
But name not *Winter-faces,* whose skin's slack;
   Lank, as an unthrift's purse; but a soul's sack;
Whose *eyes* seek light within, for all here's shade;
   Whose mouths are holes, rather worn out, than
      made;    *40*
Whose every tooth to a several place is gone,
   To vex their souls at *Resurrection;*
Name not these living *Death's-heads* unto me,
   For these, not *ancient,* but *antique* be.
I hate extremes; yet I had rather stay    *45*
   With *tombs,* than *cradles,* to wear out a day.
Since such love's natural lation° is, may still
   My love descend, and journey down the hill,
Not panting after growing beauties, so,
   I shall ebb out with them who homeward go.    *50*


# ELEGIE X

## *The Dream*

Image of her whom I love, more than she,
   Whose fair impression in my faithful heart
Makes me her medal, and makes her love me,
   As Kings do coins to which their stamps impart
The value: go, and take my heart from hence,    *5*

29 **Xerxes' strange Lydian love** Xerxes discovered a plane tree in
Greece so beautiful he adorned it with gold and appointed a
guardian for it.   47 **lation** motion.

Which now is grown too great and good for me.
Honors oppress weak spirits, and our sense
   Strong objects dull; the more, the less we see.
When you are gone, and reason gone with you,
10   Then fantasy is queen, and soul, and all;
She can present joys meaner than you do,
   Convenient, and more proportional.
So, if I dream I have you, I have you,
   For all our joys are but fantastical.
15 And so I 'scape the pain, for pain is true;
   And sleep which locks up sense, doth lock out all.
After a such fruition I shall wake,
   And, but the waking, nothing shall repent;
And shall to love more thankful sonnets make,
20   Than if more honor, tears, and pains were spent.
But dearest heart, and dearer image, stay;
   Alas, true joys at best are dream enough;
Though you stay here you pass too fast away:
   For even at first life's taper is a snuff.
25 Fill'd with her love, may I be rather grown
Mad with much heart, than idiot with none.

# ELEGIE XI

## *The Bracelet°*

### *Upon the Loss of his Mistress' Chain, for Which He Made Satisfaction*

Not that in color it was like thy hair,
For armlets° of that thou mayst let me wear:
Nor that thy hand it oft embrac'd and kiss'd,
For so it had that good, which oft I miss'd:
5 Nor for that silly old morality,
That as these links were knit, our love should be:

0 **The Bracelet** This was one of Ben Jonson's favorite poems, and, according to William Drummond of Hawthornden, he had it by heart.　　**2 armlets** cf. "The Funeral" and "The Relic."

Mourn I that I thy sevenfold chain have lost;
Nor for the luck sake, but the bitter cost.
O, shall twelve righteous Angels,° which as yet
No leaven of vile soder° did admit;                          10
Nor yet by any way have stray'd or gone
From the first state of their creation;
Angels, which heaven commanded to provide
All things to me, and be my faithful guide,
To gain new friends, to appease great enemies,             15
To comfort my soul, when I lie or rise;
Shall these twelve innocents, by thy severe
Sentence (dread judge) my sin's great burden bear?
Shall they be damn'd, and in the furnace thrown,
And punish'd for offenses not their own?                   20
They save not me, they do not ease my pains,
When in that hell they are burnt and tied in chains.
Were they but Crowns° of France, I carèd not,
For most of these their natural country's rot
I think possesseth, they come here to us,                  25
So pale, so lame, so lean, so ruinous;°
And howsoe'er French Kings most Christian be,°
Their Crowns are circumcis'd most Jewishly.°
Or were they Spanish stamps, still traveling,°
That are become as Catholic as their King,                 30
Those unlick'd bear-whelps, unfil'd pistolets°
That (more than cannon shot) avails or lets;
Which negligently left unrounded, look
Like many angled figures in the book
Of some great conjurer that would enforce                  35
Nature, as these do justice, from her course;
Which, as the soul quickens head, feet and heart,

9 **Angels** English gold coins.    10 **No leaven of vile soder** They were
pure gold. Soder: solder.    23 **Crowns** French coins.    24–26 **their
natural . . . ruinous** French coins had often been clipped or debased.
27 **most Christian be** The French royal title was "Most Christian
Majesty."    28 **Crowns . . . Jewishly** Their coins were illegally clipped
around the edges.    29 **Spanish stamps, still traveling** Stamps are dies
for striking impressions on coins. According to Grierson, the reference is to the prevalence of Spanish bribery and the policy of se-
curing paid agents in other countries.    31 **pistolets** were Spanish
coins which, used to bribe, were more efficacious than cannon.

As streams, like veins, run through the earth's every
    part,
Visit all countries, and have slyly made
40  Gorgeous France, ruin'd, ragged and decay'd;
Scotland, which knew no state, proud in one day:
And mangled seventeen-headed Belgia.
Or were it such gold as that wherewithal
Almighty chemics from each mineral,
45  Having by subtle fire a soul out-pull'd,
Are dirtily and desperately gull'd:
I would not spit to quench the fire they're in,
For they are guilty of much heinous sin.
But shall my harmless angels perish? Shall
50  I lose my guard, my ease, my food, my all?
Much hope which they should nourish will be dead,
Much of my able youth, and lustihead
Will vanish; if thou love, let them alone,
For thou will love me less when they are gone;
55  And be content that some loud squeaking crier,
Well-pleas'd with one lean thread-bare groat, for hire,
May like a devil roar through every street;
And gall the finder's conscience, if they meet.°
Or let me creep to some dread conjurer,
60  That with fantastic schemes fills full much paper;
Which hath divided heaven in tenements,
And with whores, thieves, and murderers stuff'd his
    rents,
So full, that though he pass them all in sin,
He leaves himself no room to enter in.
65  But if, when all his art and time is spent,
He say 'twill ne'er be found yet be content;
Receive from him that doom ungrudgingly,
Because he is the mouth of destiny.
    Thou say'st (alas) the gold doth still remain,
70  Though it be chang'd, and put into a chain;
So in the first fall'n Angels, resteth still

55–58 **And be content . . . meet** Instead of making me melt down my
angels to replace your bracelet, pay the town crier a pittance to
advertise your loss through the streets in the hope that the finder
may return them.

Wisdom and knowledge; but 'tis turn'd to ill:
As these should do good works and should provide
Necessities, but now must nurse thy pride.
And they are still bad angels; mine are none;                   75
For form gives being,° and their form is gone:
Pity these Angels; yet their dignities
Pass Virtues, Powers, and Principalities.°
    But thou art resolute; thy will be done!
Yet with such anguish, as her only son                          80
The mother in the hungry grave doth lay,
Unto the fire these martyrs I betray.
Good souls (for you give life to everything),
Good Angels (for good messages you bring),
Destin'd you might have been to such an one,                    85
As would have lov'd and worship'd you alone:
One that would suffer hunger, nakedness,
Yea, death, ere he would make your number less.
But, I am guilty of your sad decay;
May your few fellows longer with me stay.                       90
    But oh, thou wretched finder whom I hate
So, that I almost pity thy estate:
Gold being the heaviest metal amongst all,
May my most heavy curse upon thee fall:
Here fetter'd, manacled, and hang'd in chains,                  95
First mayst thou be; then chain'd to hellish pains;
Or be with foreign gold brib'd to betray
Thy country, and fail both of that and thy pay.
May the next thing thou stoop'st to reach, contain
Poison, whose nimble fume rot thy moist brain;                 100
Or libels, or some interdicted thing,
Which negligently kept, thy ruin bring.
Lust-bred diseases rot thee; and dwell with thee
Itching desire, and no ability.
May all the evils that gold ever wrought,                      105
All mischiefs that all devils ever thought,
Want after plenty, poor and gouty age,

---

76 **form gives being** In scholastic metaphysics substantial form in-
hering in prime matter makes a thing what it specifically is.    78
**Virtues, Powers, and Principalities** degrees of rank in the hierarchy
of angels.

The plagues of travelers, love, marriage
Afflict thee, and at thy life's last moment,
110 May thy swoll'n sins themselves to thee present.
    But I forgive; repent thee, honest man:
Gold is restorative,° restore it then:
But if from it thou beest loath to depart,
Because 'tis cordial, would 'twere at thy heart.


# ELEGIE XII

## *His Parting from Her*

Since she must go, and I must mourn, come Night,
Environ me with darkness, whilst I write:
Shadow that hell unto me, which alone
I am to suffer when my Love is gone.
5 Alas, the darkest magic cannot do it,
Thou and great Hell to boot are shadows to it.
Should Cynthia quit thee, Venus, and each star,
It would not form one thought dark as mine are.
I could lend thee obscureness now, and say,
10 Out of myself, There should be no more day,
Such is already my felt want of sight,
Did not the fires within me force a light.
Oh Love, that fire and darkness should be mix'd,
Or to thy Triumphs so strange torments fix'd?
15 Is't because thou thyself art blind, that we
Thy martyrs must no more each other see?
Or tak'st thou pride to break us on the wheel,
And view old Chaos in the pains we feel?
Or have we left undone some mutual rite,
20 Through holy fear, that merits thy despite?
No, no. The fault was mine, impute it to me,
Or rather to conspiring destiny,
Which (since I lov'd for form before) decreed,
That I should suffer when I lov'd indeed:
25 And therefore now, sooner than I can say,

112 **Gold is restorative** Gold was used medicinally.

I saw the golden fruit, 'tis rapt away.
Or as I had watch'd one drop in a vast stream,
And I left wealthy only in a dream.
Yet, Love, thou'rt blinder than thyself in this,
To vex my dove-like friend for my amiss:          30
And where my own sad truth may expiate
Thy wrath, to make her fortune run my fate:
So blinded Justice doth, when favorites fall,
Strike them, their house, their friends, their followers
     all.
Was't not enough that thou didst dart thy fires          35
Into our bloods, inflaming our desires,
And mad'st us sigh and glow, and pant, and burn,
And then thyself into our flame didst turn?
Was't not enough, that thou didst hazard us
To paths in love so dark, so dangerous:          40
And those so ambush'd round with household spies,
And over all, thy husband's towering eyes
That flam'd with oily sweat of jealousy:
Yet went we not still on with constancy?
Have we not kept our guards, like spy on spy?          45
Had correspondence whilst the foe stood by?
Stol'n (more to sweeten them) our many blisses
Of meetings, conference, embracements, kisses?
Shadow'd with negligence our most respects?
Varied our language through all dialects          50
Of becks, winks, looks, and often under-boards
Spoke dialogues with our feet far from our words?
Have we prov'd all these secrets of our art,
Yea, thy pale inwards, and thy panting heart?
And, after all this passèd purgatory,          55
Must sad divorce make us the vulgar story?
First let our eyes be riveted quite through
Our turning brains, and both our lips grow to:
Let our arms clasp like ivy, and our fear
Freeze us together, that we may stick here          60
Till Fortune, that would rive us, with the deed
Strain her eyes open, and it make them bleed:
For Love it cannot be, whom hitherto
I have accus'd, should such a mischief do.

65   Oh Fortune, thou'rt not worth my least exclaim,
     And plague enough thou hast in thy own shame.
     Do thy great worst, my friend and I have arms,
     Though not against thy strokes, against thy harms.
     Rend us in sunder, thou canst not divide
70   Our bodies so, but that our souls are tied,
     And we can love by letters still and gifts,
     And thoughts and dreams; Love never wanteth shifts.
     I will not look upon the quick'ning sun,
     But straight her beauty to my sense shall run;
75   The air shall note her soft, the fire most pure;
     Water suggest her clear, and the earth sure.
     Time shall not lose our passages; the spring
     How fresh our love was in the beginning;
     The summer how it ripened in the ear;
80   And autumn, what our golden harvests were.
     The winter I'll not think on to spite thee,
     But count it a lost season, so shall she.
     And dearest friend, since we must part, drown night
     With hope of day, burdens well borne are light.
85   Though cold and darkness longer hang somewhere,
     Yet Phoebus equally lights all the sphere.
     And what he cannot in like portions pay,
     The world enjoys in mass, and so we may.
     Be then ever yourself, and let no woe
90   Win on your health, your youth, your beauty: so
     Declare yourself base Fortune's enemy,
     No less by your contempt than constancy,
     That I may grow enamor'd on your mind,
     When my own thoughts I there reflected find.
95   For this to the comfort of my Dear I vow,
     My deeds shall still be what my words are now;
     The poles shall move to teach me ere I start;
     And when I change my love, I'll change my heart;
     Nay, if I wax but cold in my desire,
100  Think, heaven hath motion lost, and the world, fire:
     Much more I could, but many words have made
     That, oft, suspected which men would persuade;
     Take therefore all in this: I love so true,
     As I will never look for less in you.

# ELEGIE XIII

## *Julia*

Hark news, O envy, thou shalt hear descried
My *Julia;* who as yet was ne'er envied.
To vomit gall in slander, swell her veins
With calumny, that hell itself disdains,
Is her continual practice; does her best            5
To tear opinion° even out of the breast
Of dearest friends, and (which is worse than vile)
Sticks jealousy in wedlock; her own child
Scapes not the showers of envy; to repeat
The monstrous fashions, how, were, alive, to eat    10
Dear reputation. Would to God she were
But half so loath to act vice as to hear
My mild reproof. Liv'd Mantuan° now again,
That female Mastix,° to limn with his pen
This she-*Chimera* that hath eyes of fire,          15
Burning with anger, anger feeds desire,
Tongu'd like the night-crow, whose ill boding cries
Give out for nothing but new injuries,
Her breath like to the juice in Tenarus°
That blasts the springs, though ne'er so prosperous,  20
Her hands, I know not how, us'd more to spill
The food of others, then herself to fill.
But oh her mind, that Orcus, which includes
Legions of mischiefs, countless multitudes
Of formless curses, projects unmade up,              25
Abuses yet unfashion'd, thoughts corrupt,
Misshapen cavils, palpable untruths,
Inevitable errors, self-accusing oaths:
These, like those atoms swarming in the sun,
Throng in her bosom for creation.                    30
I blush to give her half her due; yet say,
No poison's half so bad as *Julia*.

6 **opinion** favorable estimation. 13 **Mantuan** Virgil. 14 **female Mastix** woman-hater. 19 **Tenarus** A sulfurous cavern at Taenarum (modern Tainaron) in southern Greece was believed in ancient times to be a passage to the underworld.

# ELEGIE XIV

### A Tale of a Citizen and His Wife

I sing no harm good sooth to any wight,
To lord or fool, cuckold, beggar or knight,
To peace-teaching lawyer, proctor, or brave
Reformèd or reducèd captain, knave,
5   Officer, juggler, or justice of peace,
Juror or judge; I touch no fat sow's grease,
I am no libeler, nor will be any,
But (like a true man) say there are too many.
I fear not *ore tenus;* for my tale,
10   Nor count nor counselor will red or pale.
A citizen and his wife the other day
Both riding on one horse, upon the way
I overtook, the wench a pretty peat,°
And (by her eye) well fitting for the feat.
15   I saw the lecherous citizen turn back
His head, and on his wife's lip steal a smack,
Whence apprehending that the man was kind,
Riding before, to kiss his wife behind,
To get acquaintance with him I began
20   To sort discourse fit for so fine a man:
I ask'd the number of the plaguy bill,°
Ask'd if the custom farmers° held out still,
Of the Virginian plot,° and whether Ward°
The traffic of the Inland seas had marr'd,
25   Whether the Britain Burse° did fill apace,

---

**13 peat** pleasure-loving woman   **21 plaguy bill** weekly list of deaths
from the plague.   **22 custom farmers** farmers of customs who col-
lected from the merchants. As they retained fees in excess of what
they had paid for their offices, there were great abuses attending the
performances of their duties.   **23 Virginian plot** Plot means plan or
scheme here. In 1609 expeditions had been sent out for the development of Virginia.   **23 Ward** a pirate with headquarters at Tunis.
The Inland seas probably refer to the Mediterranean.   **25 the
Britain Burse** an exchange consisting of shops and business establish-
ments that had been built in the Strand.

And likely were to give the Exchange disgrace;
Of new-built Algate, and the More-field crosses,
Of store of bankrupts, and poor merchants' losses
I urgèd him to speak; but he (as mute
As an old courtier worn to his last suit)                           30
Replies with only yeas and nays; at last
(To fit his element) my theme I cast
On tradesmen's gains; that set his tongue agoing:
"Alas, good sir" (quoth he) "there is no doing
In court nor city now." She smil'd and I,                           35
And (in my conscience) both gave him the lie
In one met thought: but he went on apace,
And at the present time with such a face
He rail'd, as fray'd me; for he gave no praise,
To any but my Lord of Essex' days;                                  40
Call'd those the age of action. "True" (quoth he)
"There's now as great an itch of bravery,
And heat of taking up, but cold lay down,
For, put to push of pay, away they run;
Our only city trades of hope now are                                45
Bawd, tavern-keeper, whore and scrivener;
The much of privileg'd kingsmen,° and the store
Of fresh protections° make the rest all poor;
In the first state of their creation,
Though many stoutly stand, yet proves not one                       50
A righteous pay-master." Thus ran he on
In a continued rage: so void of reason
Seem'd his harsh talk, I sweat for fear of treason.
And (troth) how could I less? when in the prayer
For the protection of the wise Lord Mayor,                          55
And his wise brethren's worships, when one pray'th,
He swore that none could say Amen with faith.
To get him off from what I glowed to hear,
(In happy time) an Angel did appear,
The bright sign of a lov'd and well-tried inn,                      60
Where many citizens with their wives have been
Well us'd and often; here I pray'd him stay,
To take some due refreshment by the way.

---

47 **kingsmen** probably noblemen who held monopolies from the
King.   48 **protections** exemptions from lawsuits, usually for debt.

Look how he look'd that hid the gold (his hope)
65 And at's return found nothing but a rope,
So he on me, refus'd, and made away,
Though willing she pleaded a weary day:
I found my miss, struck hands, and pray'd him tell
(To hold acquaintance still) where he did dwell;
70 He barely nam'd the street, promis'd the wine,
But his kind wife gave me the very sign.


# ELEGIE XV

## *The Expostulation*

To make the doubt clear, that no woman's true,
    Was it my fate to prove it strong in you?
Thought I, but one had breathèd purest air,
    And must she needs be false because she's fair?
5 Is it your beauty's mark, or of your youth,
    Or your perfection, not to study truth?
Or think you heaven is deaf, or hath no eyes?
    Or those it hath, smile at your perjuries?
Are vows so cheap with women, or the matter
10    Whereof they are made, that they are writ in water,
And blown away with wind? Or doth their breath
    (Both hot and cold at once) make life and death?
Who could have thought so many accents sweet
    Form'd into words, so many sighs should meet
15 As from our hearts, so many oaths, and tears
    Sprinkled among (all sweeter by our fears
And the divine impression of stol'n kisses,
    That seal'd the rest) should now prove empty
        blisses?
Did you draw bonds to forfeit? sign to break?
20    Or must we read you quite from what you speak,
And find the truth out the wrong way? or must
    He first desire you false, would wish you just?
O I profane, though most of women be
    This kind of beast, my thought shall except thee;

My dearest love, though froward jealousy,                    25
   With circumstance might urge thy inconstancy,
Sooner I'll think the sun will cease to cheer
   The teeming earth, and *that* forget to bear,
Sooner that rivers will run back, or Thames
   With ribs of ice in June would bind his streams,         30
Or Nature, by whose strength the world endures,
   Would change her course, before you alter yours.
But O that treacherous breast to whom weak you
   Did trust our counsels, and we both may rue,
Having his falsehood found too late, 'twas he                 35
   That made me *cast*° you guilty, and you me,
Whilst he, black wretch, betray'd each simple word
   We spake, unto the cunning of a third.
Curs'd may he be that so our love hath slain,
   And wander on the earth, wretched as Cain,                40
Wretched as he, and not deserve least pity;
   In plaguing him, let misery be witty;
Let all eyes shun him, and he shun each eye,
   Till he be noisome as his infamy;
May he without remorse deny God thrice,                       45
   And not be trusted more on his soul's price;
And after all self-torment, when he dies,
   May wolves tear out his heart, vultures his eyes,
Swine eat his bowels, and his falser tongue
   That utter'd all, be to some raven flung,                 50
And let his carrion corse be a longer feast
   To the King's dogs, than any other beast.
Now have I curs'd, let us our love revive;
   In me the flame was never more alive;
I could begin again to court and praise,                      55
   And in that pleasure lengthen the short days
Of my life's lease; like painters that do take
   Delight, not in made work, but whiles they make;
I could renew those times, when first I saw
   Love in your eyes, that gave my tongue the law            60
To like what you lik'd; and at masks and plays
   Commend the selfsame actors, the same ways;

36 **cast** to reckon, calculate astrologically.

Ask how you did, and often with intent
    Of being officious, be impertinent;
65 All which were such soft pastimes, as in these
    Love was as subtly catch'd, as a disease;
But being got it is a treasure sweet,
    Which to defend is harder than to get:
And ought not be profan'd on either part,
70     For though 'tis got by *chance*, 'tis kept by *art*.

# ELEGIE XVI

### On His Mistress

By our first strange and fatal interview,
By all desires which thereof did ensue,
By our long starving hopes, by that remorse
Which my words' masculine persuasive force
5 Begot in thee, and by the memory
Of hurts, which spies and rivals threaten'd me,
I calmly beg: but by thy father's wrath,
By all pains which want and divorcement hath,
I conjure thee, and all the oaths which I
10 And thou have sworn to seal joint constancy,
Here I unswear, and overswear them thus,
Thou shalt not love by ways so dangerous.
Temper, O fair love, love's impetuous rage,
By my true mistress still, not my feign'd page;°
15 I'll go, and, by thy kind leave, leave behind
Thee, only worthy to nurse in my mind
Thirst to come back; oh, if thou die before,
My soul from other lands to thee shall soar.
Thy (else almighty) beauty cannot move
20 Rage from the seas, nor thy love teach them love,
Nor tame wild Boreas' harshness; thou hast read
How roughly he in pieces shiverèd

14 **feign'd page** His mistress wishes to accompany him dressed as a
boy page.

Fair Orythea,° whom he swore he lov'd.
Fall ill or good, 'tis madness to have prov'd
Dangers unurg'd; feed on this flattery,                    25
That absent lovers one in the other be.
Dissemble nothing, not a boy, nor change
Thy body's habit, nor mind's; be not strange
To thyself only; all will spy in thy face
A blushing womanly discovering grace;                    30
Richly cloth'd apes are call'd apes, and as soon
Eclips'd as bright we call the moon the moon.
Men of France, changeable chameleons,
Spittles° of diseases, shops of fashions,
Love's fuelers, and the rightest company                    35
Of players, which upon the world's stage be,
Will quickly know thee, and no less, alas!°
The indifferent Italian, as we pass
His warm land, well content to think thee page,
Will hunt thee with such lust, and hideous rage,                    40
As Lot's fair guests were vex'd.° But none of these
Nor spongy hydroptic Dutch shall thee displease,
If thou stay here. O stay here; for, for thee
England is only a worthy gallery
To walk in expectation, till from thence                    45
Our greatest King call thee to his presence.
When I am gone, dream me some happiness,
Nor let thy looks our long-hid love confess.
Nor praise, nor dispraise me, nor bless, nor curse
Openly love's force, nor in bed fright thy nurse                    50
With midnight's startings, crying out, "Oh, oh
Nurse, oh my love is slain, I saw him go
O'er the white Alps alone; I saw him, I,
Assail'd, fight, taken, stabb'd, bleed, fall, and die."
Augur me better chance, except dread Jove                    55
Think it enough for me to have had thy love.

---

23 **Orythea** Boreas was god of the north wind. He loved the nymph
Orythea, but not being successful at love, he abducted her violently.
34 **Spittles** hospitals.   37 **know . . . alas** a double pun on *know*
(to have sexual knowledge) and *alas* (a lass)   41 **Lot's fair guests
were vex'd** See Genesis XIX, 1–11.

# ELEGIE XVII

## *Variety*

The heavens rejoice in motion, why should I
Abjure my so much lov'd variety,
And not with many youth and love divide?
Pleasure is none, if not diversified:
5  The sun that sitting in the chair of light
Sheds flame into what else so ever doth seem bright,
Is not contented at one sign to inn,
But ends his year and with a new begins.
All things do willingly in change delight,
10  The fruitful mother of our appetite:
Rivers the clearer and more pleasing are,
Where their fair spreading streams run wide and far;
And a dead lake that no strange bark doth greet,
Corrupts itself and what doth live in it.
15  Let no man tell me such a one is fair,
And worthy all alone my love to share.
Nature in her hath done the liberal part
Of a kind mistress, and employ'd her art
To make her lovable, and I aver
20  Him not humane that would turn back from her:
I love her well, and would, if need were, die
To do her service. But follows it that I
Must serve her only, when I may have choice
Of other beauties, and in change rejoice?
25  The law is hard, and shall not have my voice.
The last I saw in all extremes is fair,
And holds me in the sunbeams of her hair;
Her nymph-like features such agreements have
That I could venture with her to the grave:
30  Another's brown, I like her not the worse,
Her tongue is soft and takes me with discourse.
Others, for that they well descended are,
Do in my love obtain as large a share;
And though they be not fair, 'tis much with me

To win their love only for their degree.                    35
And though I fail of my required ends,
The attempt is glorious and itself commends.
How happy were our sires in ancient times,
Who held plurality of loves no crime!
With them it was accounted charity                          40
To stir up race of all indifferently;
Kindreds were not exempted from the bands:
Which with the Persian still in usage stands.
Women were then no sooner ask'd than won,
And what they did was honest and well done.                 45
But since this title honor hath been us'd,
Our weak credulity hath been abus'd;
The golden laws of nature are repeal'd,
Which our first Fathers in such reverence held;
Our liberty's revers'd, our Charter's gone,                 50
And we're made servants to opinion,
A monster in no certain shape attir'd,
And whose original is much desir'd,
Formless at first, but growing on it fashions,
And doth prescribe manners and laws to nations.             55
Here love receiv'd immedicable harms,
And was despoilèd of his daring arms.
A greater want than is his daring eyes,
He lost those awful wings with which he flies;
His sinewy bow, and those immortal darts                    60
Wherewith he is wont to bruise resisting hearts.
Only some few strong in themselves and free
Retain the seeds of ancient liberty,
Following that part of Love although depress'd,
And make a throne for him within their breast,              65
In spite of modern censures him avowing
Their sovereign, all service him allowing.
Amongst which troop although I am the least,
Yet equal in perfection with the best,
I glory in subjection of his hand,                          70
Nor ever did decline his least command:
For in whatever form the message came
My heart did open and receive the same.
But time will in his course a point descry

75   When I this lovèd service must deny,
     For our allegiance temporary is,
     With firmer age returns our liberties.
     What time in years and judgment we repos'd,
     Shall not so easily be to change dispos'd,
80   Nor to the art of several eyes obeying;
     But beauty with true worth securely weighing,
     Which being found assembled in some one,
     We'll love her ever, and love her alone.


# ELEGIE XVIII

## Love's Progress

     Whoever loves, if he do not propose
     The right true end of love, he's one that goes
     To sea for nothing but to make him sick:
     Love is a bear-whelp born, if we o'er lick
5    Our love, and force it new strange shapes to take,
     We err, and of a lump a monster make.
     Were not a calf a monster that were grown
     Face'd like a man, though better than his own?
     Perfection is in unity: prefer
10   One woman first, and then one thing in her.
     I, when I value gold, may think upon
     The ductileness, the application,
     The wholesomeness, the ingenuity,
     From rust, from soil, from fire ever free:
15   But if I love it, 'tis because 'tis made
     By our new nature (Use) the soul of trade.
        All these in women we might think upon
     (If women had them) and yet love but one.
     Can men more injure women than to say
20   They love them for that, by which they're not they?
     Makes virtue woman? must I cool my blood
     Till I both be, and find one wise and good?
     May barren Angels love so. But if we
     Make love to woman, virtue is not she:

As beauty's not, nor wealth: he that strays thus 25
From her to hers is more adulterous
Than if he took her maid. Search every sphere
And firmament, our Cupid is not there:
He's an infernal god and under ground,
With Pluto dwells, where gold and fire abound: 30
Men to such Gods, their sacrificing coals
Did not in altars lay, but pits and holes.
Although we see celestial bodies move
Above the earth, the earth we till and love:
So we her airs contemplate, words and heart 35
And virtues; but we love the centric part.

Nor is the soul more worthy, or more fit
For love, than this, as infinite as it.
But in attaining this desired place
How much they err that set out at the face? 40
The hair a forest is of ambushes,
Of springes° snares, fetters and manacles:
The brow becalms us when 'tis smooth and plain,
And when 'tis wrinkled, shipwrecks us again.
Smooth, 'tis a Paradise, where we would have 45
Immortal stay, and wrinkled, 'tis our grave.
The nose (like to the first meridian) runs
Not 'twixt an East and West, but 'twixt two suns;
It leaves a cheek, a rosy hemisphere
On either side, and then directs us where 50
Upon the Islands Fortunate° we fall,
(Not faint Canaries, but ambrosial)
Her swelling lips; to which when we are come,
We anchor there, and think ourselves at home,
For they seem all: there Sirens' songs, and there 55
Wise Delphic oracles° do fill the ear;
There in a creek where chosen pearls do swell,
The remora,° her cleaving tongue, doth dwell.

---

42 **springes** traps.   51 **the Islands Fortunate** The Fortunate Islands
or the Isles of the Blest in Greek mythology were thought to be in
the Western Ocean. The Canary Islands off the west African coast
were sometimes called the Fortunate Islands in ancient times.   56
**Delphic oracles** utterances of the priestess or oracle of Apollo at
Delphi.   58 **remora** a species of fish, known as the sucking-fish.

These, and the glorious promontory, her chin
60  O'er past; and the strait Hellespont between
The Sestos and Abydos° of her breasts,
(Not of two lovers, but two loves the nests)
Succeeds a boundless sea, but yet thine eye
Some island moles may scattered there descry;
65  And sailing towards her India, in that way
Shall at her fair Atlantic navel stay;
Though thence the current be thy pilot made,
Yet ere thou be where thou wouldst be embay'd,
Thou shalt upon another forest set,
70  Where many shipwreck, and no further get.
When thou art there, consider what this chase
Misspent by thy beginning at the face.
      Rather set out below; practice my art,
Some symmetry the foot hath with that part
75  Which thou dost seek, and is thy map for that
Lovely enough to stop, but not stay at:
Least subject to disguise and change it is;
Men say the Devil never can change his.
It is the emblem that hath figurèd
80  Firmness; 'tis the first part that comes to bed.
Civility we see refin'd: the kiss
Which at the face began, transplanted is,
Since to the hand, since to the Imperial knee,
Now at the Papal foot delights to be:
85  If Kings think that the nearer way, and do
Rise from the foot, Lovers may do so too;
For as free spheres move faster far than can
Birds, whom the air resists, so may that man
Which goes this empty and ethereal way,
90  Than if at beauty's elements he stay.
Rich Nature hath in women wisely made
Two purses, and their mouths aversely laid:
They then, which to the lower tribute owe,
That way which that exchequer looks, must go:
95  He which doth not, his error is as great,
As who by clyster° gave the stomach meat.

61 **Sestos and Abydos** cities facing each other across the Hellespont,
the Dardanelles.   96 **by clyster** by purging.

# ELEGIE XIX

## Going to Bed

Come, Madam, come, all rest my powers defy,
Until I labor, I in labor lie.
The foe oft-times having the foe in sight,
Is tir'd with standing though he never fight.
Off with that girdle, like heaven's zone glittering,     5
But a far fairer world encompassing.
Unpin that spangled breastplate which you wear,
That the eyes of busy fools may be stopp'd there.
Unlace yourself, for that harmonious chime,
Tells me from you that now it is bedtime.     10
Off with that happy busk, which I envy,
That still can be, and still can stand so nigh.
Your gown going off, such beauteous state reveals,
As when from flow'ry meads the hill's shadow steals.
Off with that wiry coronet and show     15
The hairy diadem which on you doth grow:
Now off with those shoes, and then safely tread
In this, love's hallow'd temple, this soft bed.
In such white robes, heaven's Angels us'd to be
Receiv'd by men; thou Angel bring'st with thee     20
A heaven like Mahomet's Paradise; and though
Ill spirits walk in white, we easily know,
By this these Angels from an evil sprite:
Those set our hairs, but these our flesh upright.
License my roving hands, and let them go     25
Before, behind, between, above, below.
O my America! my new-found-land,
My kingdom, safeliest when with one man mann'd,
My mine of precious stones, my empery,
How bless'd am I in this discovering thee!     30
To enter in these bonds is to be free;
Then where my hand is set, my seal shall be.
Full nakedness! All joys are due to thee,
As souls unbodied, bodies uncloth'd must be,

35 To taste whole joys. Gems which you women use
Are like Atlanta's balls,° cast in men's views,
That when a fool's eye lighteth on a gem,
His earthly soul may covet theirs, not them.
Like pictures, or like books' gay coverings made
40 For laymen, are all women thus array'd;
Themselves are mystic books, which only we
(Whom their imputed grace will dignify)
Must see reveal'd. Then, since that I may know,
As liberally, as to a midwife, show
45 Thyself: cast all, yea, this white linen hence,
There is no penance due to innocence.
    To teach thee, I am naked first; why then
What needst thou have more covering than a man.

## ELEGIE XX

### *Love's War*

Till I have peace with thee, war other men,
And when I have peace, can I leave thee then?
All other wars are scrupulous; only thou
O fair free city, mayst thyself allow
5 To any one: in Flanders, who can tell
Whether the master press; or men rebel?
Only we know, that which all idiots say,
They bear most blows which come to part the fray.
France in her lunatic giddiness did hate
10 Ever our men, yea and our God of late;
Yet she relies upon our Angels well,
Which ne'er return; no more than they which fell.
Sick Ireland is with a strange war possess'd
Like to an ague; now raging, now at rest;
15 Which time will cure: yet it must do her good
If she were purg'd, and her head vein let blood.

36 **Atlanta's balls** Atalanta was defeated in a footrace by Hippomenes
who threw three golden apples from the garden of Venus in her path,
which she turned aside to collect.

And Midas' joys our Spanish journeys give:
We touch all gold, but find no food to live.
And I should be in the hot parching clime,
To dust and ashes turn'd before my time.                    20
To mew me in a ship, is to enthrall
Me in a prison, that were like to fall;
Or in a cloister, save that there men dwell
In a calm heaven, here in a swaggering hell.
Long voyages are long consumptions,                         25
And ships are carts for executions.
Yea they are Deaths; is't not all one to fly
Into another world, as t'is to die?
Here let me war; in these arms let me lie;
Here let me parley, batter, bleed, and die.                 30
Thine arms imprison me, and mine arms thee;
Thy heart thy ransom is; take mine for me.
Other men war that they their rest may gain;
But we will rest that we may fight again.
Those wars the ignorant, these the experienc'd love,        35
There we are always under, here above.
There engines far off breed a just true fear,
Near thrusts, pikes, stabs, yea bullets hurt not here.
There lies are wrongs; here safe uprightly lie;
There men kill men, we will make one by and by.             40
Thou nothing; I not half so much shall do
In these wars, as they may which from us two
Shall spring. Thousands we see which travel not
To wars; but stay swords, arms, and shot
To make at home; and shall not I do then                    45
More glorious service, staying to make men?

# HEROICAL EPISTLE°

## Sappho to Philænis

Where is that holy fire, which Verse is said
    To have? Is that enchanting force decay'd?
Verse that draws Nature's works from Nature's law,
    Thee, her best work, to her work cannot draw.
5  Have my tears quench'd my old poetic fire;
    Why quench'd they not as well that of desire?
Thoughts, my mind's creatures, often are with thee,
    But I, their maker, want their liberty.
Only thine image in my heart doth sit,
10   But that is wax, and fires environ it.
My fires have driven, thine have drawn it hence;
    And I am robb'd of picture, heart, and sense.
Dwells with me still mine irksome memory,

0 **Heroical Epistle** The Heroic Epistle in English was modeled on
Ovid's *Heroides*. These verse letters supposed to have been
written by famous women to their lovers or husbands who had left
or deserted them. They were "heroic" because of the exalted
sentiments expressed, and because of the nobility of the speaker.
Michael Drayton had popularized the form in English, and Pope
translated Ovid's letter of Sappho to Phaon, the ferryman she was
supposed to have loved. Sappho was born on the island of Lesbos
around 600 B.C. She presided over a sorority or "Museum" of
young girls, devoted to Aphrodite and the cultivation of the arts,
especially poetry. Among the fragments of her own poetry which
have survived are many couched in terms of passionate tenderness
to the girls who were members of the circle she had drawn about
her. Donne's poem is a very good example of the Heroic Epistle in
English, but it is hardly necessary to add that the voice and approach
of Donne to his subject should not be confused with Sappho's.

Which, both to keep, and lose, grieves equally.
That tells me how fair thou art: thou art so fair,    *15*
  As gods, when gods to thee I do compare,
Are grac'd thereby; and to make blind men see
  What things gods are, I say they are like to thee.
For if we justly call each silly man
  A little world, what shall we call thee then?    *20*
Thou art not soft, and clear, and straight, and fair,
  As down, as stars, cedars, and lilies are,
But thy right hand, and cheek, and eye, only
  Are like thy other hand, and cheek, and eye.
Such was my Phao° awhile, but shall be never,    *25*
  As thou wast, art, and, oh, mayst be ever.
Here lovers swear in their idolatry
  That I am such; but grief discolors me.
And yet I grieve the less, lest grief remove
  My beauty, and make me unworthy of thy love.    *30*
Plays some soft boy with thee, oh there wants yet
  A mutual feeling which should sweeten it.
His chin, a thorny hairy unevenness
  Doth threaten, and some daily change possess.
Thy body is a natural paradise,    *35*
  In whose self, unmanur'd, all pleasure lies,
Nor needs perfection; why shouldst thou then
  Admit the tillage of a harsh rough man?
Men leave behind them that which their sin shows,
  And are as thieves trac'd, which rob when it snows.    *40*
But of our dalliance no more signs there are,
  Than fishes leave in streams, or birds in air.
And between us all sweetness may be had;
  All, all that Nature yields, or Art can add.
My two lips, eyes, thighs, differ from thy two,    *45*
  But so, as thine from one another do;
And, oh, no more; the likeness being such,
  Why should they not alike in all parts touch?
Hand to strange hand, lip to lip none denies;
  Why should they breast to breast, or thighs to
    thighs?    *50*

25 **Phao** Phaon, the youth whom Sappho was said to have loved.

Likeness begets such strange self-flattery,
   That touching myself, all seems done to thee.
Myself I embrace, and mine own hands I kiss,
   And amorously thank myself for this.
55 Me, in my glass, I call thee; but, alas,
   When I would kiss, tears d m mine eyes, and glass.
O cure this loving madness, and restore
   Me to me; thee, my half, my all, my more.
So may thy cheeks' red outwear scarlet dye,
60   And their white, whiteness of the galaxy,
So may thy mighty, amazing beauty move
   Envy in all women, and in all men, love,
And so be change, and sickness, far from thee,
   As thou by coming near, keep'st them from me.

# EPITHALAMIONS,

## OR

## MARRIAGE SONGS

### ON THE LADY ELIZABETH

*On the Lady Elizabeth, and Count Palatine
Being Married on St. Valentine's Day°*

### I.

Hail Bishop Valentine, whose day this is,
    All the air is thy diocese,
    And all the chirping choristers
And other birds are thy parishioners;
      Thou marriest every year         *5*
The lyric lark, and the grave whispering dove,
The sparrow that neglects his life for love,
The household bird with the red stomacher,
      Thou mak'st the black bird speed as soon
As doth the goldfinch, or the halcyon;      *10*
The husband cock looks out, and straight is sped,
And meets his wife, which brings her feather-bed.
This day more cheerfully than ever shine,
This day, which might enflame thyself, old Valentine.

0 **On the Lady Elizabeth . . . St. Valentine's Day** Written in commemoration of the marriage of Elizabeth, the eldest daughter of King James, to Frederick V, the Prince Palatine Elector and titular King of Bohemia.

## II.

15 Till now, thou warm'dst with multiplying loves,
      Two larks, two sparrows, or two doves;
        All that is nothing unto this,
For thou this day couplest two Phœnixes;°
        Thou mak'st a taper see
20 What the sun never saw, and what the Ark
(Which was of fowls, and beasts, the cage, and park)
Did not contain, one bed contains, through thee,
      Two Phœnixes, whose joinèd breasts
Are unto one another mutual nests,
25 Where motion kindles such fires as shall give
Young Phœnixes, and yet the old shall live.
Whose love and courage never shall decline,
But make the whole year through, thy day, O Valen-
    tine.

## III.

Up then fair Phœnix Bride, frustrate the Sun,
30       Thyself from thine affection
        Takest warmth enough, and from thine eye
All lesser birds will take their jollity.
        Up, up, fair Bride, and call
Thy stars from out their several boxes, take
35 Thy rubies, pearls, and diamonds forth, and make
Thyself a constellation of them all,
        And by their blazing, signify
That a great Princess falls, but doth not die;
Be thou a new star, that to us portends
40 Ends of much wonder; and be thou those ends.
Since thou dost this day in new glory shine,
May all men date records from this thy Valentine.

## IV.

Come forth, come forth, and as one glorious flame
      Meeting another, grows the same,

18 **Phœnixes** See note 7 to "The Canonization," page 59.

So meet thy Frederick, and so                          45
To an unseparable union grow.
      Since separation
Falls not on such things as are infinite,
Nor things which are but one, can disunite,
You are twice inseparable, great, and one;              50
      Go then to where the Bishop stays
To make you one, his way, which divers ways
Must be effected; and when all is past,
And that you are one, by hearts and hands made fast,
You two have one way left, yourselves to entwine,      55
Besides this Bishop's knot, or Bishop Valentine.

## V.

But oh, what ails the Sun, that here he stays
      Longer today, than other days?
      Stays he new light from these to get?
And finding here such store, is loath to set?          60
      And why do you two walk,
So slowly pac'd in this procession?
Is all your care but to be look'd upon,
And be to others spectacle, and talk?
      The feast, with gluttonous delays,            65
Is eaten, and too long their meat they praise,
The masquers come too late, and I think will stay,
Like fairies, till the cock crow them away.
Alas, did not antiquity assign
A night, as well as day, to thee, O Valentine?         70

## VI.

They did, and night is come; and yet we see
      Formalities retarding thee.
      What mean these ladies, which (as though
They were to take a clock in pieces) go
      So nicely about the bride;                   75
A bride, before a good night could be said,
Should vanish from her clothes into her bed,
As souls from bodies steal and are not spied.

But now she is laid, what though she be?
80  Yet there are more delays, for where is he?
He comes, and passes through sphere after sphere,
First her sheets, then her arms, then anywhere.
Let not this day, then, but this night be thine,
Thy day was but the eve to this, O Valentine.

## VII.

85  Here lies a she-Sun, and a he-Moon here,
    She gives the best light to his sphere,
    Or each is both, and all, and so
They unto one another nothing owe,
    And yet they do, but are
90  So just and rich in that coin which they pay,
That neither would, nor needs forbear, nor stay;
Neither desires to be spar'd, nor to spare,
    They quickly pay their debt, and then
Take no acquittances, but pay again;
95  They pay, they give, they lend, and so let fall
No such occasion to be liberal.
More truth, more courage in these two do shine,
Then all thy turtles have, and sparrows, Valentine.

## VIII.

And by this act of these two Phœnixes
100    Nature again restorèd is,
    For since these two are two no more,
There's but one Phœnix still, as was before.
    Rest now at last, and we
As satyrs watch the Sun's uprise, will stay
105  Waiting, when your eyes open'd, let out day,
Only desir'd, because your face we see;
    Others near you shall whispering speak,
And wagers lay, at which side day will break,
And win by observing, then, whose hand it is
110  That opens first a curtain, hers or his;
This will be tried tomorrow after nine,
Till which hour, we thy day enlarge, O Valentine.

# ECLOGUE°

## 1613. December 26.

*Allophanes, finding Idios° in the country in Christmas*
*time, reprehends his absence from court, at the*
*marriage of the Earl of Somerset; Idios gives*
*an account of his purpose therein, and*
*of his absence thence.*

*Allophanes.*

Unseasonable man, statue of ice,
    What could to country's solitude entice
Thee, in this year's cold and decrepit time?
    Nature's instinct draws to the warmer clime
Even small birds, who by that courage dare,                    5
    In numerous fleets, sail through their sea, the air.
What delicacy can in fields appear,
    Whilst Flora herself doth a freeze° jerkin wear?
Whilst winds do all the trees and hedges strip
    Of leaves, to furnish rods enough to whip                    10

0 **Eclogue** This Eclogue enclosing an Epithalamion celebrates the
marriage of Robert Ker, Earl of Somerset, with Frances Howard,
Countess of Essex, who had secured a divorce from her husband so
that she might marry her lover. The divorce proceedings had the
support and blessing of the King, whose favorite Somerset was.
Although Gosse thought Donne assisted in the divorce trial, he was
not involved in the affair beyond writing this courtier's compliment
to honor the wedding, which took place on December 26, 1613. A
year later a ruinous scandal broke over James's court when it was
revealed that Frances Howard, while still Countess of Essex, had
secured the murder by poisoning of Sir Thomas Overbury, an intimate friend of her new husband, who had violently opposed the
match. In the public trial that followed the Earl and Countess of
Somerset were spared although a number of their accomplices were
sentenced to hang. As there had been much whispered scandal about
the adulterous affair even before the divorce, the Epithalamion perhaps says more for Donne's ambition than for his sincerity.    0 **Idios**
Donne himself, who has no position at court.    8 **freeze** a punning
reference to frieze, a coarse wool cloth.

Thy madness from thee; and all springs by frost
   Have taken cold, and their sweet murmurs lost;
If thou thy faults or fortunes wouldst lament
   With just solemnity, do it in Lent;
15  At Court the spring already advancèd is,
   The sun stays longer up; and yet not his
The glory is, far other, other fires.
   First, zeal to Prince and State; then love's desires
Burn in one breast, and like heaven's two great lights,
20    The first doth govern days, the other nights.
And then that early light, which did appear
   Before the Sun and Moon created were,
The Prince's favor is diffus'd o'er all,
   From which all fortunes, names, and natures fall;
Then from those wombs of stars, the Bride's bright
25    eyes,
   At every glance, a constellation flies,
And sows the Court with stars, and doth prevent°
   In light and power, the all-ey'd firmament;
First her eyes kindle other ladies' eyes,
30    Then from their beams their jewels' lusters rise,
And from their jewels torches do take fire,
   And all is warmth, and light, and good desire;
Most other Courts, alas, are like to hell,
   Where in dark plots, fire without light doth dwell:
35  Or but like stoves, for lust and envy get
   Continual, but artificial heat;
Here zeal and love grown one, all clouds disgest,
   And make our Court an everlasting East.
And canst thou be from thence?

*Idios.*               No, I am there.
40   As heaven, to men dispos'd, is everywhere,
So are those Courts, whose Princes animate,
   Not only all their house, but all their State.
Let no man think, because he is full, he hath all;
   Kings (as their pattern, God) are liberal
45  Not only in fullness, but capacity,

27 **prevent** anticipate.

Enlarging narrow men, to feel and see,
And comprehend the blessings they bestow.
So reclus'd hermits oftentimes do know
More of heaven's glory than a worldling can.
    As man is of the world, the heart of man,          *50*
Is an epitome of God's great book
    Of creatures, and man need no farther look;
So is the country of Courts, where sweet peace doth,
    As their one common soul, give life to both—;
I am not then from Court.

*Allophanes.*                    Dreamer, thou art.          *55*
    Think'st thou, fantastic, that thou hast a part
In the East-Indian fleet, because thou hast
    A little spice, or amber° in thy taste?
Because thou art not frozen, art thou warm?
    Seest thou all good because thou seest no harm?          *60*
The earth doth in her inward bowels hold
    Stuff well dispos'd, and which would fain be gold,
But never shall, except it chance to lie,
    So upward, that heaven gild it with his eye;
As for divine things, faith comes from above,          *65*
    So, for best civil use, all tinctures° move
From higher powers; from God religion springs,
    Wisdom, and honor from the use of Kings.
Then unbeguile thyself, and know with me,
    That Angels, though on earth employ'd they be,          *70*
Are still in heav'n, so is he still at home
    That doth, abroad, to honest actions come.
Chide thyself then, O fool, which yesterday
    Might'st have read more than all thy books bewray;
Hast thou a history° which doth present          *75*
    A Court, where all affections do assent
Unto the King's, and that, that King's are just?
    And where it is no levity to trust?
Where there is no ambition, but to obey,
    Where men need whisper nothing, and yet may;          *80*

58 **amber** ambergris, used as an ingredient in cooking.   66 **tinctures**
principles causing modifications in things or persons.   75 **history**
a book of history.

Where the King's favors are so plac'd, that all
    Find that the King therein is liberal
To them, in him, because his favors bend
    To virtue, to the which they all pretend?
85  Thou hast no such; yet here was this, and more,
    An earnest lover,° wise then, and before.
Our little Cupid hath suèd livery,
    And is no more in his minority;
He is admitted now into that breast°
90      Where the King's counsels and his secrets rest.
What hast thou lost, O ignorant man?

*Idios.*                                    I knew
    All this, and only therefore I withdrew.
To know and feel all this, and not to have
    Words to express it, makes a man a grave
95  Of his own thoughts; I would not therefore stay
    At a great feast, having no grace to say.
And yet I scap'd not here; for being come
    Full of the common joy, I utter'd some;
Read then this nuptial song, which was not made
100     Either the Court or men's hearts to invade,
But since I am dead, and buried, I could frame
    No epitaph, which might advance my fame
So much as this poor song, which testifies
    I did unto that day some sacrifice.

---

86 **An earnest lover** the Earl of Somerset, wise both before he lost
his heart, and after he had fallen in love with Frances Howard.
89 **breast** Cupid, dwelling in Somerset's breast, learns new wisdom
from the proximity, ceases to be a child, and sues livery, i.e., demands
the legal delivery of his inheritance, having reached his majority.

# EPITHALAMION

## I.

### *The Time of the Marriage*

Thou art repriev'd old year, thou shalt not die,     *105*
    Though thou upon thy death bed lie,
    And shouldst within five days expire,
Yet thou art rescu'd by a mightier fire
    Than thy old soul, the Sun,
When he doth in his largest circle run.     *110*
The passage of the West or East would thaw,
And open wide their easy liquid jaw
To all our ships, could a Promethean art
Either unto the Northern Pole impart
The fire of these inflaming eyes, or of this loving heart.   *115*

## II.

### *Equality of Persons*

But undiscerning Muse, which heart, which eyes,
    In this new couple, dost thou prize,
    When his eye as inflaming is
As hers, and her heart loves as well as his?
    Be tried by beauty, and then     *120*
The bridegroom is a maid, and not a man.
If by that manly courage they be tried
Which scorns unjust opinion, then the bride
Becomes a man. Should chance or envy's art
Divide these two, whom nature scarce did part?     *125*
Since both have both the inflaming eyes, and both the
    loving heart.

## III.

### Raising of the Bridegroom

Though it be some divorce to think of you
  Singly, so much one are you two,
   Yet let me here contemplate thee,
130 First, cheerful Bridegroom, and first let me see,
   How thou prevent'st the Sun,
And his red foaming horses dost outrun,
How, having laid down in thy Sovereign's breast
  All businesses, from thence to reinvest
135 Them, when these triumphs cease, thou forward art
  To show to her, who doth the like impart,
The fire of thy inflaming eyes, and of thy loving heart.

## IV.

### Raising of the Bride

But now, to thee, fair Bride, it is some wrong,
  To think thou wert in bed so long,
140   Since soon thou liest down first, 'tis fit
Thou in first rising shouldst allow for it.
   Powder thy radiant hair,
Which if without such ashes thou wouldst wear,
Thou, which to all which come to look upon,
145 Art meant for Phœbus, wouldst be Phaëton.°
For our ease, give thine eyes the unusual part
  Of joy, a tear; so quench'd, thou mayst impart,
To us that come, thy inflaming eyes, to him, thy loving
  heart.

---

145 **Phaëton** Apollo's son, who being unable to manage his father's
horses, scorched the earth by driving the sun-chariot too near.
Donne's meaning in these lines is that the sunlike radiance of
Frances Howard's hair, unless dimmed by powder, will scorch her
admirers. The ensuing images follow this line.

## V.

### *Her Appareling*

Thus thou descend'st to our infirmity,
    Who can the Sun in water see.                      *150*
    So dost thou, when in silk and gold,
Thou cloud'st thyself; since we which do behold,
    Are dust, and worms, 'tis just
Our objects be the fruits of worms and dust;
Let every jewel be a glorious star,                         *155*
Yet stars are not so pure, as their spheres° are.
And though thou stoop, to appear to us in part,
Still in that picture thou entirely art,
Which thy inflaming eyes have made within his loving
    heart.

## VI.

### *Going to the Chapel*

Now from your Easts° you issue forth, and we,               *160*
    As men which through a cypress° see
    The rising sun, do think it two,
So, as you go to church, do think of you,
    But that veil being gone,
By the Church rites you are from thenceforth one.          *165*
The Church Triumphant made this match before,
And now the Militant doth strive no more;
Then, reverend priest, who God's recorder art,
Do, from his dictates, to these two impart
All blessings, which are seen, or thought, by Angel's
    eye or heart.                                       *170*

---

156 **spheres** the crystalline spheres in which the planets were set.
160 **Now from your Easts** Since Somerset and his new countess are
both compared to the sun, each one rises from his respective East
to meet at the church.   161 **cypress** Donne apparently means that
the sun, veiled behind the foliage of a tree, appears to be larger
because the leaves disperse its light.

## VII.

### *The Benediction*

Bless'd pair of Swans, oh may you interbring
    Daily new joys, and never sing,
      Live, till all grounds of wishes fail,
Till honor, yea till wisdom grow so stale,
175       That, new great heights to try,
It must serve your ambition, to die;
Raise heirs, and may here to the world's end, live
Heirs from this King, to take thanks, you, to give,
Nature and grace do all, and nothing art.
180 May never age, or error overthwart
With any West, these radiant eyes, with any North, this
    heart.

## VIII.

### *Feasts and Revels*

But you are over-bless'd. Plenty this day
    Injures; it causeth time to stay;
      The tables groan, as though this feast
185 Would, as the flood, destroy all fowl and beast.
      And were the doctrine new
That the earth mov'd, this day would make it true;
For every part to dance and revel goes.
They tread the air, and fall not where they rose.
190 Though six hours since, the Sun to bed did part,
The masks and banquets will not yet impart
A sunset to these weary eyes, a center to this heart.

## IX.

### *The Bride's Going to Bed*

What mean'st thou, Bride, this company to keep?
    To sit up, till thou fain wouldst sleep?
195      Thou mayst not, when thou art laid, do so.

Thyself must to him a new banquet grow,
    And you must entertain
And do all this day's dances o'er again.
Know that if Sun and Moon together do
Rise in one point, they do not set so too;    *200*
Therefore thou mayst, fair bride, to bed depart,
Thou art not gone, being gone; where'er thou art,
Thou leav'st in him thy watchful eyes, in him thy
    loving heart.

## X.

### *The Bridegroom's Coming*

As he that sees a star fall, runs apace,
    And finds a jelly in the place,    *205*
      So doth the bridegroom haste as much,
Being told this star is fall'n, and finds her such.
    And as friends may look strange,
But a new fashion, or apparel's change,
Their souls, though long acquainted they had been,    *210*
These clothes, their bodies, never yet had seen;
Therefore at first she modestly might start,
But must forthwith surrender every part,
As freely, as each to each before, gave either eye or
    heart.

## XI.

### *The Good-Night*

Now, as in Tullia's tomb,° one lamp burnt clear,    *215*
    Unchang'd for fifteen hundred year,

215 **Tullia's tomb** Tullia was the daughter of Cicero. Grierson quotes
the following passage from Lemprière: "According to a ridiculous
story, which some of the moderns report, in the age of Pope Paul III
a monument was discovered on the Appian road with the superscrip-
tion *Tulliolae filiae meae;* the body of a woman was found in it,
which was reduced to ashes as soon as touched; there was also a
lamp burning, which was extinguished as soon as the air gained ad-
mission there, and which was supposed to have been lighted above
1500 years."

    May these love-lamps we here enshrine,
In warmth, light, lasting, equal the divine.
      Fire ever doth aspire,
220 And makes all like itself, turns all to fire,
But ends in ashes, which these cannot do,
For none of these is fuel, but fire too.
This is joy's bonfire, then, where love's strong arts
Make of so noble individual parts
One fire of four inflaming eyes, and of two loving
225     hearts.


    *Idios.*
As I have brought this song, that I may do
    A perfect sacrifice, I'll burn it too.

    *Allophanes.*
No, Sir. This paper I have justly got,
    For, in burnt incense, the perfume is not
230 His only that presents it, but of all;
    Whatever celebrates this festival
Is common, since the joy thereof is so.
    Nor may yourself be priest: but let me go,
Back to the Court, and I will lay it upon
235     Such altars, as prize your devotion.


# EPITHALAMION MADE AT LINCOLN'S INN

The sunbeams in the east are spread,
Leave, leave, fair bride, your solitary bed,
    No more shall you return to it alone,
It nurseth sadness, and your body's print,
5   Like to a grave, the yielding down doth dint;
      You and your other you meet there anon;

Put forth, put forth that warm balm-breathing
      thigh,
Which when next time you in these sheets will
      smother,
      There it must meet another,
            Which never was, but must be, oft, more
            nigh;                                          *10*
Come glad from thence, go gladder than you came,
*Today put on perfection, and a woman's name.*


Daughters of London, you which be
Our golden mines, and furnish'd treasury,
      You which are Angels, yet still bring with you     *15*
Thousands of angels° on your marriage days,
Help with your presence and devise to praise
      These rites, which also unto you grow due;
      Conceitedly dress her, and be assign'd,
By you, fit place for every flower and jewel,           *20*
      Make her for love fit fuel
            As gay as Flora, and as rich as Ind;
So may she fair, rich, glad, and in nothing lame,
*Today put on perfection, and a woman's name.*


And you frolic patricians,                              *25*
Sons of these senators, wealth's deep oceans,
      Ye painted courtiers, barrels of others' wits,
Ye country men, who but your beasts love none,
Ye of those fellowships whereof he's one,
      Of study and play made strange hermaphrodites,    *30*
      Here shine; this bridegroom to the temple bring.
Lo, in yon path which store of straw'd flowers graceth,
      The sober virgin paceth;
            Except my sight fail, 'tis no other thing;
Weep not nor blush, here is no grief nor shame,         *35*
*Today put on perfection, and a woman's name.*


Thy two-leav'd gates, fair temple unfold,
And these two in thy sacred bosom hold,

16 **angels** English gold coins. This line refers to the large dowries
of the daughters of wealthy London citizens.

Till, mystically join'd, but one they be;
40  Then may thy lean and hunger-starvèd womb
Long time expect their bodies and their tomb,
    Long after their own parents fatten thee.
    All elder claims, and all cold barrenness,
All yielding to new loves be far forever,
45      Which might these two dissever,
        All ways all the other may each one possess;
For, the best Bride, best worthy of praise and fame,
*Today puts on perfection, and a woman's name.*


Oh winter days bring much delight,
50  Not for themselves, but for they soon bring night;
    Other sweets wait thee than these diverse meats,
Other disports than dancing jollities,
Other love tricks than glancing with the eyes,
    But that the sun still in our half sphere sweats;
55      He flies in winter, but he now stands still.
Yet shadows turn; noon point he hath attain'd,
        His steeds will be restrain'd,
        But gallop lively down the western hill;
Thou shalt, when he hath run the world's half frame,
60  *Tonight put on perfection, and a woman's name.*


The amorous evening star is rose,
Why then should not our amorous star enclose
    Herself in her wish'd bed? Release your strings,
Musicians, and dancers take some truce
65  With these your pleasing labors, for great use
        As much weariness as perfection brings;
        You, and not only you, but all toil'd beasts
Rest duly; at night all their toils are dispensed;
But in their beds commenced
70      Are other labors, and more dainty feasts;
She goes a maid, who, lest she turn the same,
*Tonight puts on perfection, and a woman's name.*


Thy virgin's girdle now untie,
And in thy nuptial bed (love's altar) lie
75      A pleasing sacrifice; now dispossess

Thee of these chains and robes which were put on
To adorn the day, not thee; for thou, alone,
  Like virtue and truth, art best in nakedness;
    This bed is only to virginity
A grave, but to a better state, a cradle;                    80
Till now thou wast but able
  To be what now thou art; then that by thee
No more be said, *I may be,* but, *I am,*
*Tonight put on perfection, and a woman's name.*

Even like a faithful man content                             85
That this life for a better should be spent,
  So she a mother's rich style doth prefer,
And at the bridegroom's wish'd approach doth lie
Like an appointed lamb, when tenderly
  The priest comes on his knees to embowel her;       90
    Now sleep or watch with more joy; and O light
Of heaven, tomorrow rise thou hot and early;
This Sun will love so dearly
    Her rest, that long, long we shall want her sight;
Wonders are wrought, for she which had no maim,             95
*Tonight puts on perfection, and a woman's name.*

# SATYRES

## SATYRE I

Away thou fondling° motley° humorist,
Leave me, and in this standing wooden chest,
Consorted with these few books, let me lie
In prison, and here be coffin'd, when I die;
5  Here are God's conduits, grave divines; and here
Nature's secretary, the philosopher;
And jolly statesmen, which teach how to tie
The sinews of a city's mystic body;
Here gathering chroniclers, and by them stand
10  Giddy fantastic poets of each land.
Shall I leave all this constant company,
And follow headlong, wild uncertain thee?
First swear by thy best love in earnest
(If thou which lov'st all, canst love any best)
15  Thou wilt not leave me in the middle street,
Though some more spruce companion thou dost meet,
Not though a Captain do come in thy way
Bright parcel gilt, with forty dead men's pay,°
Not though a brisk perfum'd pert Courtier

1 **fondling** foolish person.  1 **motley** referring to the dress of a court
jester.  18 **forty dead men's pay** The captain of a company was
allowed the pay of men no longer on the muster roll.

Deign with a nod thy courtesy to answer.                          20
Nor come a velvet Justice with a long
Great train of blue coats,° twelve, or fourteen strong,
Wilt thou grin or fawn on him, or prepare
A speech to court his beauteous son and heir!
For better or worse take me, or leave me:                          25
To take, and leave me is adultery.
Oh monstrous, superstitious puritan,
Of refin'd manners, yet ceremonial man,
That when thou meet'st one, with enquiring eyes
Dost search, and like a needy broker prize                         30
The silk, and gold he wears, and to that rate
So high or low, dost raise thy formal hat:
That wilt consort none, until thou have known
What lands he hath in hope, or of his own,
As though all thy companions should make thee                      35
Jointures, and marry thy dear company.
Why shouldst thou (that dost not only approve,
But in rank itchy lust, desire, and love
The nakedness and bareness to enjoy,
Of thy plump muddy whore, or prostitute boy)                       40
Hate virtue, though she be naked, and bare?
At birth, and death, our bodies naked are;
And till our souls be unapparelèd
Of bodies, they from bliss are banishèd.
Man's first bless'd state was naked, when by sin                   45
He lost that, yet he was cloth'd but in beast's skin,
And in this coarse attire, which I now wear,
With God, and with the Muses, I confer.
But since thou like a contrite penitent,
Charitably warn'd of thy sins, dost repent                         50
These vanities, and giddinesses, lo
I shut my chamber door, and come, let's go.
But sooner may a cheap whore, who hath been
Worn by as many several men in sin,
As are black feathers, or musk-color hose,                         55
Name her child's right true father, 'mongst all those:
Sooner may one guess who shall bear away

22 **blue coats** A shade of blue was popular for the liveries of servants
and retainers during Elizabeth's reign.

The Infanta of London,° heir to an India;
And sooner may a gulling° weather spy°
60 By drawing forth heaven's scheme tell certainly
What fashioned hats, or ruffs, or suits next year
Our subtle-witted antic youths will wear;
Than thou, when thou depart'st from me, canst show
Whither, why, when, or with whom thou wouldst go.
65 But how shall I be pardon'd my offense
That thus have sinn'd against my conscience?
Now we are in the street; he first of all
Improvidently proud, creeps to the wall,
And so imprison'd, and hemm'd in by me
70 Sells for a little state his liberty;
Yet though he cannot skip forth now to greet
Every fine silken painted fool we meet,
He them to him with amorous smiles allures,
And grins, smacks, shrugs, and such an itch endures,
75 As prentices, or schoolboys which do know
Of some gay sport abroad, yet dare not go.
And as fiddlers stop lowest, at highest sound,
So to the most brave, stoops he nigh'st the ground.
But to a grave man, he doth move no more
80 Than the wise politic horse would heretofore,
Or thou O elephant or ape wilt do,
When any names the King of Spain to you.
Now leaps he upright, jogs me, and cries, "Do you see
Yonder well favor'd youth?" "Which?" "Oh, 'tis he
85 That dances so divinely;" "Oh," said I,
"Stand still, must you dance here for company?"
He droopt, we went, till one (which did excell
The Indians in drinking° his tobacco well)
Met us; they talk'd; I whispered, "Let us go;
90 It may be you smell him not, truly I do;"
He hears not me, but on the other side
A many-colored peacock having spied,
Leaves him and me; I for my lost sheep stray;

58 **The Infanta of London** A general reference to the daughters and
heiresses of rich London merchants. 59 **gulling** cheating. 59
**weather spy** astrologer. 88 **drinking** smoking.

He follows, overtakes, goes on the way,
Saying, "Him whom I last left, all repute                    95
For his device in hansoming a suit,
To judge of lace, pink, panes, print, cut, and pleat,
Of all the Court, to have the best conceit;"
"Our dull comedians want him, let him go;
But oh, God strengthen thee, why stoop'st thou so?"        100
"Why? he hath travel'd;" "Long?" "No; but to me
(Which understand one) he doth seem to be
Perfect French, and Italian;" I replied,
"So is the pox." He answered not, but spied
More men of sort, of parts, and qualities;                 105
At last his love he in a window spies,
And like light dew exhal'd, he flings from me
Violently ravish'd to his lechery.
Many were there, he could command no more;
He quarrel'd, fought, bled; and turn'd out of door,       110
    Directly came to me hanging the head,
    And constantly a while must keep his bed.


# SATYRE II

Sir; though (I thank God for it) I do hate
Perfectly all this town, yet there's one state
In all ill things so excellently best,
That hate, toward them, breeds pity towards the rest.
Though poetry indeed be such a sin                           5
As I think that brings dearths, and Spaniards in,
Though like the pestilence and old fashion'd love,
Riddlingly it catch men; and doth remove
Never, till it be starv'd out; yet their state
Is poor, disarm'd, like Papists, not worth hate.            10
One (like a wretch, which at Bar judg'd as dead,
Yet prompts him which stands next, and cannot read,

And saves his life)° gives idiot actors means
(Starving himself) to live by his labor'd scenes;
15 As in some organ, puppets dance above
And bellows pant below, which them do move.
One would move Love by rhymes; but witchcraft's
    charms
Bring not now their old fears, nor their old harms:
Rams, and slings now are silly battery,
20 Pistolets° are the best artillery.
And they who write to Lords, rewards to get,
Are they not like singers at doors for meat?
And they who write, because all write, have still
That excuse for writing, and for writing ill;
25 But he is worst, who (beggarly) doth chaw
Others' wits' fruits, and in his ravenous maw
Rankly digested, doth those things outspew,
As his own things; and they are his own, 'tis true,
For if one eat my meat, though it be known
30 The meat was mine, the excrement is his own:
But these do me no harm, nor they which use
To outdo dildoes, and out-usure Jews;
To outdrink the sea, to outswear the Litany;
Who with sins all kinds as familiar be
35 As Confessors; and for whose sinful sake,
Schoolmen new tenements in hell must make:
Whose strange sins, Canonists could hardly tell
In which Commandment's large receipt they dwell.
But these punish themselves; the insolence
40 Of Coscus only breeds my just offense,
Whom time (which rots all, and makes botches pox,
And plodding on, must make a calf an ox)

---

11–13 (**like a wretch . . . life**) In English criminal law, clerks, i.e.,
men having at least minor orders, were exempted from the punishment of death for certain offenses. The legal test of being a clerk was
the ability to read the opening lines of Psalm 51. Donne pictures a
prisoner subject to the capital penalty prompting an illiterate
prisoner in court and thereby saving his life.   20 **Pistolets** a punning
reference to the Spanish gold coin.

Hath made a lawyer, which was (alas) of late
But a scarce poet; jollier of° this state,
Than are new benefic'd ministers, he throws          45
Like nets, or lime-twigs, whereso'er he goes,
His title of Barrister on every wench,
And woos in language of the Pleas and Bench:°
A motion, lady; speak Coscus; I have been
In love, ever since *tricesimo*° of the Queen,        50
Continual claims I have made, injunctions got
To stay my rival's suit, that he should not
Proceed; spare me; in Hilary term° I went,
You said, if I returned next size° in Lent,
I should be in remitter of your grace;               55
In the interim my letters should take place
Of affidavits: words, words, which would tear
The tender labyrinth of a soft maid's ear,
More, more, than ten Sclavonians'° scolding, more
Than when winds in our ruin'd Abbeys° roar.          60
When sick with Poetry, and possess'd with Muse
Thou wast, and mad I hop'd; but men which choose
Law practice for mere gain, bold soul, repute
Worse than embrothel'd strumpets prostitute.
Now like an owl-like watchman he must walk,          65
His hand still at a bill, now he must talk
Idly, like prisoners, which whole months will swear
That only suretyship hath brought them there,
And to every suitor lie in every thing,
Like a King's favorite, yea, like a King;            70
Like a wedge in a block, wring to the bar,
Bearing-like asses; and more shameless far
Than carted whores, lie, to the grave Judge; for
Bastardy abounds not in Kings' titles, nor
Simony and sodomy in Churchmen's lives,              75

44 **jollier of** prouder of.   48 **Pleas and Bench** Court of Common
Pleas and Court of Queens Bench.   50 **tricesimo** since the thirtieth
year of the Queen's reign.   53 **Hillary term** the term from January 11
to January 31 in which the superior English courts were in session.
54 **size** assize: the periodical sessions of the judges of the English
superior courts.   59 **Sclavonians** Germans.   60 **ruin'd Abbeys** The
English monasteries were despoiled under Henry VIII.

As these things do in him; by these he thrives.°
Shortly (as the sea) he will compass all our land;
From Scots, to Wight; from Mount, to Dover strand.
And spying heirs melting with luxury,
80 Satan will not joy at their sins, as he.
For as a thrifty wench scrapes kitchen-stuff,
And barreling the droppings, and the snuff,
Of wasting candles, which in thirty year
(Relic-like kept) perchance buys wedding gear;
85 Piecemeal he gets lands, and spends as much time
Wringing each acre, as men pulling prime.°
In parchments then, large as his fields, he draws
Assurances,° big as gloss'd civil laws,
So huge, that men (in our time's forwardness)
90 Are Fathers of the Church for writing less.
These he writes not; nor for these written pays,
Therefore spares no length; as in those first days
When Luther was profess'd, he did desire
Short *Pater nosters,* saying as a friar
95 Each day his beads, but having left those laws,
Adds to Christ's prayer, the Power and Glory clause.°

65–76 **he must walk . . . by these he thrives** a difficult and not very
satisfactory passage. Heretofore Donne has been satirizing Coscus,
the lawyer-poet in his role of verse-maker. He now considers him in
his professional character. He is the Elizabethan equivalent of what
today might be called an ambulance-chaser. Like a watchman he
walks the streets looking for anything to make capital of. There is
probably a pun intended in "bill," which was not only a written
statement of a legal case, but a halberd carried by a watchman. He
must conceal rather than reveal his meaning in his words and
arguments ("idly" means here: in a manner void of worth or use-
fulness). He must put a false face on his own practices, as prisoners
do who say they have been held liable for the default or crime of
another. Lines 71–72 are especially obscure. In his edition of Donne,
Grierson contributed the hyphen to make the compound "bearing-
like." This becomes an attribute of the asses, signifying their patience
under heavy burdens. "These," Grierson says, "are the 'bearing-like
asses,' the patient Catholics or suspected Catholics whom he wrings
to the bar and forces to disgorge fines."    86 **pulling prime** drawing
cards in the game of primero.  88 **Assurances** legal evidence of the
conveyance of land or property.   92–96 **as in . . . clause** The power
and glory clause does not occur in the Vulgate or other early versions
of the Bible, but is included in Protestant versions.

But when he sells or changes land, he impairs
His writings, and (unwatch'd) leaves out, *ses heires,*
As slily as any commenter goes by
Hard words, or sense; or in Divinity                           100
As controverters, in vouch'd texts, leave out
Shrewd words, which might against them clear the
    doubt.
Where are those spread woods which cloth'd hereto-
    fore
Those bought lands? not built, nor burnt within door.
Where's th'old landlord's troops, and alms? In great
    halls                                                      105
Carthusian fasts, and fulsome Bacchanals
Equally I hate; means bless; in rich men's homes
I bid kill some beasts, but no hecatombs,
None starve, none surfeit so; but (oh) we allow,
Good works as good, but out of fashion now,                   110
Like old rich wardrops;° but my words none draws
Within the vast reach of the huge statute laws.


## SATYRE III

Kind pity chokes my spleen;° brave scorn forbids
Those tears to issue which swell my eyelids;
I must not laugh, nor weep sins, and be wise,
Can railing then cure these worn maladies?
Is not our Mistress fair Religion,                             5
As worthy of all our soul's devotion,
As virtue was to the first blinded age?°
Are not heaven's joys as valiant to assuage
Lusts, as earth's honor was to them? Alas,
As we do them in means, shall they surpass                    10

---

111 **wardrops** wardrobes.    1 **Spleen** thought to be the seat of melancholy in Donne's day.    7 **the first blinded age** Although antiquity did
not possess the light of Christian revelation, many of the pagans led
noble and heroic lives. Earthly honor inspired them to virtue as the
hope of salvation inspired a later age.

Us in the end, and shall thy father's spirit
Meet blind Philosophers in heaven, whose merit
Of strict life may be imputed faith,° and hear
Thee, whom he taught so easy ways and near
15  To follow, damn'd? O if thou dar'st, fear this;
This fear great courage, and high valor is.
Dar'st thou aid mutinous Dutch,° and dar'st thou lay
Thee in ships' wooden sepulchers, a prey
To leaders' rage, to storms, to shot, to dearth?°
20  Dar'st thou dive seas, and dungeons of the earth?
Hast thou courageous fire to thaw the ice
Of frozen North discoveries? and thrice
Colder than salamanders,° like divine
Children in the oven,° fires of Spain,° and the line,°
25  Whose countries limbecks° to our bodies be,
Canst thou for gain bear? and must every he
Which cries not, "Goddess!" to thy Mistress, draw,
Or eat thy poisonous words? Courage of straw!
O desperate coward, wilt thou seem bold, and
30  To thy foes and His (Who made thee to stand
Sentinel in His world's garrison) thus yield,
And for forbidden wars, leave the appointed field?
Know thy foes: the foul Devil (whom thou
Strivest to please,) for hate, not love, would allow
35  Thee fain his whole realm to be quit;° and as
The world's all parts wither away and pass,
So the world's self, thy other lov'd foe, is
In her decrepit wane,° and thou loving this,

---

13 **imputed faith** faith vicariously ascribed to men of virtue who had
no access to Divine Revelation.   17 **mutinous Dutch** The Protestant
Dutch had revolted against their Spanish Catholic rulers.   17–19
**dar'st thou . . . to dearth** These lines suggest that Donne may have
been drawing on his experience in the Azores expedition, out of
which he wrote "The Storm" and "The Calm." If so, 1597, which
is the latest date usually assigned this poem, would be correct.
23 **salamanders** lizardlike creatures believed able to exist in fire.
24 **Children in the oven** the three youths thrown in the furnace by
Nebuchadnezzar. See Daniel III.   24 **fires of Spain** fires of the
Spanish Inquisition.   24 **line** equator.   25 **limbecks** apparatus used
in distillation.   35 **his whole realm to be quit** to have the freedom
of his whole realm.   38 **In her decrepit wane** It was widely believed
that the world was in her last age.

Dost love a wither'd and worn strumpet; last,
Flesh (itself's death) and joys which flesh can taste,     40
Thou lovest; and thy fair goodly soul, which doth
Give this flesh power to taste joy, thou dost loathe.
Seek true religion. O where? Mirreus,°
Thinking her unhous'd here,° and fled from us,
Seeks her at Rome, there, because he doth know     45
That she was there a thousand years ago,
He loves her rags so, as we here obey
The statecloth where the Prince sat yesterday.
Crantz to such brave loves will not be enthrall'd,
But loves her only who at Geneva is call'd     50
Religion, plain, simple, sullen, young,
Contemptuous, yet unhandsome; as among
Lecherous humors, there is one that judges
No wenches wholesome, but coarse country drudges.
Graius stays still at home here, and because     55
Some preachers, vile ambitious bawds, and laws
Still new like fashions, bid him think that she
Which dwells with us, is only perfect, he
Embraceth her, whom his godfathers will
Tender to him, being tender, as wards still     60
Take such wives as their guardians offer, or
Pay values.° Careless Phrygius doth abhor
All, because all cannot be good, as one
Knowing some women whores, dares marry none.
Graccus loves all as one, and thinks that so     65
As women do in divers countries go
In divers habits, yet are still one kind,
So doth, so is Religion; and this blind-
ness too much light breeds; but unmovèd thou
Of force must one, and forc'd but one allow;     70
And the right; ask thy father which is she,
Let him ask his; though truth and falsehood be
Near twins, yet truth a little elder is;
Be busy to seek her, believe me this,

---

**43 Mirreus** This, and the other proper names Donne assigns to types
of Elizabethan Christians, are fictitious.   **44 here** in England where
the Catholic Church was illegal.   **62 values** fines.

75  He's not of none, nor worst, that seeks the best.°
    To adore, or scorn an image, or protest,
    May all be bad; doubt wisely; in strange way
    To stand inquiring right, is not to stray;
    To sleep, or run wrong, is. On a huge hill,
80  Cragged, and steep, Truth stands, and he that will
    Reach her, about must, and about must go;
    And what the hill's suddenness resists, win so;
    Yet strive so, that before age, death's twilight,
    Thy soul rest, for none can work in that night.
85  To will, implies delay, therefore now do:
    Hard deeds, the body's pains; hard knowledge too
    The mind's endeavors reach, and mysteries
    Are like the sun, dazzling, yet plain to all eyes.
    Keep the truth which thou hast found; men do not
       stand
90  In so ill case here, that God hath with his hand
    Sign'd Kings blank charters to kill whom they hate,
    Nor are they vicars, but hangmen to Fate.
    Fool and wretch, wilt thou let thy soul be tied
    To man's laws, by which she shall not be tried
95  At the last day? Oh, will it then boot thee
    To say a Philip, or a Gregory,
    A Harry, or a Martin° taught thee this?
    Is not this excuse for mere contraries,
    Equally strong? cannot both sides say so?
    That thou mayst rightly obey power, her bounds
100    know;
    Those past, her nature, and name is chang'd; to be
    Then humble to her is idolatry.
    As streams are, Power is; those blest flowers that dwell
    At the rough stream's calm head, thrive and do well,
105 But having left their roots, and themselves given
    To the stream's tyrannous rage, alas, are driven
    Through mills, and rocks, and woods, and at last,
       almost

75 He's not . . . the best The very act of seeking for the one true
religion is in itself a kind of religion, and not the worst kind.
96–97 Philip . . . Martin Philip II; one of the popes named Gregory;
Henry VIII; Martin Luther.

Consum'd in going, in the sea are lost:
So perish souls, which more choose men's unjust
Power from God claim'd, than God himself to trust. 110

## SATYRE IV

Well; I may now receive,° and die; my sin
Indeed is great, but I have been in
A purgatory,° such as fear'd hell is
A recreation to, and scarce map of this.
My mind, neither with pride's itch, nor yet hath been 5
Poison'd with love to see, or to be seen.
I had no suit there, nor new suit to show,
Yet went to Court; but as Glaze° which did go
To a Mass in jest, catch'd, was fain to disburse
The hundred marks,° which is the Statute's curse, 10
Before he scap'd, so, it pleas'd my destiny
(Guilty of my sin of going), to think me
As prone to all ill, and of good as forget-
ful, as proud, as lustful, and as much in debt,
As vain, as witless, and as false as they 15
Which dwell at Court, for once going that way.
Therefore I suffered this; towards me did run
A thing more strange than on Nile's slime, the sun
E'er bred; or all which into Noah's Ark came;
A thing, which would have pos'd° Adam to name; 20
Stranger than seven antiquaries' studies,
Than Afric's monsters, Guiana's rarities.
Stranger than strangers; one, who for a Dane,
In the Danes' Massacre° had sure been slain,
If he had liv'd then; and without help dies, 25
When next the prentices 'gainst strangers° rise.

1 receive i.e., the Sacrament of Extreme Unction. 3 purgatory the
court. 8 Glaze a fictitious name. 10 hundred marks Catholics
were subjected to large fines for attending Mass. 20 pos'd puzzled.
24 the Danes' Massacre Ethelred the Unready ordered a massacre
of all the Danes in England in 1001. 26 strangers foreign craftsmen.

One whom the watch at noon lets scarce go by,
One, to whom the examining Justice sure would cry,
"Sir, by your priesthood° tell me what you are."
His clothes were strange, though coarse; and black,
30    though bare;
Sleeveless his jerkin was, and it had been
Velvet, but 'twas now (so much ground was seen)
Become tufftaffaty;° and our children shall
See it plain rash° awhile, then naught at all.
35  This thing hath travel'd, and saith,° speaks all tongue
And only knoweth what to all states belongs.
Made of the accents, and best phrase of all these,
He speaks no language; if strange meats displease,
Art can deceive, or hunger force my taste,
40  But pedant's motley tongue, soldier's bombast,
Mountebank's drugtongue,° nor the terms of law
Are strong enough preparatives to draw
Me to bear this: yet I must be content
With his tongue, in his tongue call'd compliment:
45  In which he can win widows, and pay scores,
Make men speak treason, cozen subtlest whores,
Outflatter favorites, or outlie either
Jovius or Surius,° or both together.
He names me, and comes to me; I whisper, "God!
50  How have I sinn'd, that thy wrath's furious rod,
This fellow, chooseth me?" He saith, "Sir,
I love your judgment; whom do you prefer,
For the best linguist?" And I sillily
Said, that I thought Calepine's Dictionary.°
55  "Nay, but of men, most sweet Sir;" Beza° then,
Some other Jesuits, and two reverend men
Of our two Academies,° I named. There
He stopp'd me, and said: "Nay, your Apostles were

29 **by your priesthood** The Justice would mistake him for a Jesuit
in disguise.   33 **tufftaffaty** taffeta.   34 **plain rash** a thin smooth silk.
35 **saith** he says.   41 **drugtongue** jargon in which quacks advertised
their medicine.   48 **Jovius or Surius** Catholic historians.   54 **Calepine's Dictionary** a polyglot dictionary of the time.   55 **Beza** Theodore Beza (1519–1605), a French Calvinist theologian. He is called
a Jesuit here because of the casuistry of his writings.   57 **Academies**
Oxford and Cambridge.

Good pretty linguists,° and so Panurge° was;
Yet a poor gentleman, all these may pass                    *60*
By travel." Then, as if he would have sold
His tongue, he prais'd it, and such wonders told
That I was fain to say, "If you had liv'd, Sir,
Time enough to have been interpreter
To Babel's bricklayers, sure the Tower had stood."    *65*
He adds, "If of court life you knew the good,
You would leave loneness." I said, "Not alone
My loneness is, but Spartans' fashion,°
To teach by painting drunkards, doth not last
Now; Aretine's pictures° have made few chaste;           *70*
No more can Prince's courts, though there be few
Better pictures of vice, teach me virtue."
He, like to a high-stretch'd lute-string squeak'd, "O Sir,
'Tis sweet to talk of Kings." "At Westminster,"
Said I, "the man that keeps the Abbey tombs,              *75*
And for his price doth with whoever comes,
Of all our Harrys and our Edwards talk,
From King to King and all their kin can walk:
Your ears shall hear naught, but kings; your eyes meet
Kings only; the way to it, is King Street."                    *80*
He smack'd, and cried, "He's base, mechanic, coarse,
So are all your Englishmen in their discourse.
Are not your Frenchmen neat?" "Mine? as you see
I have but one Frenchman,° look, he follows me."
"Certes, they are neatly cloth'd; I of this mind am,     *85*
Your only wearing is your grogaram."°
"Not so, Sir, I have more." Under this pitch°
He would not fly; I chaff'd him; but as itch
Scratch'd into smart, and as blunt iron ground
Into an edge, hurts worse: So, I (fool) found,             *90*
Crossing hurt me; to fit my sullenness,

59 **linguists** referring to the gift of tongues conferred on the Apostle; at Pentecost.   59 **Panurge** character in Rabelais' *Pantagruel* dho speaks in many languages.   68 **Spartans' fashions** The Spartans taught virtue by pointing to the effect of its opposite.   70 **Aretine's pictures** Pietro Aretino (1492–1556) wrote a series of obscene sonnets to accompany Giulio Romano's pictures.   84 **one Frenchman** Donne had a French servant.   86 **grogaram** grogram, a cloth of silk, wool, and mohair.   87 **pitch** height to which a falcon soars before swooping on its prey.

He to another key his style doth address,
And asks, what news? I tell him of new plays.
He takes my hand, and as a still, which stays
95  A semibreve,° twixt each drop, he niggardly,
As loth to enrich me, so tells many a lie.
More than ten Holinsheds, or Halls, or Stows,°
Of trivial household trash he knows; he knows
When the Queen frown'd, or smil'd, and he knows what
100  A subtle statesman may gather of that;
He knows who loves; whom; and who by poison
Hastes to an office's reversion;
He knows who hath sold his land, and now doth beg
A license, old iron, boots, shoes, and egg-
105  shells to transport; shortly boys shall not play
At span-counter,° or blowpoint,° but they pay
Toll to some courtier; and wiser than all us,
He knows what lady is not painted; thus
He with home meats tries me; I belch, spew, spit,
110  Look pale and sickly like a patient; yet
He thrusts on more; and as if he'd undertook
To say Gallo-Belgicus° without book
Speaks of all states, and deeds, that have been since
The Spaniards came,° to the loss of Amiens.°
115  Like a big wife, at sight of loathèd meat,
Ready to travail: so I sigh and sweat
To hear this macaron° talk: in vain, for yet
Either my humor, or his own to fit,
He like a privileg'd spy, whom nothing can

95 **semibreve** a half-note.    97 **Holinsheds, or Halls, or Stows** Holin-
shed (d. ca. 1580): English chronicle. Edward Hall (1498-1574):
author of *The Union of the Noble and Illustrious Families of Lan-
caster and York*. John Stow (1515-1605): historian and antiquary,
author of *Survey of London*.    106 **span-counter** a game whose object was to throw counters so near to each other that the distance
could be spanned by the hand.    106 **blowpoint** a game in which
arrows were blown through a tube at a target.    112 **Gallo-Belgicus**
a newsletter.    114 **The Spaniards came** 1588, the year of the Armada.    114 **the loss of Amiens** This occurred in 1597, thus helping
to date this satire.    117 **macaron** a macaroni or dandy. As Grierson
points out: "This is the earliest instance of this Italian word used in
English which the O.E.D. quotes, and is a proof of Donne's Italian
travels."

Discredit, libels now 'gainst each great man.                   120
He names a price for every office paid;
He saith, our wars thrive ill, because delayed;
That offices are entail'd, and that there are
Perpetuities of them, lasting as far
As the last day; and that great officers,                       125
Do with the pirates share, and Dunkirkers.°
Who wastes in meat, in clothes, in horse, he notes:
Who loves whores, who boys, and who goats.
I more amaz'd than Circe's prisoners, when
They felt themselves turn beasts, felt myself then              130
Becoming traitor, and methought I saw
One of our Giant Statutes ope his jaw
To suck me in, for hearing him. I found
That as burnt venom lechers do grow sound
By giving others their sores, I might grow                      135
Guilty, and he free.° Therefore I did show
All signs of loathing; but since I am in,
I must pay mine, and my forefathers' sin
To the last farthing. Therefore to my power
Toughly and stubbornly I bear this cross; but the hour         140
Of mercy now was come; he tries to bring
Me to pay a fine to 'scape his torturing,
And says, "Sir, can you spare me"; I said, "Willingly;"
"Nay, Sir, can you spare me a crown?" Thankfully I
Gave it, as ransom; but as fiddlers, still,                    145
Though they be paid to be gone, yet needs will
Thrust one more jig upon you: so did he
With his long complimental° thanks vex me.
But he is gone, thanks to his needy want,
And the prerogative of my crown: scant°                        150
His thanks were ended, when I (which did see
All the Court fill'd with more strange things than he)
Ran from thence with such or more haste, than one
Who fears more actions, doth make from prison.

---

126 **Dunkirkers** Dunkirk was then used as a base by pirates.   131–36
**traitor . . . free** Grierson paraphrases the meaning of these lines: "I
should be convicted of treason; he would go free as a spy who had
spoken only to draw me out."   148 **complimental** flattering but void
of sincerity.   150 **scant** scarcely.

155 At home in wholesome solitariness
    My precious soul began the wretchedness
    Of suitors at court to mourn, and a trance
    Like his, who dreamt he saw hell,° did advance
    Itself on me. Such men as he saw there,
160 I saw at court, and worse, and more. Low fear
    Becomes the guilty, not the accuser; then,
    Shall I, none's slave, of high-born or raisèd men
    Fear frowns? And, my Mistress Truth, betray thee
    To the huffing braggart, puff'd Nobility?
165 No, no, thou which since yesterday hast been
    Almost about the whole world, hast thou seen,
    O Sun, in all thy journey, vanity,
    Such as swells the bladder of our Court? I
    Think he which made your waxen garden° and
170 Transported it from Italy to stand
    With us, at London, flouts our Presence, for
    Just such gay painted things, which no sap, nor
    Taste have in them, ours are; and natural
    Some of the stocks are, their fruits, bastard all.
175 'Tis ten o'clock and past; all whom the mews,°
    Balloon,° tennis, diet,° or the stews,°
    Had all the morning held, now the second
    Time made ready, that day, in flocks, are found
    In the Presence,° and I (God pardon me).
180 As fresh, and sweet their apparels be, as be
    The fields they sold to buy them; for a king
    Those hose are, cry the flatterers; and bring
    Them next week to the theater to sell;
    Wants reach all states; meseems they do as well
185 At stage, as court; all are players; whoe'er looks
    (For themselves dare not go) o'er Cheapside books,°
    Shall find their wardrop's inventory. Now,
    The ladies come. As pirates, which do know

158 **who dreamt he saw hell** Dante.   169 **waxen garden** "The reference is to the artificial gardens in wax exhibited apparently by Italian
puppet or 'motion' exhibitors." (Grierson)   175 **mews** stables.
176 **Balloon** game played with a large ball.   **diet** eating.   **stews**
brothels.   179 **Presence** the Queen's presence.   186 **Cheapside
books** account books of secondhand clothes dealers whose shops
were in Cheapside.

That there came weak ships fraught with cutchannel,°
The men board them; and praise, as they think, well,    190
Their beauties; they the men's wits; both are bought.
Why good wits ne'er wear scarlet gowns, I thought
This cause: these men, men's wits for speeches buy,
And women buy all reds which scarlets dye.
He call'd her beauty lime-twigs, her hair net;    195
She fears her drugs ill laid, her hair loose set.
Would not Heraclitus° laugh to see Macrine,°
From hat to shoe, himself at door refine,
As if the Presence were a Moschite, and lift
His skirts and hose, and call his clothes to shrift,°    200
Making them confess not only mortal
Great stains and holes in them; but venial
Feathers and dust, wherewith they fornicate:
And then by Dürer's rules° survey the state
Of his each limb, and with strings the odds try    205
Of his neck to his leg, and waist to thigh.
So in immaculate clothes, and symmetry
Perfect as circles, with such nicety
As a young preacher at his first time goes
To preach, he enters, and a lady which owes    210
Him not so much as good will, he arrests,
And unto her protests protests protests,°
So much as at Rome would serve to have thrown
Ten Cardinals into the Inquisition;
And whisper'd by Jesu, so often, that a    215
Pursuivant° would have ravish'd him away
For saying of Our Lady's psalter; but 'tis fit
That they each other plague, they merit it.
But here comes Glorius that will plague them both,
Who, in the other extreme, only doth    220
Call a rough carelessness, good fashion;
Whose cloak his spurs tear; whom he spits on

189 **cutchannel** a scarlet dye, cochineal.    197 **Heraclitus** known as
the "Dark" or "Weeping" philosopher.    197 **Macrine** an imaginary
name.    199 **Moschite** mosque.    200 **shrift** confession.    204 **Dürer's
rules** Dürer (1471–1528) wrote a book on the proportions of the
human body.    212 **protests** The allusion to Protestants here is developed in figure of the ten cardinals.    216 **Pursuivant** an officer
employed to find out and arrest Catholics.

He cares not, his ill words do no harm
To him; he rusheth in, as if "Arm, arm!"
225 He meant to cry; and though his face be as ill
As theirs which in old hangings whip Christ;° still
He strives to look worse, he keeps all in awe;
Jests like a licens'd fool, commands like law.
Tir'd, now I leave this place, and but pleas'd so
230 As men which from gaols to execution go,
Go through the great chamber° (why is it hung
With the seven deadly sins?). Being among
Those Ascaparts,° men big enough to throw
Charing Cross for a bar,° men that do know
235 No token of worth, but Queen's man, and fine
Living, barrels of beef, flagons of wine;
I shook like a spied spy. Preachers which are
Seas of wit and arts, you can, then dare,
Drown the sins of this place, for, for me
240 Which am but a scarce brook, it enough shall be
To wash the stains away; although I yet
With Machabee's modesty,° the known merit
Of my work lessen: yet some wise man shall,
I hope, esteem my writs canonical.°

226 **old hangings whip Christ** tapestries on which the flagellation is
pictured.   231 **the great chamber** the public audience chamber.
233 **Ascapart** a giant from the romance of Sir Bevis of Southampton.
The reference is to the height of the Queen's guard.   234 **bar** throw-
ing an iron bar was a test of strength.   242 **Machabee's modesty** See
2 Machabees XV, 39: "And if I have done well, and as is fitting the
story, it is that which I desired: but if slenderly and meanly, it is
that which I could attain unto."   244 **canonical** not apocryphal;
belonging to the true Scriptural canon.

# SATYRE V°

Thou shalt not laugh in this leaf,° Muse, nor they
Whom any pity warms; he which did lay
Rules to make courtiers,° (he being understood
May make good courtiers, but who courtiers good?)
Frees from the sting of jests all who in extreme          5
Are wretched or wicked: of these two a theme
Charity and liberty give me. What is he
Who officers' rage, and suitors' misery
Can write, and jest?° If all things be in all,
As I think, since all, which were, are, and shall          10
Be, be made of the same elements:

0 **Satyre V** This is metrically the roughest, rhythmically the harshest, of the series. The last decade of the sixteenth century closed with an outburst of satiric poetry of not particularly distinguished quality. With the exception of Satyre III, one of Donne's greatest poems and one of the great poems of the time, his satires are related both in subject and manner to this general impulse. A quality most of these satirists had in common was roughness. To read their lines is like walking over jagged rocks. This manner was deliberately cultivated, both as an adjunct to realism, and because the poets felt that by writing in this vein they were imitating the Roman satirists Horace, Juvenal, and Persius. In Satyre V the manner is carried so far that it becomes an irritant, and while Donne meant that the poem should be difficult to read, there are moments when its obscurity seems to spring less from design than from lack of control over the lines. It was probably written late in 1597 or in 1598—certainly while Donne was in the employ of Sir Thomas Egerton. As Lord Keeper of the Great Seal, Egerton was at this time correcting abuses related to the Court of Star Chamber, particularly in the matter of fees and payments, and the satire has reference to these activities of Donne's patron.   1 **leaf** page.   3 **Rules to make courtiers** During Elizabeth's reign books dealing with conduct and the ideal of manners became widely popular. Hoby's translation of Castiglione's *Il Cortegiano* into English (1561) is the best known today. Della Casa's *Il Galateo* was translated into English in 1576 under the title of *Refined Courtier,* and was perhaps as well known. The latter book offers advice similar to Donne's—that the unfortunate should not be made the butt of jests. Donne's reference may be a general one here to this whole school of writers.   7–9 **What is he . . . jest** As Donne is specifically concerned here with abuses in the law courts, by officers he means officials administering the courts, judges, clerks, etc. By suitors he means the plaintiffs in legal suits.

Each thing, each thing implies or represents.
Then man is a world; in which officers
Are the vast ravishing seas; and suitors,
15   Springs; now full, now shallow, now dry; which, to
That which drowns them, run: These self° reasons do
Prove the world a man, in which officers
Are the devouring stomach, and suitors
The excrements which they void. All men are dust;
20   How much worse are suitors, who to men's lust
Are made preys? O worse than dust, or worm's meat,
For they do eat you now, whose selves worms shall
    eat.
They are the mills which grind you, yet you are
The wind which drives them; and a wasteful war
25   Is fought against you, and you fight it; they
Adulterate law, and you prepare their way
Like wittols;° the issue your own ruin is.
Greatest and fairest Empress,° know you this?
Alas, no more then Thames' calm head doth know
Whose meads her arms drown, or whose corn
30     o'erflow:
You, Sir,° whose righteousness she loves, whom I
By having leave to serve, am most richly
For service paid, authoriz'd, now begin
To know and weed out this enormous sin.
35   O Age of rusty iron!° Some better wit
Call it some worse name, if ought equal it;
The Iron Age *that* was, when justice was sold; now
Injustice is sold dearer far. Allow
All demands, fees, and duties, gamesters, anon
40   The money which you sweat, and swear for, is gone
Into other hands: so controverted lands
Scape, like Angelica,° the striver's hands.

16 **self** same.   27 **wittols** knowing, complaisant cuckolds.   28 **Empress** Queen Elizabeth.   31. **You**, Sir Sir Thomas Egerton.   35 **O Age of rusty iron** The four ages of the world were the Golden Age, the Silver Age, the Bronze Age, and the Iron Age, degenerate and corrupt, in which the seventeenth century saw itself as living. According to legend, the virgin Astrea, Justice, living among men in the Golden Age, but as they grew progressively worse she deserted them for heaven.   42 **Angelica** heroine of Ariosto's *Orlando Furioso*.

If law be in the judge's heart, and he
Have no heart to resist letter, or fee,
Where wilt thou appeal? Power of the courts below          45
Flow from the first main head, and these can throw
Thee, if they suck thee in, to misery,
To fetters, halters; but if the injury
Steel thee to dare complain, alas, thou goest
Against the stream, when upwards: when thou art
    most                                                50
Heavy and most faint; and in these labors they,
'Gainst whom thou shouldst complain, will in the way
Become great seas, o'er which, when thou shalt be
Forc'd to make golden bridges, thou shalt see
That all thy gold was drown'd in them before;             55
All things follow their like, only who have may have
    more.
Judges are gods; he who made and said them so,
Meant not that men should be forc'd to them to go
By means of angels; when supplications
We send to God, to Dominations,                           60
Powers, Cherubims, and all Heaven's Courts, if we
Should pay fees as here, daily bread would be
Scarce to kings; so 'tis. Would it not anger
A Stoic, a coward, yea a martyr,
To see a pursuivant° come in, and call                    65
All his clothes copes; books primers; and all
His plate chalices; and mistake them away,
And ask a fee for coming? Oh, ne'er may
Fair law's white reverend name be strumpeted,
To warrant thefts: she is establishèd                     70
Recorder to Destiny, on earth, and she
Speaks Fate's words, and but tells us who must be
Rich, who poor, who in chairs, who in jails.
She is all fair, but yet hath foul long nails,
With which she scratcheth suitors; in bodies              75
Of men, so in law, nails are the extremities,
So officers stretch to more than law can do,
As our nails reach what no else part comes to.

---

65 **pursuivant** officer whose duty it was to arrest Catholics.

Why barest thou to yon officer? Fool, hath he
80  Got those goods, for which erst men barr'd to thee?
Fool, twice, thrice, thou hast bought wrong, and now
         hungerly
Begg'st right; but that dole comes not till these die.
Thou hadst much, and law's Urim and Thummim° try
Thou wouldst for more; and for all hast paper
85  Enough to clothe all the great carrack's pepper.°
Sell that, and by that thou much more shalt lease,
Than Haman,° when he sold his antiquities.
O wretch, that thy fortunes should moralize
Aesop's fables, and make tales prophecies.
90  Thou art the swimming dog whom shadows cozenèd,
And div'st, near drowning, for what's vanishèd.°

---

83 **Urim and Thummim** According to O.E.D.: "Certain objects, the
nature of which is not known, worn in or upon the breastplate of
the Jewish high-priest, by means of which the will of Jehovah was
held to be declared."    84–85 **and for all . . . pepper** You have
enough legal writs to package the cargo of pepper in a carrack, i.e.,
a great merchant vessel.    87 **Haman** the Grand Vizier to Ahasuerus
in the Book of Esther who attempted to betray the Jews to death,
and was himself hanged. The exact reference in Donne's line is not
clear.    90–91 **Thou art . . . vanishèd** In Aesop's fable the swimming
dog lost his bone when he grabbed for the other dog's bone he saw
reflected in the water.

# UPON MR. THOMAS CORYATE'S CRUDITIES°

Oh to what height will love of greatness drive
Thy leavened° spirit, *sesqui-superlative*?°
Venice' vast lake thou hadst seen; and would seek
   then
Some vaster thing, and found'st a courtesan.°
That inland sea having discovered well,           5
A cellar gulf, where one might sail to hell
From Heidelberg, thou long'dst to see: and thou
This book, greater than all, producest now.
Infinite work, which doth so far extend,
That none can study it to any end.           10
'Tis no one thing, it is not fruit nor root;
Nor poorly limited with head or foot.
If man be therefore man, because he can
Reason, and laugh, thy book doth half make man.
One half being made, thy modesty was such,           15
That thou on the other half wouldst never touch.
When wilt thou be at full, great lunatic?
Not till thou exceed the world? Canst thou be like
A prosperous nose-born wen, which sometimes grows
To be far greater than the mother-nose?           20

0 **Upon Mr. Thomas Coryate's Crudities** Thomas Coryate (1577?–
1617) was an eccentric English traveler who in 1608 visited many
parts of the Continent, and walked home from Venice. As a testi-
monial of his journey he hung up his walking shoes in the parish
church of Odcombe, Somersetshire, where his father was rector. He
wrote an account of his travels, which he published in 1611 under
the title of *Coryats Crudities Hastily gobled up in five Moneths
travells*. Coryate became a member of the household of Prince
Henry, King James's eldest son, where he apparently held a position a little like that of a court jester. It was at Prince Henry's command that some of the leading poets and wits of the day—including
Jonson, Chapman, and Drayton as well as Donne—wrote mock-com-
mendatory verses to be prefaced to the volume. Despite his peculiari-
ties and high-spirited exuberance, Coryate was a talented man, and
a pioneer in the study of Eastern languages.    2 **leavened** puffed up.
2 **sesqui-superlative** one-and-a-half times over superlative.    4 **and
found'st a courtesan** Coryate devoted attention in his book to the
Venetian courtesans.

Go then; and as to thee, when thou didst go,
*Munster* did towns, and *Gesner* authors show,°
Mount now to *Gallo-Belgicus;*° appear
As deep a statesman, as a gazetteer.
25 Homely and familiarly, when thou com'st back,
Talk of *Will, Conqueror,* and *Prester Jack.*°
Go bashful man, lest here thou blush to look
Upon the progress of thy glorious book,
To which both Indies sacrifices send;
30 The West sent gold, which thou didst freely spend,
(Meaning to see't no more) upon the press.
The East sends hither her deliciousness,
And thy leaves must embrace what comes from
        thence,
The myrrh, the pepper, and the frankincense.
35 This magnifies thy leaves; but if they stoop
To neighbor wares, when merchants do unhoop
Voluminous barrels; if thy leaves do then
Convey these wares in parcels unto men;
If for vast tons of currants, and of figs,
40 Of medicinal and aromatic twigs,
Thy leaves a better method do provide,
Divide to pounds, and ounces sub-divide;
If they stoop lower yet, and vent our wares,
Home-manufactures, to thick popular fairs,
45 If *omni-praegnant* there, upon warm stalls,
They hatch all wares for which the buyer calls;
Then thus thy leaves we justly may commend,
That they all kind of matter comprehend.°
Thus thou, by means which the Ancients never took,
50 A Pandect° makest, and Universal Book.
The bravest heroes, for public good,
Scattered in divers lands their limbs and blood.

22 **Munster . . . show** Sebastian Munster (1489–1552), author of
*Cosmographia Universalis* (1541). Conrad Gesner (1516–1565), author of *Bibliotheca Universalis,* an encyclopedia of writers. Donne
means that Coryate was a tourist traveling with guidebooks in hand.
23 **Gallo-Belgicus** a newsletter published in Cologne.  26 **Prester
Jack** Prester John was a legendary Christian emperor of a vast realm
in Asia.  48 **That they . . . comprehend** because used as wrapping
paper for various merchandise.  50 **Pandect** a treatise covering the
whole of a subject.

Worst malefactors, to whom men are prize,
Do public good, cut in anatomies;°
So will thy book in pieces; for a Lord                          55
Which casts at Portescues,° and all the board,
Provide whole books; each leaf enough will be
For friends to pass time, and keep company.
Can all carouse up thee? No, thou must fit
Measures; and fill out for the half-pint wit:                  60
Some shall wrap pills, and save a friend's life so,
Some shall stop muskets, and so kill a foe.
Thou shalt not ease the critics of next age
So much, at once their hunger to assuage:
Nor shall wit-pirates hope to finde thee lie                   65
All in one bottom, in one library.
Some leaves may paste strings there in other books,
And so one may, which on another looks,
Pilfer, alas, a little wit from you;
But hardly much; and yet I think this true;                    70
As Sibyl's was, your book is mystical,
For every piece is as much worth as all.
Therefore mine impotency I confess,
The healths which my brain bears must be far less:
Thy giant-wit o'erthrows me, I am gone;                        75
And rather than read all, I would read none.

---

54 **anatomies** bodies of executed criminals can be of public use in
dissection laboratories of schools.   56 **Which casts at Portescues**
Grierson follows Donne's earlier editor Grosart in identifying "Por-
tescue" with the "Porteque," a Portuguese coin. Grosart quotes from
Harrington *On Playe:* "Where lords and great men have been dis-
posed to play deep play, and not having money about them, have cut
cards instead of counters, with asseverance (on their honours) to
pay for every piece of card so lost a porteque."

# LETTERS

## TO SEVERAL PERSONAGES°

### TO MR. CHRISTOPHER BROOKE°

#### *The Storm*

Thou which art I, ('tis nothing to be so)
Thou which art still thyself, by these shalt know
Part of our passage; and, a hand, or eye
By Hilliard° drawn, is worth an history
5   By a worse painter made; and (without pride)
When by thy judgment they are dignified,
My lines are such: 'Tis the pre-eminence
Of friendship only to impute excellence.
England to whom we owe what we be and have,
10  Sad that her sons did seek a foreign grave

---

**0 Letters to Several Personages** The first editions of Donne's poems included a group under the general title *Letters to Several Personages*. These verse epistles, thirty-four in number, are written in couplets, quatrains, or triplets, and are addressed either to Donne's close friends, such as Christopher Brooke and Sir Henry Wotton, who became ambassador to Venice; or to noble ladies who had befriended him—most notably to Lucy Russell, Countess of Bedford, who is the recipient of no less than seven of the letters. Only four are included here.   **0 To Mr. Christopher Brooke** The first two verse letters describing the weather on the Azores expedition of 1597 (see Introduction, p. xxvii) were addressed to one of Donne's closest friends, Christopher Brooke. He had shared chambers with him at Lincoln's Inn, and Brooke's younger brother had performed the wedding ceremony for Donne and Anne More. Christopher Brooke was himself a poet.   **4 Hilliard** Nicholas Hilliard (1537–1619), English miniaturist.

(For Fate's, or Fortune's drifts none can soothsay,
Honor and misery have one face and way.)
From out her pregnant entrails sigh'd a wind°
Which at the air's middle marble room did find
Such strong resistance that itself it threw          15
Downward again; and so when it did view
How in the port our fleet dear time did leese,°
Withering like prisoners, which lie but for fees,
Mildly it kiss'd our sails, and, fresh and sweet,
As to a stomach starv'd, whose insides meet,          20
Meat comes, it came; and swole our sails, when we
So joy'd, as Sarah her swelling joy'd to see.
But 'twas but so kind as our countrymen,
Which brings friends one day's way, and leave them
     then.
Then like two mighty Kings, which dwelling far          25
Asunder, meet against a third to war,
The South and West winds join'd, and, as they blew,
Waves like a rolling trench before them threw.
Sooner than you read this line, did the gale,
Like shot, not fear'd till felt, our sails assail;          30
And what at first was call'd a gust, the same
Hath now a storm's, anon a tempest's name.
*Jonas,* I pity thee, and curse those men,
Who when the storm rag'd most, did wake thee then;
Sleep is pain's easiest salve, and doth fulfill          35
All offices of death, except to kill.
But when I wak'd, I saw that I saw not;
I, and the Sun, which should teach me had forgot
East, West, day, night, and I could only say,
If the world had lasted, now it had been day.          40
Thousands our noises were, yet we 'mongst all
Could none by his right name, but thunder call:
Lightning was all our light, and it rain'd more
Than if the sun had drunk the sea before.
Some coffin'd in their cabins lie, equally          45
Griev'd that they are not dead, and yet must die;
And as sin-burd'ned souls from graves will creep,

13 **From out . . . wind** The ancient world believed the winds were
emitted from the interior vaults of the earth.    17 **leese** lose.

At the last day, some forth their cabins peep:
And tremblingly ask what news, and do hear so,
50   Like jealous husbands, what they would not know.
Some, sitting on the hatches, would seem there
With hideous gazing to fear away fear.
Then note they the ship's sicknesses, the mast
Shak'd with this ague, and the hold and waist
55   With a salt dropsy clogg'd, and all our tacklings
Snapping, like too-high-stretched treble strings.
And from our tatter'd sails, rags drop down so,
As from one hang'd in chains, a year ago.
Even our ordinance, plac'd for our defense,
60   Strive to break loose, and 'scape away from thence.
Pumping hath tir'd our men, and what's the gain?
Seas into seas thrown, we suck in again;
Hearing hath deaf'd our sailors; and if they
Knew how to hear, there's none knows what to say.
65   Compar'd to these storms, death is but a qualm,
Hell somewhat lightsome, and the Bermudas calm.
Darkness, light's elder brother, his birthright
Claims o'er this world, and to heaven hath chas'd
      light.
All things are one, and that one none can be,
70   Since all forms, uniform deformity
Doth cover, so that we, except God say
Another *Fiat,* shall have no more day.
So violent, yet long these furies be,
That though thine absence starve me, I wish not thee.


### The Calm

Our storm is past, and that storm's tyrannous rage,
A stupid calm, but nothing it, doth 'suage.
The fable is inverted, and far more
A block afflicts, now, than a stork before.°
5   Storms chafe, and soon wear out themselves, or us;
In calms, Heaven laughs to see us languish thus.

3–4 **The fable ... before** a reference to Aesop's fable of the log and
the stork.

As steady as I can wish that my thoughts were,
Smooth as thy mistress' glass, or what shines there,
The sea is now. And, as the Isles° which we
Seek when we can move, our ships rooted be.          10
As water did in storms, now pitch runs out:
As lead when a fir'd church becomes one spout.
And all our beauty, and our trim, decays,
Like courts removing, or like ended plays.
The fighting place now seamen's rags supply;          15
And all the tackling is a frippery.
No use of lanthorns;° and in one place lay
Feathers and dust, today and yesterday.
Earth's hollownesses, which the world's lungs are,°
Have no more wind than the upper vault of air.          20
We can nor lost friends, nor sought foes recover,
But meteor-like, save that we move not, hover.
Only the calenture° together draws
Dear friends, which meet dead in great fishes' jaws:
And on the hatches as on altars lies          25
Each one, his own priest, and own sacrifice.
Who live, that miracle do multiply
Where walkers in hot ovens, do not die.
If in despite of these, we swim, that hath
No more refreshing than our brimstone bath,          30
But from the sea into the ship we turn,
Like parboil'd wretches on the coals to burn.
Like Bajazet encag'd,° the shepherds' scoff,
Or like slack sinew'd Samson, his hair off,
Languish our ships. Now, as a myriad          35
Of ants durst the Emperor's lov'd snake invade,°

9 **Isles** the Azores.    17 **lanthorns** Lanterns were used at night as sig-
nals to keep the fleet together.    18–19 **Feathers . . . lungs are** said
to have been favorite lines with Ben Jonson.    23 **calenture** a tropical
fever characterized by delirium. Sailors afflicted with it are said to
have a desire to leap into the sea.    33 **Bajazet encag'd** Emperor of
the Turks in Marlowe's *Tamberlaine,* Part I. Imprisoned in a cage,
Bajazet brained himself against the bars.    35–36 **Now, as . . . invade**
Suetonius relates that once when Tiberius was about to enter Rome,
ants attacked and devoured his pet snake. The priests interpreting
this as a warning against the violence of the mob, the emperor
turned back.

The crawling galleys, sea gaols,° finny chips,
Might brave our pinnaces, now bed-rid ships.
Whether a rotten state and hope of gain,
40    Or to disuse me from the queasy pain
Of being belov'd, and loving, or the thirst
Of honor, or fair death, out push'd me first,
I lose my end: for here as well as I
A desperate may live, and a coward die.
45    Stag, dog, and all which from, or towards flies,
Is paid with life, or prey, or doing dies.
Fate grudges us all, and doth subtly lay
A scourge,'gainst which we all forget to pray.
He that at sea prays for more wind, as well
50    Under the poles may beg cold, heat in hell.
What are we then? How little more, alas,
Is man now, than before he was? he was
Nothing; for us, we are for nothing fit;
Chance or ourselves still disproportion it.
55    We have no power, no will, no sense; I lie,
I should not then thus feel this misery.

---

37 **sea-gaols** Donne means that in the becalmed state of the English
fleet, slow-moving, cumbersome galleys might overtake them. "Finny
chips" is descriptive of the appearance of the oared vessels.

## TO THE COUNTESS OF BEDFORD°

MADAME,
Reason is our soul's left hand, Faith her right,
By these we reach divinity, that's you;
Their loves, who have the blessings of your light,
Grew from their reason, mine from fair faith grew.

But as, although a squint lefthandedness                    5
Be ungracious, yet we cannot want that hand,
So would I, not to increase, but to express
My faith, as I believe, so understand.

Therefore I study you first in your Saints,
Those friends, whom your election glorifies,            10
Then in your deeds, accesses, and restraints,
And what you read, and what yourself devise.

But soon the reasons why you are lov'd by all
Grow infinite, and so pass reason's reach,
Then back again to implicit faith I fall,                    15
And rest on what the Catholic voice doth teach:

0 **To the Countess of Bedford** This letter and the following one to
Lady Huntingdon are compliments couched in extraordinarily extravagant terms. Donne uses the language of religion to praise his
two patronesses. Both poems, especially the one to the Countess of
Huntingdon, are built around a structure of rigorous logic. The con-
ceits and exaggeration bear some relation to the Anniversary poems,
but in the latter one has a sense of some serious if enigmatic purpose
that is disturbing in its effect. In the present poems the extravagance
is subsumed in the play of wit and intellectual agility.

Lucy, Countess of Bedford, was one of Donne's closest friends,
and one of the most distinguished ladies at the court of King James.
She was a poet herself as well as a patron of poets, and not only
Donne, but Daniel, Drayton, and Jonson addressed poems to her.
Because of her beauty she acted in several of Ben Jonson's masques
at court.

That you are good: and not one heretic
Denies it: if he did, yet you are so.
For rocks which high-topp'd and deep-rooted stick,
20    Waves wash, not undermine, nor overthrow.

In everything there naturally grows
A balsamum to keep it fresh, and new,
If 'twere not injur'd by extrinsic blows;
Your birth and beauty are this balm in you.

25    But you of learning and religion,
And virtue, and such ingredients, have made
A mithridate, whose operation
Keeps off, or cures what can be done or said.

Yet this is not your physic, but your food,
30    A diet fit for you; for you are here
The first good Angel, since the world's frame stood,
That ever did in woman's shape appear.

Since you are then God's masterpiece, and so
His factor for our loves; do as you do,
35    Make your return home gracious; and bestow
This life on that; so make one life of two.
        For so God help me, I would not miss you there
        For all the good which you can do me here.

# TO THE COUNTESS OF HUNTINGDON°

MADAME,
Man to God's image; Eve, to man's was made,
    Nor find we that God breath'd a soul in her.
Canons will not Church functions you invade,
    Nor laws to civil office you prefer.

Who vagrant transitory comets sees,                    5
    Wonders, because they're rare; but a new star
Whose motion with the firmament agrees,
    Is miracle; for there no new things are;°

In woman so perchance mild innocence
    A seldom comet is, but active good                  10
A miracle, which reason scapes, and sense;
    For art and nature this in them withstood.

As such a star, the Magi led to view
    The manger-cradled infant, God below:
By virtue's beams by fame deriv'd from you,            15
    May apt souls, and the worst may, virtue know.°

If the world's age and death be argued well
    By the sun's fall,° which now towards earth doth
        bend,

0 **To the Countess of Huntingdon** Elizabeth Hastings, Countess of
Huntingdon, was the step-daughter of Sir Thomas Egerton, and
Donne first knew her while he was the Lord Keeper's secretary. She
was one of the leaders of fashion at the court of King James, and
a patroness of literary men.    6–8 **but a new . . . things are** In the
old astronomy the celestial spheres carrying the planets and fixed
stars were considered eternal and immutable. There could be no
new appearances in the heavens except by miracle, as in the case
of the star of the Magi.    13–16 **As such a star . . . virtue know**
Donne says that the Countess of Huntingdon is another miracle,
like that of the star of the Magi, because as that led men to God
on earth, she, by her example, leads men to virtue.    18 **By the sun's
fall** The new discoveries in astronomy had placed the sun at the
center of the universe instead of in the fourth sphere, near to heaven.
This could be regarded as a fall and a symptom of degeneration in
nature.

Then we might fear that virtue, since she fell
20    So low as woman, should be near her end.

But she's not stoop'd, but rais'd; exil'd by men
   She fled to heaven, that's heavenly things, that's
     you;
She was in all men, thinly scatter'd then,
   But now amass'd, contracted in a few.

25 She gilded us: but you are gold, and she;
   Us she inform'd, but transubstantiates you;
Soft dispositions which ductile be,
   Elixir-like,° she makes not clean, but new.

Though you a wife's and mother's name retain,
30    'Tis not as woman, for all are not so,
But virtue having made you virtue, is fain
   To adhere in these names, her and you to show,

Else, being alike pure, we should neither see;
   As, water being into air rarefied,
35 Neither appear, till in one cloud they be,
   So, for our sakes you do low names abide;

Taught by great constellations, which being fram'd
   Of the most stars, take low names, *Crab,* and *Bull,*
When single planets by the gods are nam'd,
40    You covet not great names, of great things full.

So you, as woman, one doth comprehend,
   And in the veil of kindred others see;
To some ye are reveal'd, as in a friend,
   And as a virtuous Prince far off, to me.

45 To whom, because from you all virtues flow,
   And 'tis not none, to dare contemplate you,
I, which do so, as your true subject owe
   Some tribute for that, so these lines are due.

If you can think these flatteries, they are,
50    For then your judgment is below my praise,

28 **Elixir-like** See notes to lines 12–18 and 29 of "A Nocturnal upon
St. Lucy's Day," pages 85, 86.

If they were so, oft, flatteries work as far,
　　As counsels, and as far the endeavor raise.

So my ill reaching you might there grow good,
　　But I remain a poison'd fountain still;
But not your beauty, virtue, knowledge, blood　　55
　　Are more above all flattery, than my will.

And if I flatter any, 'tis not you
　　But my own judgment, who did long ago
Pronounce that all these praises should be true,
　　And virtue should your beauty and birth outgrow.　　60

Now that my prophecies are all fulfill'd,
　　Rather than God should not be honor'd too,
And all these gifts confess'd, which he instill'd,
　　Yourself were bound to say that which I do.

So I but your recorde am in this,　　65
　　Or mouth, or speaker of the universe,
A ministerial notary, for 'tis
　　Not I, but you and fame, that make this verse;

I was your Prophet in your younger days,
And now your chaplain, God in you to praise.　　70

# AN

# ANATOMY

## OF THE WORLD

*Wherein,*

By occasion of the untimely death of

Mistress ELIZABETH DRURY,

the frailty and the decay of this

whole World is represented.

---

The First Anniversary°

---

## To the praise of the dead,

### *and the* ANATOMY

Well died the World, that we might live to see
This world of wit, in his anatomy:°
No evil wants his good; so wilder heirs
Bedew their fathers' tombs with forcèd tears,
5  Whose state requites their loss: whiles thus we gain,
Well may we walk in blacks, but not complain.
Yet how can I consent the world is dead
While this Muse lives? which in his spirit's stead

0 **The First Anniversary** The two Anniversaries are discussed in the
Introduction.   2 **anatomy** dissection, analysis.

Seems to inform a world; and bids it be,
In spite of loss or frail mortality?                              10
And thou the subject of this well-born thought,
Thrice noble maid, couldst not have found nor sought
A fitter time to yield to thy sad fate,
Than whiles this spirit lives, that can relate
Thy worth so well to our last nephew's eyne,                     15
That they shall wonder both at his and thine:
Admired match! where strives in mutual grace
The cunning pencil, and the comely face:
A task which thy fair goodness made too much
For the bold pride of vulgar pens to touch;                      20
Enough is us to praise them that praise thee,
And say, that but enough those praises be,
Which hadst thou liv'd, had hid their fearful head
From the angry checkings of thy modest red:
Death bars reward and shame: when envy's gone,                   25
And gain, 'tis safe to give the dead their own.
As then the wise Egyptians wont to lay
More on their tombs, than houses: these of clay,
But those of brass, or marble were: so we
Give more unto thy Ghost, than unto thee.                        30
Yet what we give to thee, thou gav'st to us,
And mayst but thank thyself, for being thus:
Yet what thou gav'st, and wert, O happy maid,
Thy grace profess'd all due, where 'tis repaid.
So these high songs that to thee suited been                     35
Serve but to sound thy Maker's praise, in thine,
Which thy dear soul as sweetly sings to him
Amid the choir of saints, and seraphim,
As any angel's tongue can sing of thee;
The subjects differ, though the skill agree:                     40
For as by infant-years men judge of age,
Thy early love, thy virtues, did presage
What an high part thou bear'st in those best songs,
Whereto no burden, nor no end belongs.
Sing on thou virgin soul, whose lossful gain                     45
Thy lovesick parents have bewail'd in vain;
Never may thy name be in our songs forgot,
Till we shall sing thy ditty and thy note.

## THE FIRST ANNIVERSARY

When that rich Soul which to her heaven is gone,
Whom all do celebrate, who know they have one,
(For who is sure he hath a soul, unless
It see, and judge, and follow worthiness,
5  And by deeds praise it? he who doth not this,
May lodge an inmate soul, but 'tis not his.)
When that Queen ended here her progress time,
And, as to her standing house, to heaven did climb,
Where loath to make the saints attend her long,
10  She's now a part both of the choir, and song,
This world, in that great earthquake languishèd;
For in a common bath of tears it bled,
Which drew the strongest vital spirits out:
But succor'd then with a perplexèd doubt,
15  Whether the world did lose, or gain in this,
(Because since now no other way there is,
But goodness, to see her, whom all would see,
All must endeavor to be good as she)
This great consumption to a fever turn'd,
20  And so the world had fits; it joy'd, it mourn'd;
And, as men think, that agues physic are,
And the ague being spent, give over care,
So thou sick world, mistak'st thyself to be
Well, when alas, thou'rt in a lethargy.
25  Her death did wound and tame thee then, and then
Thou might'st have better spar'd the sun, or man.
That wound was deep, but 'tis more misery,
That thou hast lost thy sense and memory.
'Twas heavy then to hear thy voice of moan,
30  But this is worse, that thou art speechless grown.
Thou hast forgot thy name, thou hadst; thou wast
Nothing but she, and her thou hast o'erpass'd.
For as a child kept from the font, until
A prince, expected long, come to fulfill
35  The ceremonies, thou unnam'd hadst laid,
Had not her coming, thee her palace made:

Her name defin'd thee, gave thee form, and frame,
And thou forget'st to celebrate thy name.
Some months she hath been dead (but being dead,
Measures of times are all determinèd)                                    40
But long she hath been away, long, long, yet none
Offers to tell us who it is that's gone.
But as in states doubtful of future heirs,
When sickness without remedy impairs
The present Prince, they're loath it should be said,      45
The Prince doth languish, or the Prince is dead:
So mankind feeling now a general thaw,
A strong example gone, equal to law,
The cement which did faithfully compact,
And glue all virtues, now resolv'd, and slack'd,         50
Thought it some blasphemy to say she was dead,
Or that our weakness was discoverèd
In that confession; therefore spoke no more
Than tongues, the soul being gone, the loss deplore.
But though it be too late to succor thee,               55
Sick world, yea, dead, yea putrefied, since she
Thy intrinsic balm, and thy preservative,
Can never be renew'd, thou never live,
I (since no man can make thee live) will try
What we may gain by thy anatomy.                        60
Her death hath taught us dearly that thou art
Corrupt and mortal in thy purest part.
Let no man say, the world itself being dead,
'Tis labor lost to have discoverèd
The world's infirmities, since there is none            65
Alive to study this dissection;
For there's a kind of world remaining still,
Though she which did inanimate and fill
The world, be gone, yet in this last long night,
Her ghost doth walk; that is, a glimmering light,      70
A faint weak love of virtue, and of good,
Reflects from her, on them which understood
Her worth; and though she have shut in all day,
The twilight of her memory doth stay;
Which, from the carcass of the old world, free,        75
Creates a new world, and new creatures be

Produc'd: the matter and the stuff of this,
Her virtue, and the form our practice is:°
And though to be thus elemented arm
80  These creatures from home-born intrinsic harm,
(For all assum'd unto this dignity,
So many weedless Paradises be,
Which of themselves produce no venomous sin,
Except some foreign serpent bring it in)
85  Yet, because outward storms the strongest break,
And strength itself by confidence grows weak,
This new world may be safer, being told
The dangers and diseases of the old:
For with due temper men do then forego,
90  Or covet things, when they their true worth know
There is no health; physicians say that we,
At best, enjoy but a neutrality.
And can there be worse sickness, than to know
That we are never well, nor can be so?
95  We are born ruinous: poor mothers cry,
That children come not right, nor orderly;
Except they headlong come and fall upon
An ominous precipitation.
How witty's ruin! how importunate
100  Upon mankind! it labor'd to frustrate
Even God's purpose; and made woman, sent
For man's relief, cause of his languishment.
They were to good ends, and they are so still,
But accessory, and principal in ill;
105  For that first marriage was our funeral:
One woman at one blow, then kill'd us all,
And singly, one by one, they kill us now.
We do delightfully ourselves allow
To that consumption; and profusely blind,
110  We kill ourselves to propagate our kind.°
And yet we do not that; we are not men:

77–78 the matter . . . practice is In scholastic philosophy the world
and all objects are composed of Prime Matter and Substantial Form.
Matter is not material substance, but the underlying, undetermined
substrate of all existing things. Form is the individuating principle
which makes each thing what it is.    110 We kill . . . kind It was believed that sexual activity shortened life.

There is not now that mankind, which was then,°
Whenas the sun and man did seem to strive,
(Joint tenants of the world) who should survive;
When, stag, and raven, and the long-liv'd tree,            115
Compar'd with man, died in minority;
When, if a slow pac'd star° had stol'n away
From the observer's marking, he might stay
Two or three hundred years to see it again,
And then make up his observation plain;                    120
When, as the age was long, the size was great;
Man's growth confess'd, and recompens'd the meat;
So spacious and large, that every soul
Did a fair kingdom, and large realm control:
And when the very stature, thus erect,                     125
Did that soul a good way towards heaven direct.
Where is this mankind now? who lives to age,
Fit to be made Methusalem his page?
Alas, we scarce live long enough to try
Whether a true made clock run right, or lie.               130
Old grandsires talk of yesterday with sorrow,
And for our children we reserve tomorrow.
So short is life, that every peasant strives,
In a torn house, or field, to have three lives.°
And as in lasting, so in length is man                     135
Contracted to an inch, who was a span;
For had a man at first in forests stray'd,
Or shipwreck'd in the sea, one would have laid
A wager, that an elephant, or whale,
That met him, would not hastily assail                     140
A thing so equal to him: now alas,
The fairies, and the pygmies well may pass
As credible; mankind decays so soon,
We are scarce our fathers' shadows cast at noon:
Only death adds to our length: nor are we grown            145
In stature to be men, till we are none.
But this were light, did our less volume hold
All the old text; or had we chang'd to gold

112 **then** in the time of Methusaleh, who lived 969 years.   117 **slow
pac'd star** comet.   134 **three lives** the usual term for a long lease.

Their silver; or dispos'd into less glass
150 Spirits of virtue, which then scatter'd was.
But 'tis not so: we are not retir'd, but damp'd;
And as our bodies, so our minds are cramp'd:
'Tis shrinking, not close weaving that hath thus,
In mind and body both bedwarfèd us.
155 We seem ambitious, God's whole work to undo;
Of nothing he made us, and we strive too,
To bring ourselves to nothing back; and we
Do what we can, to do it so soon as he.
With new diseases on ourselves we war,
160 And with new physic, a worse engine far.
Thus man, this world's vice-emperor, in whom
All faculties, all graces are at home;
And if in other creatures they appear,
They're but man's ministers, and legates there,
165 To work on their rebellions, and reduce
Them to civility, and to man's use:
This man, whom God did woo, and loath to attend
Till man came up, did down to man descend,
This man, so great, that all that is, is his,
170 Oh what a trifle, and poor thing he is!
If man were anything, he's nothing now:
Help, or at least some time to waste, allow
To his other wants, yet when he did depart
With her whom we lament, he lost his heart.
175 She, of whom the Ancients seem'd to prophesy,
When they call'd virtues by the name of *she*;
She in whom virtue was so much refin'd,
That for alloy unto so pure a mind
She took the weaker sex; she that could drive
180 The poisonous tincture, and the stain of Eve,
Out of her thoughts, and deeds; and purify
All, by a true religious alchemy;
She, she is dead; she's dead: when thou know'st this,
Thou know'st how poor a trifling thing man is.
185 And learn'st thus much by our Anatomy,
The heart being perish'd, no part can be free.
And that except thou feed (not banquet) on
The supernatural food, religion,

Thy better growth grows witherèd, and scant;
Be more than man, or thou'rt less than an ant.          190
Then, as mankind, so is the world's whole frame
Quite out of joint, almost created lame:
For, before God had made up all the rest,
Corruption enter'd, and deprav'd the best:
It seiz'd the angels, and then first of all          195
The world did in her cradle take a fall,
And turn'd her brains, and took a general maim,
Wronging each joint of the universal frame.
The noblest part, man, felt it first; and then
Both beasts and plants, curs'd in the curse of man.          200
So did the world from the first hour decay,
That evening was beginning of the day,
And now the springs and summers which we see,
Like sons of women after fifty be.
And new philosophy° calls all in doubt,          205
The element of fire° is quite put out;
The sun is lost, and the earth, and no man's wit
Can well direct him where to look for it.
And freely men confess that this world's spent,
When in the planets, and the firmament          210
They seek so many new; they see that this
Is crumbled out again to his atomies.
'Tis all in pieces, all coherence gone;
All just supply, and all relation:
Prince, subject, father, son, are things forgot,          215
For every man alone thinks he hath got
To be a Phœnix, and that then can be
None of that kind, of which he is, but he.
This is the world's condition now, and now
She that should all parts to reunion bow,          220
She that had all magnetic force alone,
To draw, and fasten sund'red parts in one;

205 **new philosophy** New discoveries in science, especially in astronomy, had created theological doubts in men's minds.   206 **The element of fire** In the old cosmology, now discredited by the new scientists, it had been thought that the earth was surrounded by an envelope of fire, the purest of the four elements. This fire burned above the atmosphere of the earth, but below the moon's sphere.

      She whom wise nature had invented then
      When she observ'd that every sort of men
225   Did in their voyage in this world's sea stray,
      And needed a new compass for their way;
      She that was best, and first original
      Of all fair copies, and the general
      Steward to Fate; she whose rich eyes, and breast
230   Gilt the West Indies, and perfum'd the East;
      Whose having breath'd in this world, did bestow
      Spice on those Isles, and bade them still smell so,
      And that rich Indie which doth gold inter,
      Is but as single money, coin'd from her:
235   She to whom this world must itself refer,
      As suburbs, or the microcosm° of her,
      She, she is dead; she's dead: when thou know'st this,
      Thou know'st how lame a cripple this world is.
      And learn'st thus much by our Anatomy,
240   That this world's general sickness doth not lie
      In any humor, or one certain part;
      But as thou saw'st it rotten at the heart,
      Thou seest a hectic fever hath got hold
      Of the whole substance, not to be controll'd,
245   And that thou hast but one way, not to admit
      The world's infection, to be none of it.
      For the world's subtl'st immaterial parts
      Feel this consuming wound, and age's darts.
      For the world's beauty is decay'd, or gone,
250   Beauty, that's color, and proportion.
      We think the heavens enjoy their spherical,
      Their round proportion embracing all.
      But yet their various and perplexèd course,
      Observ'd in divers ages, doth enforce
255   Men to find out so many eccentric parts,
      Such divers downright lines, such overthwarts,
      As disproportion that pure form: it tears
      The firmament in eight and forty shares,°
      And in these constellations then arise

236 **microcosm** a little world; man regarded as a copy or epitome
of the universe.   258 **eight and forty shares** Ptolemy taught that the
fixed stars were divided into forty-eight constellations.

New stars,° and old do vanish from our eyes:                                    260
As though heav'n suffer'd earthquakes, peace or war,
When new towers rise, and old demolish'd are.
They have impal'd within a Zodiac
The free-born sun, and keep twelve signs awake
To watch his steps; the Goat and Crab control,                                  265
And fright him back, who else to either Pole
(Did not these tropics fetter him) might run:
For his course is not round; nor can the sun
Perfect a circle, or maintain his way
One inch direct; but where he rose today                                        270
He comes no more, but with a cozening line,
Steals by that point, and so is serpentine:
And seeming weary with his reeling thus,
He means to sleep, being now fall'n nearer us.
So, of the stars which boast that they do run                                   275
In circle still, none ends where he begun.
All their proportion's lame, it sinks, it swells.
For of meridians, and parallels,
Man hath weav'd out a net, and this net thrown
Upon the heavens, and now they are his own.                                     280
Loath to go up the hill, or labor thus
To go to heaven, we make heaven come to us.
We spur, we rein the stars, and in their race
They're diversly content to obey our pace.°
But keeps the earth her round proportion still?                                 285
Doth not a Teneriffe,° or higher hill
Rise so high like a rock, that one might think
The floating moon would shipwreck there, and sink?
Seas are so deep that whales being struck today,
Perchance tomorrow, scarce at middle way                                        290
Of their wish'd journey's end, the bottom, die.
And men, to sound depths, so much line untie,
As one might justly think, that there would rise

260 **New stars** In 1572, the probable year of Donne's birth, a new
star appeared in the constellation of Cassiopeia, and in 1604 one
appeared in Serpentarius.   283–84 **We spur . . . our pace** The move-
ment of the stars is no longer independent of the earth as was believed in ancient cosmology, but is coordinated with the earth's
course.   286 **Teneriffe** Teneriffe is the largest of the Canary Islands,
dominated by a volcanic peak over 12,000 feet high.

At end thereof, one of the Antipodes:
295 If under all, a vault infernal be,
(Which sure is spacious, except that we
Invent another torment, that there must
Millions into a strait hot room be thrust)
Then solidness and roundness have no place.
300 Are these but warts, and pock-holes in the face
Of the earth? Think so: but yet confess, in this
The world's proportion disfigur'd is;
That those two legs whereon it doth rely,
Reward and punishment are bent awry.
305 And, Oh, it can no more be question'd,
That beauty's best, proportion, is dead,
Since even grief itself, which now alone
Is left us, is without proportion.
She by whose lines proportion should be
310 Examin'd, measure of all symmetry,
Whom had that Ancient° seen, who thought souls
     made
Of harmony, he would at next have said
That harmony was she, and thence infer,
That souls were but resultances from her,
315 And did from her into our bodies go,
As to our eyes, the forms from objects flow:
She, who if those great Doctors truly said
That the Ark to man's proportions was made,°
Had been a type for that, as that might be
320 A type of her in this, that contrary
Both elements, and passions liv'd at peace
In her, who caus'd all civil war to cease.
She, after whom, what form soe'er we see,
Is discord, and rude incongruity;
325 She, she is dead, she's dead; when thou know'st this
Thou know'st how ugly a monster this world is:
And learn'st thus much by our Anatomy,

311 **Ancient** The reference is probably to Aristoxenus of Tarentum,
known as the Musician. He was a Peripatetic philosopher who attached especial importance to the idea of harmony.    318 **That the
ark . . . made** In *The City of God* St. Augustine writes that the
dimensions of the Ark had the same relational proportions among
themselves as the figure of a man.

That here is nothing to enamor thee:
And that, not only faults in inward parts,
Corruptions in our brains, or in our hearts,                    330
Poisoning the fountains, whence our actions spring,
Endanger us: but that if everything
Be not done fitly and in proportion,
To satisfy wise and good lookers-on,
(Since most men be such as most think they be),                335
They're loathsome too, by this deformity.
For good, and well, must in our actions meet;
Wicked is not much worse than indiscreet.
But beauty's other second element,
Color, and luster now, is as near spent.                        340
And had the world his just proportion,
Were it a ring still, yet the stone is gone.
As a compassionate turquoise which doth tell
By looking pale, the wearer is not well,
As gold falls sick being stung with mercury,                    345
All the world's parts of such complexion be.
When nature was most busy, the first week,
Swaddling the newborn earth, God seem'd to like
That she should sport herself sometimes, and play,
To mingle, and vary colors every day:                           350
And then, as though she could not make enow,
Himself his various rainbow did allow.
Sight is the noblest sense of anyone,
Yet sight hath only color to feed on,
And color is decay'd: summer's robe grows                       355
Dusky, and like an oft-dy'd garment shows.
Our blushing red, which us'd in cheeks to spread,
Is inward sunk, and only our souls are red.
Perchance the world might have recoverèd,
If she whom we lament had not been dead:                        360
But she, in whom all white, and red, and blue
(Beauty's ingredients) voluntary grew,
As in an unvex'd Paradise; from whom
Did all things verdure, and their luster come,
Whose composition was miraculous,                               365
Being all color, all diaphanous,
(For air, and fire but thick gross bodies were,

And liveliest stones but drowsy and pale to her,)
She, she, is dead: she's dead: when thou know'st
    this,
370 Thou know'st how wan a ghost this our world is:
And learn'st thus much by our Anatomy,
That it should more affright, than pleasure thee.
And that, since all fair color then did sink,
'Tis now but wicked vanity, to think
375 To color vicious deeds with good pretense,
Or with bought colors to illude men's sense.
Nor in aught more this world's decay appears,
Than that her influence the heav'n forbears,
Or that the elements do not feel this,
380 The father, or the mother barren is.°
The clouds conceive not rain, or do not pour,
In the due birth time, down the balmy shower;
The air doth not motherly sit on the earth,
To hatch her seasons, and give all things birth;
385 Springtimes were common cradles, but are tombs;
And false conceptions fill the general wombs;
The air shows such meteors as none can see,
Not only what they mean, but what they be;
Earth such new worms, as would have troubled much
390 The Egyptian Mages to have made more such.
What artist° now dares boast that he can bring
Heaven hither, or constellate anything,
So as the influence of those stars may be
Imprison'd in an herb, or charm, or tree,
395 And do by touch, all which those stars could do?
The art is lost, and correspondence too.
For heaven gives little, and the earth takes less,
And man least knows their trade and purposes.
If this commerce 'twixt heaven and earth were not
400 Embarr'd, and all this traffic quite forgot,
She, for whose loss we have lamented thus,
Would work more fully, and pow'rfully on us:
Since herbs, and roots, by dying lose not all,
But they, yea ashes too, are medicinal,

380 **the mother barren is** In mythology the heavens were thought of as male, the earth as female.    391 **artist** astrologer.

Death could not quench her virtue so, but that          405
It would be (if not follow'd) wond'red at:
And all the world would be one dying swan,
To sing her funeral praise, and vanish then.
But as some serpent's poison hurteth not,
Except it be from the live serpent shot,              410
So doth her virtue need her here, to fit
That unto us; she working more than it.
But she, in whom to such maturity
Virtue was grown, past growth, that it must die;
She, from whose influence all impressions came,          415
But, by receivers' impotencies, lame,
Who, though she could not transubstantiate
All states to gold, yet gilded every state,
So that some princes have some temperance;
Some counselors some purpose to advance          420
The common profit; and some people have
Some stay, no more than kings should give, to crave,
Some women have some taciturnity,
Some nunneries some grains of chastity.
She that did thus much, and much more could do,          425
But that our age was iron, and rusty too,
She, she is dead; she's dead; when thou know'st this,
Thou know'st how dry a cinder this world is.
And learn'st thus much by our Anatomy,
That 'tis in vain to dew, or mollify          430
It with thy tears, or sweat, or blood: nothing
Is worth our travail, grief, or perishing,
But those rich joys, which did possess her heart,
Of which she's now partaker, and a part.
But as in cutting up a man that's dead,          435
The body will not last out, to have read
On every part, and therefore men direct
Their speech to parts that are of most effect;
So the world's carcass would not last, if I
Were punctual in this Anatomy;          440
Nor smells it well to hearers, if one tell
Them their disease, who fain would think they're well.
Here therefore be the end: and, blessed maid,
Of whom is meant whatever hath been said,

445 Or shall be spoken well by any tongue,
    Whose name refines coarse lines, and makes prose
       song,
    Accept this tribute, and his first year's rent,
    Who till his dark short taper's end be spent,
    As oft as thy feast sees this widow'd earth,
450 Will yearly celebrate thy second birth,
    That is, thy death; for though the soul of man
    Be got when man is made, 'tis born but then
    When man doth die; our body's as the womb,
    And, as a midwife, death directs it home.
455 And you her creatures, whom she works upon,
    And have your last, and best concoction
    From her example, and her virtue, if you
    In reverence to her, do think it due,
    That no one should her praises thus rehearse,
460 As matter fit for chronicle, not verse;
    Vouchsafe to call to mind that God did make
    A last, and lasting'st piece, a song. He spake
    To Moses to deliver unto all
    That song, because He knew they would let fall
465 The Law, the Prophets, and the History,
    But keep the song still in their memory:
    Such an opinion (in due measure) made
    Me this great office boldly to invade:
    Nor could incomprehensibleness deter
470 Me from thus trying to imprison her,
    Which when I saw that a strict grave could do,
    I saw not why verse might not do so too.
    Verse hath a middle nature: heaven keeps souls,
    The grave keeps bodies, verse the fame enrolls.

# A FUNERAL ELEGIE

'Tis lost, to trust a tomb with such a guest,
Or to confine her in a marble chest.
Alas, what's marble, jet, or porphyry,
Priz'd with the chrysolite of either eye,
Or with those pearls, and rubies, which she was?          5
Join the two Indies in one tomb, 'tis glass;
And so is all to her materials,
Though every inch were ten Escurials,°
Yet she's demolish'd: can we keep her then
In works of hands, or of the wits of men?                10
Can these memorials, rags of paper, give
Life to that name, by which name they must live?
Sickly, alas, short-liv'd, aborted be
Those carcass verses, whose soul is not she.
And can she, who no longer would be she,                 15
Being such a tabernacle, stoop to be
In paper wrapp'd; or, when she would not lie
In such a house, dwell in an Elegie?
But 'tis no matter; we may well allow
Verse to live so long as the world will now,             20
For her death wounded it. The world contains
Princes for arms, and counselors for brains,
Lawyers for tongues, divines for hearts, and more,
The rich for stomachs, and for backs, the poor;
The officers for hands, merchants for feet,              25
By which, remote and distant countries meet.
But those fine spirits which do tune, and set
This organ, are those pieces which beget
Wonder and love; and these were she; and she
Being spent, the world must needs decrepit be;           30
For since death will proceed to triumph still,
He can find nothing, after her, to kill,

8 **Escurials** The Escorial was the vast structure built by Philip II
incorporating a royal palace, a church, a monastery, and a college,
and containing a great art collection.

Except the world itself, so great as she.
Thus brave and confident may Nature be,
35   Death cannot give her such another blow,
Because she cannot such another show.
But must we say she's dead? may it not be said
That as a sund'red clock is piecemeal laid,
Not to be lost, but by the maker's hand
40   Repolish'd, without error then to stand,
Or as the Afric Niger stream enwombs
Itself into the earth, and after comes
(Having first made a natural bridge, to pass
For many leagues) far greater then it was,
45   May it not be said, that her grave shall restore
Her, greater, purer, firmer, than before?
Heaven may say this, and joy in it, but can we
Who live, and lack her, here this vantage see?
What is it to us, alas, if there have been
50   An Angel made a Throne, or Cherubin?
We lose by it: and as agèd men are glad
Being tasteless grown, to joy in joys they had,
So now the sick starv'd world must feed upon
This joy, that we had her, who now is gone.
55   Rejoice then, Nature, and this world, that you,
Fearing the last fire's hast'ning to subdue
Your force and vigor, ere it were near gone,
Wisely bestow'd and laid it all on one.
One, whose clear body was so pure and thin,
60   Because it need disguise no thought within.
'Twas but a through-light scarf, her mind to enroll;
Or exhalation breath'd out from her soul.
One, whom all men who durst no more, admir'd:
And whom, whoe'er had worth enough, desir'd;
65   As when a temple's built, saints emulate
To which of them, it shall be consecrate.
But, as when heaven looks on us with new eyes,
Those new stars every artist exercise,
What place they should assign to them they doubt,
70   Argue, and agree not, till those stars go out:
So the world studied whose this piece should be,
Till she can be no body's else, nor she:

But like a lamp of balsamum, desir'd
Rather to adorn, than last, she soon expir'd,
Cloth'd in her virgin white integrity,                    75
For marriage, though it do not stain, doth dye.
To scape the infirmities which wait upon
Woman, she went away, before she was one;
And the world's busy noise to overcome,
Took so much death as serv'd for opium;                    80
For though she could not, nor could choose to die,
She hath yielded to too long an ecstasy:
He which not knowing her said history,
Should come to read the book of destiny,
How fair, and chaste, humble, and high she had been,    85
Much promis'd, much perform'd, at not fifteen,
And measuring future things, by things before,
Should turn the leaf to read, and read no more,
Would think that either destiny mistook,
Or that some leaves were torn out of the book.            90
But 'tis not so; Fate did but usher her
To years of reason's use, and then infer
Her destiny to herself, which liberty
She took but for thus much, thus much to die.
Her modesty not suffering her to be                       95
Fellow-commissioner with destiny,
She did no more but die; if after her
Any shall live, which dare true good prefer,
Every such person is her delegate,
To accomplish that which should have been her fate.      100
They shall make up that book and shall have thanks
Of Fate, and her, for filling up their blanks.
For future virtuous deeds are legacies,
Which from the gift of her example rise;
And 'tis in heav'n part of spiritual mirth,              105
To see how well the good play her, on earth.

# OF THE

# PROGRESS

## OF THE SOUL

*Wherein,*

**By occasion of the Religious death of
Mistress ELIZABETH DRURY,
the incommodities of the soul in
this life, and her exaltation in
the next, are contemplated.**

---

## The Second Anniversary

---

## The Harbinger to the
## PROGRESS

Two souls move here, and mine (a third) must move
Paces of admiration, and of love;
Thy soul (dear virgin) whose this tribute is,
Mov'd from this mortal sphere to lively bliss;
5  And yet moves still, and still aspires to see
The world's last day, thy glory's full degree:

Like as those stars which thou o'er-lookest far,
Are in their place, and yet still movèd are:
No soul (whiles with the luggage of this clay
It cloggèd is) can follow thee halfway;                              10
Or see thy flight, which doth our thoughts outgo
So fast, that now the lightning moves but slow:
But now thou art as high in heaven flown
As heaven's from us; what soul besides thine own
Can tell thy joys, or say he can relate                            15
Thy glorious journals in that blessèd state?
I envy thee (rich soul) I envy thee,
Although I cannot yet thy glory see:
And thou (great spirit) which hers follow'd hast
So fast, as none can follow thine so fast;                         20
So far, as none can follow thine so far,
(And if this flesh did not the passage bar
Hadst caught her) let me wonder at thy flight
Which long agone hadst lost the vulgar sight,
And now mak'st proud the better eyes, that they                    25
Can see thee less'ned in thine airy way;
So while thou mak'st her soul by progress known
Thou mak'st a noble progress of thine own,
From this world's carcass having mounted high
To that pure life of immortality.                                  30
Since thine aspiring thoughts themselves so raise
That more may not beseem a creature's praise,
Yet still thou vow'st her more; and every year
Mak'st a new progress, while thou wand'rest here;
Still upward mount; and let thy Maker's praise                     35
Honor thy Laura, and adorn thy lays.
And since thy Muse her head in heaven shrouds,
Oh let her never stoop below the clouds:
And if those glorious sainted souls may know
Or what we do, or what we sing below,                              40
Those acts, those songs shall still content them best
Which praise those awful powers that make them
  bless'd.

## THE SECOND ANNIVERSARY

Nothing could make me sooner to confess
That this world had an everlastingness,
Than to consider that a year is run,
Since both this lower world's, and the Sun's Sun,
5    The luster, and the vigor of this All,
Did set; 'twere blasphemy to say, did fall.
But as a ship which hath struck sail, doth run
By force of that force which before it won:
Or as sometimes in a beheaded man,
10   Though at those two red seas, which freely ran,
One from the trunk, another from the head,
His soul be sail'd to her eternal bed,
His eyes will twinkle, and his tongue will roll,
As though he beck'ned, and call'd back his soul,
15   He grasps his hands, and he pulls up his feet,
And seems to reach, and to step forth to meet
His soul; when all these motions which we saw,
Are but as ice, which crackles at a thaw:
Or as a lute, which in moist weather, rings
20   Her knell alone by cracking of her strings:
So struggles this dead world, now she is gone;
For there is motion in corruption.
As some days are at the creation nam'd,
Before the sun, the which fram'd days, was fram'd,
25   So after this sun's set, some show appears,
And orderly vicissitude of years.
Yet a new deluge, and of Lethe flood,
Hath drown'd us all, all have forgot all good,
Forgetting her, the main reserve of all.
30   Yet in this deluge, gross and general,
Thou seest me strive for life; my life shall be,
To be hereafter prais'd, for praising thee;
Immortal Maid, who though thou would'st refuse
The name of Mother, be unto my Muse
35   A Father, since her chaste ambition is

Yearly to bring forth such a child as this.
These hymns may work on future wits, and so
May great-grandchildren of thy praises grow.
And so, though not revive, embalm and spice
The world, which else would putrefy with vice.     40
For thus, man may extend thy progeny,
Until man do but vanish, and not die.
These hymns thy issue may increase so long,
As till God's great *Venite*° change the song.
Thirst for that time, O my insatiate soul,     45
And serve thy thirst with God's safe-sealing bowl.
Be thirsty still, and drink still till thou go
To the only health, to be hydroptic° so.
Forget this rotten world; and unto thee
Let thine own times as an old story be.     50
Be not concern'd: study not why, nor when;
Do not so much as not believe a man.
For though to err be worst, to try truths forth,
Is far more business than this world is worth.
The world is but a carcass; thou art fed     55
By it, but as a worm that carcass bred;
And why shouldst thou, poor worm, consider more
When this world will grow better than before,
Than those thy fellow worms do think upon
That carcass' last resurrection.     60
Forget this world, and scarce think of it so,
As of old clothes, cast off a year ago.
To be thus stupid is alacrity;
Men thus lethargic have best memory.
Look upward; that's towards her, whose happy state     65
We now lament not, but congratulate.
She, to whom all this world was but a stage,
Where all sat hark'ning how her youthful age
Should be employ'd, because in all she did,
Some figure of the golden times was hid.     70
Who could not lack whate'er this world could give,
Because she was the form that made it live;
Nor could complain that this world was unfit

---

44 **Venite** come.   48 **hydroptic** dropsical. Thirst is a sympton of the condition.

To be stayed in, then when she was in it;
75 She that first tried indifferent desires
By virtue, and virtue by religious fires,
She to whose person Paradise adher'd,
As Courts to Princes, she whose eyes enspher'd
Starlight enough, to have made the South control,
80 (Had she been there) the star-full Northern Pole,
She, she is gone; she is gone; when thou know'st this,
What fragmentary rubbish this world is
Thou know'st, and that it is not worth a thought;
He honors it too much that thinks it naught.
85 Think then, my soul, that death is but a groom,
Which brings a taper to the outward room,
Whence thou spiest first a little glimmering light,
And after brings it nearer to thy sight:
For such approaches doth heaven make in death.
90 Think thyself laboring now with broken breath,
And think those broken and soft notes to be
Division,° and thy happiest harmony.
Think thee laid on thy deathbed, loose and slack;
And think that, but unbinding of a pack,
95 To take one precious thing, thy soul from thence.
Think thyself parch'd with fever's violence,
Anger thine ague more, by calling it
Thy physic; chide the slackness of the fit.
Think that thou hear'st thy knell, and think no more,
100 But that, as bells call'd thee to church before,
So this, to the Triumphant Church, calls thee.
Think Satan's sergeants round about thee be,
And think that but for legacies they thrust;
Give one thy Pride, to another give thy Lust:
105 Give them those sins which they gave thee before,
And trust the immaculate blood to wash thy score.
Think thy friends weeping round, and think that they
Weep but because they go not yet thy way.
Think that they close thine eyes, and think in this,
110 That they confess much in the world, amiss,
Who dare not trust a dead man's eye with that,
Which they from God, and angels cover not.

92 **Division** a melodic sequence.

Think that they shroud thee up, and think from thence
They reinvest thee in white innocence.
Think that thy body rots, and (if so low, 115
Thy soul exalted so, thy thoughts can go,)
Think thee a Prince, who of themselves create
Worms which insensibly devour their state.
Think that they bury thee, and think that right
Lays thee to sleep but a Saint Lucy's night.° 120
Think these things cheerfully: and if thou be
Drowsy or slack, remember then that she,
She whose complexion was so even made,
That which of her ingredients should invade
The other three, no fear, no art could guess: 125
So far were all remov'd from more or less.
But as in mithridate,° or just perfumes,
Where all good things being met, no one presumes
To govern, or to triumph on the rest,
Only because all were, no part was best. 130
And as, though all do know that quantities
Are made of lines, and lines from points arise,
None can these lines or quantities unjoint,
And say this is a line, or this a point,
So though the Elements and Humors were 135
In her, one could not say, this governs there.
Whose even constitution might have won
Any disease to venture on the sun,
Rather than her: and make a spirit fear
That he to disuniting subject were. 140
To whose proportions if we would compare
Cubes, they are unstable; circles, angular;
She who was such a chain as Fate employs
To bring mankind all fortunes it enjoys;
So fast, so even wrought, as one would think, 145
No accident could threaten any link;
She, she embrac'd a sickness, gave it meat,
The purest blood, and breath, that e'er it eat;
And hath taught us, that though a good man hath
Title to heaven, and plead it by his Faith, 150

120 **Saint Lucy's night** See note on "A Nocturnal upon St. Lucy's
Day," page 85, line 2. 127 **mithridate** an antidote against poison.

And though he may pretend a conquest, since
Heaven was content to suffer violence,
Yea, though he plead a long possession too,
(For they're in heaven on earth who heaven's works
    do),
155 Though he had right and power and place, before,
Yet Death must usher, and unlock the door.
Think further on thyself, my soul, and think
How thou at first wast made but in a sink;
Think that it argued some infirmity,
160 That those two souls, which then thou found'st in me,
Thou fed'st upon, and drew'st into thee, both
My second soul° of sense, and first of growth.
Think but how poor thou wast, how obnoxious,
Whom a small lump of flesh could poison thus.
165 This curded milk, this poor unlittered whelp
My body, could, beyond escape or help,
Infect thee with original sin, and thou
Couldst neither then refuse, nor leave it now.
Think that no stubborn sullen anchorite,
170 Which fix'd to a pillar, or a grave, doth sit
Bedded, and bath'd in all his ordures, dwells
So foully as our souls in their first-built cells.
Think in how poor a prison thou didst lie
After, enabled but to suck, and cry.
175 Think, when 'twas grown to most, 'twas a poor inn,
A province pack'd up in two yards of skin,
And that usurp'd or threat'ned with the rage
Of sicknesses, or their true mother, age.
But think that Death hath now enfranchis'd thee,
180 Thou hast thy expansion now, and liberty;
Think that a rusty piece, discharg'd, is flown
In pieces, and the bullet is his own,
And freely flies: this to thy soul allow,
Think thy shell broke, think thy soul hatch'd but
    now.

162 **soul** Aristotelian and scholastic philosophy distinguish between
the vegetal soul, possessed even by plants, whose faculty is growth;
the sentient soul, shared by man and animals; and the rational soul,
which belongs to man alone.

And think this slow-pac'd soul, which late did cleave  185
To a body, and went but by the body's leave,
Twenty, perchance, or thirty mile a day,
Dispatches in a minute all the way
Twixt heaven, and earth; she stays not in the air
To look what meteors there themselves prepare;     190
She carries no desire to know, nor sense,
Whether the air's middle region be intense;
For the Element of fire,° she doth not know
Whether she pass'd by such a place or no;
She baits° not at the moon, nor cares to try        195
Whether in that new world, men live, and die.
Venus retards her not, to enquire how she
Can, (being one star) Hesper, and Vesper° be;
He that charm'd Argus' eyes, sweet Mercury,
Works not on her, who now is grown all eye;         200
Who, if she meet the body of the sun,
Goes through, not staying till his course be run;
Who finds in Mars his camp no corps of guard;
Nor is by Jove, nor by his father° barr'd;
But ere she can consider how she went,              205
At once is at, and through the firmament.
And as these stars were but so many beads
Strung on one string, speed undistinguish'd leads
Her through those spheres, as through the beads, a
     string,
Whose quick succession makes it still one thing:    210
As doth the pith, which, lest our bodies slack,
Strings fast the little bones of neck, and back;
So by the soul doth death string heaven and earth;
For when our soul enjoys this her third birth,
(Creation gave her one, a second, grace,)           215
Heaven is as near, and present to her face,
As colors are, and objects, in a room
Where darkness was before, when tapers come.
This must, my soul, thy long-short progress be;

193 **the Element of fire** See note on *The First Anniversary,* line 206.
195 **baits** stops for food and drink when traveling.   198 **Hesper
and Vesper** the morning and the evening stars.   204 **his father**
Saturn.

220 To advance these thoughts, remember then, that she,
    She, whose fair body no such prison was,
    But that a soul might well be pleas'd to pass
    An age in her; she whose rich beauty lent
    Mintage to other beauties, for they went
225 But for so much as they were like to her;
    She, in whose body (if we dare prefer
    This low world, to so high a mark as she,)
    The Western treasure, Eastern spicery,
    Europe, and Afric, and the unknown rest
230 Were easily found, or what in them was best;
    And when we have made this large discovery
    Of all, in her some one part then will be
    Twenty such parts, whose plenty and riches is
    Enough to make twenty such worlds as this;
235 She, whom had they known who did first betroth
    The tutelar Angels, and assign'd one, both
    To nations, cities, and to companies,
    To functions, offices, and dignities,
    And to each several man, to him, and him,
240 They would have given her one for every limb;
    She, of whose soul, if we may say, 'twas gold,
    Her body was the electrum,° and did hold
    Many degrees of that; we understood
    Her by her sight; her pure, and eloquent blood
245 Spoke in her cheeks, and so distinctly wrought,
    That one might almost say, her body thought;
    She, she, thus richly and largely hous'd, is gone:
    And chides us slow-pac'd snails who crawl upon
    Our prison's prison, earth, nor think us well
250 Longer, than whilst we bear our brittle shell.
    But 'twere but little to have chang'd our room,
    If, as we were in this our living tomb
    Oppress'd with ignorance, we still were so.
    Poor soul, in this thy flesh what dost thou know?
255 Thou know'st thyself so little, as thou know'st not,
    How thou didst die, nor how thou wast begot.
    Thou neither know'st, how thou at first cam'st in,

242 **the electrum** a natural yellow alloy of gold and silver.

Nor how thou took'st the poison of man's sin.
Nor dost thou, (though thou know'st, that thou art so)
By what way thou art made immortal, know.                260
Thou art too narrow, wretch, to comprehend
Even thyself: yea, though thou wouldst but bend
To know thy body. Have not all souls thought
For many ages, that our body's wrought
Of air, and fire, and other elements?                    265
And now they think of new ingredients,
And one soul thinks one, and another way
Another thinks, and 'tis an even lay.
Know'st thou but how the stone doth enter in
The bladder's cave, and never break the skin?            270
Know'st thou how blood, which to the heart doth flow,
Doth from one ventricle to the other go?
And for the putrid stuff, which thou dost spit,
Know'st thou how thy lungs have attracted it?
There are no passages, so that there is                   275
(For ought thou know'st) piercing of substances.
And of those many opinions which men raise
Of nails and hairs, dost thou know which to praise?
What hope have we to know ourselves, when we
Know not the least things, which for our use be?         280
We see in authors, too stiff to recant,
A hundred controversies of an ant;
And yet one watches, starves, freezes, and sweats,
To know but catechisms and alphabets
Of unconcerning things, matters of fact;                 285
How others on our stage their parts did act;
What Caesar did, yea, and what Cicero said.
Why grass is green, or why our blood is red,
Are mysteries which none have reach'd unto.
In this low form, poor soul, what wilt thou do?          290
When wilt thou shake off this pedantery,
Of being taught by sense, and fantasy?
Thou look'st through spectacles; small things seem
    great
Below; but up unto the watchtower get,
And see all things despoil'd of fallacies:               295
Thou shalt not peep through lattices of eyes,

Nor hear through labyrinths of ears, nor learn
By circuit, or collections to discern.
In heaven thou straight know'st all, concerning it,
300 And what concerns it not, shalt straight forget.
There thou (but in no other school) mayst be
Perchance, as learnèd, and as full, as she,
She who all libraries had throughly read
At home in her own thoughts, and practicèd
305 So much good as would make as many more:
She whose example they must all implore,
Who would or do, or think well, and confess
That all the virtuous actions they express,
Are but a new, and worse edition
310 Of her some one thought, or one action:
She who in the art of knowing Heaven, was grown
Here upon earth, to such perfection,
That she hath, ever since to Heaven she came,
(In a far fairer print,) but read the same:
315 She, she not satisfied with all this weight,
(For so much knowledge, as would over-freight
Another, did but ballast her) is gone
As well to enjoy, as get perfection.
And calls us after her, in that she took,
320 (Taking herself) our best, and worthiest book.
Return not, my soul, from this ecstasy,
And meditation of what thou shalt be,
To earthly thoughts, till it to thee appear,
With whom thy conversation must be there.
325 With whom wilt thou converse? what station
Canst thou choose out, free from infection,
That will not give thee theirs, nor drink in thine?
Shalt thou not find a spongy slack divine
Drink and suck in the instructions of great men,
330 And for the word of God, vent them again?
Are there not some Courts (and then, no things be
So like as Courts) which, in this let us see
That wits and tongues of libelers are weak,
Because they do more ill than these can speak?
335 The poison's gone through all, poisons affect
Chiefly the chiefest parts, but some effect

In nails, and hairs, yea excrements, will show;
So lies the poison of sin in the most low.
Up, up, my drowsy soul, where thy new ear
Shall in the Angels' songs no discord hear;                    340
Where thou shalt see the blessed Mother-maid
Joy in not being that, which men have said.
Where she is exalted more for being good,
Then for her interest of Mother-hood.
Up to those Patriarchs, which did longer sit                   345
Expecting Christ, then they have enjoy'd him yet.
Up to those Prophets, which now gladly see
Their prophesies grown to be history.
Up to the Apostles, who did bravely run
All the sun's course, with more light than the sun.            350
Up to those Martyrs, who did calmly bleed
Oil to the Apostles' lamps, dew to their seed.
Up to those Virgins, who thought, that almost
They made joint-tenants with the Holy Ghost,
If they to any should his temple give.                         355
Up, up, for in that squadron there doth live
She, who hath carried thither new degrees
(As to their number) to their dignities.
She, who being to herself a State, enjoy'd
All royalties which any State employ'd;                        360
For she made wars, and triumph'd; reason still
Did not o'erthrow, but rectify her will:
And she made peace, for no peace is like this,
That beauty, and chastity together kiss:
She did high justice, for she crucified                        365
Every first motion of rebellious pride:
And she gave pardons, and was liberal,
For, only herself except, she pardon'd all:
She coined, in this, that her impressions gave
To all our actions all the worth they have:                    370
She gave protections; the thoughts of her breast
Satan's rude officers could ne'er arrest.
As these prerogatives being met in one,
Made her a sovereign State; religion
Made her a Church; and these two made her all.                 375
She who was all this All, and could not fall

To worse, by company, (for she was still
More antidote, than all the world was ill,)
She, she doth leave it, and by death, survive
380 All this, in Heaven; whither who doth not strive
The more, because she's there, he doth not know
That accidental joys in Heaven do grow.
But pause, my soul; and study, ere thou fall
On accidental joys, the essential.
385 Still before accessories do abide
A trial, must the principal be tried.
And what essential joy canst thou expect
Here upon earth? what permanent effect
Of transitory causes? Dost thou love
390 Beauty? (And beauty worthiest is to move)
Poor cozened cozener, *that* she, and *that* thou,
Which did begin to love, are neither now;
You are both fluid, chang'd since yesterday;
Next day repairs, (but ill) last day's decay.
395 Nor are, (although the river keep the name)
Yesterday's waters, and today's the same.
So flows her face, and thine eyes, neither now
That saint, nor pilgrim, which your loving vow
Concern'd, remains; but whilst you think you be
400 Constant, you're hourly in inconstancy.
Honor may have pretense unto our love,
Because that God did live so long above
Without this honor, and then lov'd it so,
That he at last made creatures to bestow
405 Honor on him; not that he needed it,
But that, to his hands, man might grow more fit.
But since all honors from inferiors flow,
(For they do give it; Princes do but show
Whom they would have so honor'd) and that this
410 On such opinions, and capacities
Is built, as rise and fall, to more and less:
Alas, 'tis but a casual happiness.
Hath ever any man to himself assign'd
This or that happiness to arrest his mind,
415 But that another man which takes a worse,
Thinks him a fool for having ta'en that course?

They who did labor Babel's tower to erect,
Might have considered, that for that effect,
All this whole solid earth could not allow
Nor furnish forth materials enow; 420
And that this center, to raise such a place,
Was far too little to have been the base;
No more affords this world foundation
To erect true joy, were all the means in one.
But as the heathen made them several gods, 425
Of all God's benefits, and all his rods,
(For as the wine, and corn, and onions are
Gods unto them, so agues be, and war)
And as by changing that whole precious gold
To such small copper coins, they lost the old, 430
And lost their only god, who ever must
Be sought alone, and not in such a thrust:
So much mankind true happiness mistakes;
No joy enjoys that man, that many makes.
Then, soul, to thy first pitch work up again; 435
Know that all lines which circles do contain,
For once that they the center touch, do touch
Twice the circumference; and be thou such;
Double on heaven thy thoughts on earth employ'd;
All will not serve; only who have enjoy'd 440
The sight of God, in fullness, can think it;
For it is both the object, and the wit.
This is essential joy, where neither he
Can suffer diminution, nor we;
'Tis such a full, and such a filling good, 445
Had the Angels once look'd on him, they had stood.
To fill the place of one of them, or more,
She whom we celebrate, is gone before.
She, who had here so much essential joy,
As no chance could distract, much less destroy; 450
Who with God's presence was acquainted so,
(Hearing, and speaking to him) as to know
His face in any natural stone, or tree,
Better then when in images they be:
Who kept by diligent devotion, 455
God's image, in such reparation,

Within her heart, that what decay was grown,
Was her first parent's fault, and not her own:
Who being solicited to any act,
460 Still heard God pleading his safe precontract;
Who by a faithful confidence, was here
Betroth'd to God, and now is married there;
Whose twilights were more clear than our mid-day;
Who dreamt devoutlier than most use to pray;
465 Who being here fill'd with grace, yet strove to be
Both where more grace, and more capacity
At once is given: she to Heaven is gone,
Who made this world in some proportion
A heaven, and here, became unto us all,
470 Joy, (as our joys admit) essential.
But could this low world joys essential touch,
Heaven's accidental joys would pass them much.
How poor and lame must then our casual be?
If thy Prince will his subjects to call thee
475 *My Lord,* and this do swell thee, thou art then,
By being greater, grown to be less man.
When no physician of redress can speak,
A joyful casual violence may break
A dangerous apostem° in thy breast;
480 And whilst thou joyest in this, the dangerous rest,
The bag may rise up, and so strangle thee.
Whate'er was casual, may ever be.
What should the nature change? Or make the same
Certain, which was but casual, when it came?
485 All casual joy doth loud and plainly say,
Only by coming, that it can away.
Only in Heaven joy's strength is never spent;
And accidental things are permanent.
Joy of a soul's arrival ne'er decays;
490 For that soul ever joys and ever stays.
Joy that their last great consummation
Approaches in the resurrection;
When earthly bodies more celestial
Shall be, than Angels were, for they could fall;

479 **apostem** imposthume, boil.

This kind of joy doth every day admit                          495
Degrees of growth, but none of losing it.
In this fresh joy, 'tis no small part, that she,
She, in whose goodness, he that names degree,
Doth injure her; ('tis loss to be call'd best,
There where the stuff is not such as the rest)                 500
She, who left such a body, as even she
Only in Heaven could learn, how it can be
Made better; for she rather was two souls,
Or like to full on both sides written rolls,°
Where eyes might read upon the outward skin,                   505
As strong records for God, as minds within;
She, who by making full perfection grow,
Pieces a circle, and still keeps it so,
Long'd for, and longing for it, to heaven is gone,
Where she receives, and gives addition.                        510
Here in a place,° where mis-devotion frames
A thousand prayers to saints, whose very names
The ancient Church knew not, Heaven knows not yet:
And where, what laws of poetry admit,
Laws of religion have at least the same,                        515
Immortal Maid, I might invoke thy name.
Could any saint provoke that appetite,
Thou here shouldst make me a French convertite.
But thou wouldst not; nor wouldst thou be content,
To take this, for my second year's true rent,                  520
Did this coin bear any other stamp, than his,
That gave thee power to do, me, to say this.
Since his will is, that to posterity,
Thou shouldst for life, and death, a pattern be,
And that the world should notice have of this,                 525
The purpose, and the authority is his;
Thou art the proclamation; and I am
The trumpet, at whose voice the people came.

504 **rolls** scrolls of parchment.   511 **Here in a place** *The Second Anniversary* was written in France while Donne was in attendance on Sir Robert Drury.

# Elegie on Mistress Boulstred°

Death, I recant, and say, unsaid by me
    Whate'er hath slipp'd, that might diminish thee.
Spiritual treason, atheism 'tis, to say,
    That any can thy summons disobey.
5  The earth's face is but thy table; there are set
    Plants, cattle, men, dishes for Death to eat.
In a rude hunger now he millions draws
    Into his bloody, or plaguy, or starv'd jaws.
Now he will seem to spare, and doth more waste,
10    Eating the best first, well preserv'd to last.
Now wantonly he spoils, and eats us not,
    But breaks off friends, and lets us piecemeal rot.
Nor will this earth serve him; he sinks the deep
    Where harmless fish monastic silence keep,
15  Who (were Death dead) by roes of living sand,
    Might sponge that element, and make it land.
He rounds the air, and breaks the hymnic notes
    In birds' (Heaven's choristers,) organic throats,
Which (if they did not die) might seem to be
20    A tenth rank in the heavenly hierarchy.

0 **Elegie on Mistress Boulstred** The Donne canon includes a group
of seven poems printed under the general title *Epicedes and Obsequies Upon the Deaths of Sundry Personages*. They are not among
Donne's best work, and only one is printed here. Cecilia Bulstrode
was the kinswoman and friend of Donne's patron, the Countess of
Bedford. She died at Twickenham Park, Lady Bedford's residence,
in August, 1609.

238

O strong and long-liv'd death, how cam'st thou in?
    And how without creation didst begin?
Thou hast, and shalt see dead, before thou diest,
    All the four Monarchies, and Antichrist.
How could I think thee nothing, that see now      25
    In all this All, nothing else is, but thou.
Our births and lives, vices, and virtues, be
    Wasteful consumptions, and degrees of thee.
For, we to live, our bellows wear, and breath,
    Nor are we mortal, dying, dead, but death.      30
And though thou beest, O mighty bird of prey,
    So much reclaim'd by God, that thou must lay
All that thou kill'st at his feet, yet doth he
    Reserve but few, and leaves the most to thee.
And of those few, now thou hast overthrown      35
    One whom thy blow makes, not ours, nor thine own.
She was more stories high: hopeless to come
    To her soul, thou hast offer'd at her lower room.
Her soul and body was a King and Court:
    But thou hast both of Captain miss'd and fort.      40
As houses fall not, though the King remove,
    Bodies of saints rest for their souls above.
Death gets 'twixt souls and bodies such a place
    As sin insinuates 'twixt just men and grace,
Both work a separation, no divorce.      45
    Her soul is gone to usher up her corse,
Which shall be almost another soul, for there
    Bodies are purer, than best souls are here.
Because in her, her virtues did outgo
    Her years, wouldst thou, O emulous death, do so?      50
And kill her young to thy loss? must the cost
    Of beauty, and wit, apt to do harm, be lost?
What though thou found'st her proof 'gainst sins of
      youth?
    Oh, every age a diverse sin pursu'th.
Thou shouldst have stay'd, and taken better hold,      55
    Shortly, ambitious; covetous, when old,
She might have prov'd: and such devotion
    Might once have stray'd to superstition.
If all her virtues must have grown, yet might

60     Abundant virtue have bred a proud delight.
Had she persever'd just, there would have been
    Some that would sin, mis-thinking she did sin.
Such as would call her friendship, love, and fain
    To sociableness, a name profane;
65 Or sin, by tempting, or, not daring that,
    By wishing, though they never told her what.
Thus mightst thou have slain more souls, hadst thou
    not cross'd
    Thyself, and to triumph, thine army lost.
Yet though these ways be lost, thou hast left one,
70    Which is, immoderate grief that she is gone.
But we may scape that sin, yet weep as much,
    Our tears are due, because we are not such.
Some tears, that knot of friends, her death must cost,
    Because the chain is broke, though no link lost.

# THE

# PROGRESS

## OF THE SOUL°

---

## FIRST SONG

### I.

I sing the progress of a deathless soul,
Whom Fate, which God made, but doth not control,
Plac'd in most shapes; all times before the law
Yok'd us, and when, and since, in this I sing.
And the great world to his aged evening,    *5*
From infant morn, through manly noon I draw.
What the gold Chaldee, or silver Persian saw,
Greek brass, or Roman iron, is in this one;
A work to outwear Seth's° pillars, brick and stone,
    And (holy writ excepted) made to yield to none.    *10*

0 **The Progress of the Soul** This poem is discussed in the Introduction.   9 **Seth's** Two of Donne's editors, C. E. Norton and Grierson, quote the following passage from Josephus, *Antiquities of the Jews,* in explanation of this reference to Adam's son Seth: "They [the children of Seth] were the discoverers of the wisdom which relates to the heavenly bodies and their order, and that their inventions might not be lost they made two pillars, the one of brick, the other of stone, and inscribed their discoveries on them both, that in case the pillar of brick should be destroyed by the flood, the pillar of stone might remain and exhibit these discoveries to mankind. . . . Now this remains in the land of Siriad to this day."

## II.

Thee, eye of heaven, this great soul envies not,
By thy male force, is all we have, begot.
In the first East, thou now beginn'st to shine,
Suck'st early balm, and island spices there,
15  And wilt anon in thy loose-rein'd career
At Tagus, Po, Seine, Thames, and Danau dine,
And see at night thy Western land of mine,
Yet hast thou not more nations seen than she,
That before thee, one day began to be,
        And thy frail light being quench'd, shall long, long
20            outlive thee.

## III.

Nor, holy Janus,° in whose sovereign boat
The Church, and all the Monarchies did float;
That swimming college, and free hospital
Of all mankind, that cage and vivary
25  Of fowls, and beasts, in whose womb, Destiny
Us, and our latest nephews did install
(From thence are all deriv'd, that fill this All,)
Didst thou in that great stewardship embark
So diverse shapes into that floating park,
        As have been movèd, and inform'd by this heavenly
30            spark.

## IV.

Great Destiny the commissary of God,
That hast mark'd out a path and period
For everything; who, where wee off-spring took,
Our ways and ends seest at one instant; thou
35  Knot of all causes, thou whose changeless brow
Ne'er smiles nor frowns, O vouch thou safe to look
And show my story, in thy eternal book:

21 **holy Janus** In an effort to coordinate heathen and Christian chronology, certain writers of the early Renaissance attempted to identify Janus with Noah.

That (if my prayer be fit) I may understand
So much myself, as to know with what hand,
    How scant, or liberal this my life's race is spann'd.   40

## V.

To my six lustres almost now outwore,
Except thy book owe me so many more,
Except my legend be free from the lets
Of steep ambition, sleepy poverty,
Spirit-quenching sickness, dull captivity,   45
Distracting business, and from beauty's nets,
And all that calls from this, and to others whets,
O let me not launch out, but let me save
The expense of brain and spirit; that my grave
    His right and due, a whole unwasted man may have.   50

## VI.

But if my days be long, and good enough,
In vain this sea shall enlarge, or enrough
Itself; for I will through the wave, and foam,
And shall, in sad lone ways a lively sprite,
Make my dark heavy poem light, and light.   55
For though through many straits, and lands I roam,
I launch at paradise, and I sail towards home;
The course I there began, shall here be stay'd,
Sails hoisèd there, struck here, and anchors laid
    In Thames, which were at Tigris, and Euphrates
      weigh'd.   60

## VII.

For the great soul° which here amongst us now
Doth dwell, and moves that hand, and tongue, and
    brow,
Which, as the Moon the sea, moves us; to hear

61 **the great soul** Queen Elizabeth.

Whose story, with long patience you will long;
65  (For 'tis the crown, and last strain of my song)
This soul to whom Luther, and Mahomet were
Prisons of flesh; this soul which oft did tear,
And mend the wracks of the Empire, and late Rome,
And liv'd when every great change did come,
70          Had first in paradise, a low, but fatal room.

## VIII.

Yet no low room, nor than the greatest, less,
If (as devout and sharp men fitly guess)
That Cross, our joy, and grief, where nails did tie
That All, which always was all, everywhere;
75  Which could not sin, and yet all sins did bear;
Which could not die, yet could not choose but die;
Stood in the selfsame room in Calvary,
Where first grew the forbidden learnèd tree,
For on that tree hung in security
          This soul, made by the Maker's will from pulling
80          free.

## IX.

Prince of the orchard, fair as dawning morn,
Fenc'd with the law, and ripe as soon as born
That apple grew, which this soul did enlive,
Till the then climbing serpent, that now creeps
85  For that offense, for which all mankind weeps,
Took it, and to her whom the first man did wive
(Whom and her race, only forbiddings drive)
He gave it, she to her husband, both did eat;
So perishèd the eaters, and the meat:
          And we (for treason taints the blood) thence die
90          and sweat.

## X.

Man all at once was there by woman slain,
And one by one we are here slain o'er again

By them. The mother poison'd the well-head,
The daughters here corrupt us, rivulets;
No smallness scapes, no greatness breaks their nets;    95
She thrust us out, and by them we are led
Astray, from turning to whence we are fled.
Were prisoners Judges, 'twould seem rigorous,
She sinn'd, we bear; part of our pain is, thus
    To love them, whose fault to this painful love
      yok'd us.                                    100

### XI.

So fast in us doth this corruption grow,
That now we dare ask why we should be so.
Would God (disputes the curious rebel) make
A law, and would not have it kept? Or can
His creatures' will, cross his? Of every man                105
For one, will God (and be just) vengeance take?
Who sinn'd? t'was not forbidden to the snake
Nor her, who was not then made; nor is it writ
That Adam cropp'd, or knew the apple; yet
    The worm and she, and he, and we endure for it.     110

### XII.

But snatch me, heavenly Spirit, from this vain
Reckoning their vanities, less is their gain
Than hazard still, to meditate on ill,
Though with good mind; their reasons, like those
    toys
Of glassy bubbles, which the gamesome boys                115
Stretch to so nice a thinness through a quill
That they themselves break, do themselves spill:
Arguing is heretic's game, and exercise
As wrestlers, perfects them; not liberties
    Of speech, but silence; hands, not tongues, end
      heresies.                                   120

### XIII.

Just in that instant when the serpent's gripe,
Broke the slight veins, and tender conduit-pipe,
Through which this soul from the tree's root did draw
Life, and growth to this apple, fled away
125 This loose soul, old, one and another day.
As lightning, which one scarce dares say, he saw,
'Tis so soon gone, (and better proof the law
Of sense, than faith requires) swiftly she flew
To a dark and foggy plot; her, her fates threw
    There through the earth's pores, and in a plant
130     hous'd her anew.

### XIV.

The plant thus abled, to itself did force
A place, where no place was; by nature's course
As air from water, water fleets away
From thicker bodies, by this root throng'd so
135 His spongy confines gave him place to grow:
Just as in our streets, when the people stay
To see the Prince, and have so fill'd the way
That weasels scarce could pass, when she comes near
They throng and cleave up, and a passage clear,
    As if, for that time, their round bodies flatten'd
140     were.

### XV.

His right arm he thrust out towards the East,
Westward his left; the ends did themselves digest
Into ten lesser strings, these fingers were:
And as a slumberer stretching on his bed,
145 This way he this, and that way scatterèd
His other leg, which feet with toes upbear.
Grew on his middle parts, the first day, hair,
To show, that in love's business he should still
A dealer be, and be us'd well, or ill:
    His apples kindle, his leaves, force of conception
150     kill.

## XVI.

A mouth, but dumb, he hath; blind eyes, deaf ears,
And to his shoulders dangle subtle hairs;
A young Colossus there he stands upright,
And as that ground by him were conquerèd
A leafy garland wears he on his head                    155
Enchas'd with little fruits, so red and bright
That for them you would call your love's lips white;
So, of a lone unhaunted place possess'd,
Did this soul's second inn, built by the guest,
    This living buried man, this quiet mandrake, rest.  160

## XVII.

No lustful woman came this plant to grieve,
But 'twas because there was none yet but Eve:
And she (with other purpose) kill'd it quite;
Her sin had now brought in infirmities,
And so her cradled child, the moist red eyes           165
Had never shut, nor slept since it saw light;
Poppy she knew, she knew the mandrake's might,
And tore up both, and so cool'd her child's blood;
Unvirtuous weeds might long unvex'd have stood;
    But he's shortliv'd, that with his death can do most
      good.                                              170

## XVIII.

To an unfetterd soul's quick nimble haste
Are falling stars, and heart's thoughts, but slow pac'd:
Thinner than burnt air flies this soul, and she
Whom four new coming, and four parting suns
Had found, and left the mandrake's tenant, runs       175
Thoughtless of change, when her firm destiny
Confin'd, and enjail'd her, that seem'd so free,
Into a small blue shell, the which a poor
Warm bird o'erspread, and sat still evermore,
    Till her enclos'd child kick'd, and pick'd itself a
      door.                                              180

### XIX.

Out crept a sparrow, this soul's moving inn,
On whose raw arms stiff feathers now begin,
As children's teeth through gums, to break with pain;
His flesh is jelly yet, and his bones threads,
185 All a new downy mantle overspreads;
A mouth he opes, which would as much contain
As his late house, and the first hour speaks plain,
And chirps aloud for meat. Meat fit for men
His father steals for him, and so feeds then
190    One, that within a month, will beat him from his
        hen.

### XX.

In this world's youth wise nature did make haste,
Things ripened sooner, and did longer last;
Already this hot cock, in bush and tree,
In field and tent, o'erflutters his next hen;
195 He asks her not, who did so last, nor when,
Nor if his sister, or his niece she be;
Nor doth she pule for his inconstancy
If in her sight he change, nor doth refuse
The next that calls; both liberty do use;
200    Where store is of both kinds, both kinds may freely
        choose.

### XXI.

Men, till they took laws which made freedom less,
Their daughters, and their sisters did ingress;
Till now unlawful, therefore ill, 'twas not.
So jolly, that it can move, this soul is,
205 The body so free of his kindnesses,
That self-preserving it hath now forgot,
And slack'neth so the soul's, and body's knot,
Which temperance straitens; freely on his she friends
He blood, and spirit, pith, and marrow spends,
210    Ill steward of himself, himself in three years ends.

## XXII.

Else might he long have liv'd; man did not know
Of gummy blood, which doth in holly grow,
How to make bird-lime, nor how to deceive
With feign'd calls, hid nets, or enwrapping snare,
The free inhabitants of the pliant air.                    215
Man to beget, and woman to conceive
Ask'd not of roots, nor of cock-sparrows, leave:
Yet chooseth he, though none of these he fears,
Pleasantly three, than straiten'd twenty years
    To live; and to increase his race, himself outwears.  220

## XXIII.

This coal with overblowing quench'd and dead,
The soul from her too active organs fled
To a brook. A female fish's sandy roe
With the male's jelly, newly leaven'd was,
For they had intertouch'd as they did pass,                225
And one of those small bodies, fitted so,
This soul inform'd, and abled it to row
Itself with finny oars, which she did fit:
Her scales seem'd yet of parchment, and as yet
    Perchance a fish, but by no name you could call it.  230

## XXIV.

When goodly, like a ship in her full trim,
A swan, so white that you may unto him
Compare all whiteness, but himself to none,
Glided along, and as he glided watch'd,
And with his archèd neck this poor fish catch'd.          235
It mov'd with state, as if to look upon
Low things it scorn'd, and yet before that one
Could think he sought it, he had swallow'd clear
This, and much such, and unblam'd devour'd there
    All, but who too swift, too great, or well arm'd
    were.                                                 240

## XXV.

Now swam a prison in a prison put,
And now this soul in double walls was shut,
Till melted with the swan's digestive fire,
She left her house the fish, and vapor'd forth;
245 Fate not affording bodies of more worth
For her as yet, bids her again retire
To another fish, to any new desire
Made a new prey; for, he that can to none
Resistance make, nor complaint, sure is gone.
250     Weakness invites, but silence feasts oppression.

## XXVI.

Pace with her native stream, this fish doth keep,
And journeys with her, towards the glassy deep,
But oft retarded, once with a hidden net
Though with great windows, for when need first taught
255 These tricks to catch food, then they were not wrought
As now, with curious greediness to let
None scape, but few, and fit for use, to get,
As, in this trap a ravenous pike was ta'en,
Who, though himself distress'd, would fain have slain
260     This wretch; so hardly are ill habits left again.

## XXVII.

Here by her smallness she two deaths o'erpass'd,
Once innocence scap'd, and left the oppressor fast.
The net through-swum, she keeps the liquid path,
And whether she leap up sometimes to breath
265 And suck in air, or find it underneath,
Or working parts like mills or limbecks hath
To make the water thin, and airlike, faith
Cares not; but safe the place she's come unto
Where fresh with salt waves meet, and what to do
        She knows not, but between both makes a board
270     or two.

## XXVIII.

So far from hiding her guests, water is,
That she shows them in bigger quantities
Than they are. Thus doubtful of her way,
For game and not for hunger a sea pie
Spied through this traitorous spectacle, from high,    *275*
The silly fish where it disputing lay,
And to end her doubts and her, bears her away:
Exalted she is, but to the exalter's good,
As are by great ones, men which lowly stood.
    It's rais'd, to be the raiser's instrument and food.    *280*

## XXIX.

Is any kind subject to rape like fish?
Ill unto man, they neither do, nor wish:
Fishers they kill not, nor with noise awake,
They do not hunt, nor strive to make a prey
Of beasts, nor their young sons to bear away;    *285*
Fowls they pursue not, nor do undertake
To spoil the nests industrious birds do make;
Yet them all these unkind kinds feed upon,
To kill them is an occupation,
    And laws make fasts, and Lents for their destruc-
      tion.    *290*

## XXX.

A sudden stiff land-wind in that self hour
To sea-ward forc'd this bird, that did devour
The fish; he cares not, for with ease he flies,
Fat gluttony's best orator: at last
So long he hath flown, and hath flown so fast    *295*
That many leagues at sea, now tir'd he lies,
And with his prey, that till then languish'd, dies:
The souls no longer foes, two ways did err,
The fish I follow, and keep no calendar
    Of the other; he lives yet in some great officer.    *300*

### XXXI.

Into an embryon fish, our soul is thrown,
And in due time thrown out again, and grown
To such vastness as, if unmanaclèd
From Greece, Morea were, and that by some
305 Earthquake unrooted, loose Morea swum,
Or seas from Afric's body had severèd
And torn the hopeful promontory's head,
This fish would seem these, and, when all hopes fail,
A great ship overset, or without sail
    Hulling, might (when this was a whelp) be like
310     this whale.

### XXXII.

At every stroke his brazen fins do take,
More circles in the broken sea they make
Than cannons' voices, when the air they tear:
His ribs are pillars, and his high arch'd roof
315 Of bark that blunts best steel, is thunder-proof:
Swim in him swallow'd dolphins, without fear,
And feel no sides, as if his vast womb were
Some inland sea, and ever as he went
He spouted rivers up, as if he meant
320    To join our seas, with seas above the firmament.

### XXXIII.

He hunts not fish, but as an officer,
Stays in his court, at his own net, and there
All suitors of all sorts themselves enthrall;
So on his back lies this whale wantoning,
325 And in his gulf-like throat, sucks everything
That passeth near. Fish chaseth fish, and all,
Flyer and follower, in this whirlpool fall;
O might not states of more equality
Consist? and is it of necessity
    That thousand guiltless smalls, to make one great,
330     must die?

## XXXIV.

Now drinks he up seas, and he eats up flocks,
He jostles lands, and he shakes firm rocks.
Now in a roomful house this soul doth float,
And like a Prince she sends her faculties
To all her limbs, distant as provinces.                    *335*
The sun hath twenty times both crab and goat
Parch'd, since first launch'd forth this living boat;
'Tis greatest now, and to destruction
Nearest; there's no pause at perfection;
   Greatness a period hath, but hath no station.        *340*


## XXXV.

Two little fishes whom he never harm'd,
Nor fed on their kind, two not throughly arm'd
With hope that they could kill him, nor could do
Good to themselves by his death (they did not eat
His flesh, nor suck those oils, which thence outstreat)      *345*
Conspir'd against him, and it might undo
The plot of all, that the plotters were two,
But that they fishes were, and could not speak
How shall a tyrant wise strong projects break,
   If wretches can on them the common anger wreak?      *350*


## XXXVI.

The flail-finn'd thresher, and steel-beak'd swordfish
Only attempt to do, what all do wish.
The thresher backs him, and to beat begins;
The sluggard whale yields to oppression,
And to hide himself from shame and danger, down            *355*
Begins to sink; the swordfish upward spins,
And gores him with his beak; his staff-like fins,
So well the one, his sword the other plies,
That now a scoff, and prey, this tyrant dies,
   And (his own dole) feeds with himself all com-
panies.                                                      *360*

## XXXVII.

Who will revenge his death? or who will call
Those to account, that thought, and wrought his fall?
The heirs of slain kings, we see are often so
Transported with the joy of what they get,
365 That they, revenge and obsequies forget,
Nor will against such men the people go,
Because he is now dead, to whom they should show
Love in that act; some kings by vice being grown
So needy of subjects' love, that of their own
370     They think they lose, if love be to the dead Prince
      shown.

## XXXVIII.

This soul, now free from prison, and passion,
Hath yet a little indignation
That so small hammers should so soon down beat
So great a castle. And having for her house
375 Got the strait cloister of a wretched mouse
(As basest men that have not what to eat,
Nor enjoy ought, do far more hate the great
Than they, who good repos'd estates possess)
This soul, late taught that great things might by less
380     Be slain, to gallant mischief doth herself address.

## XXXIX.

Nature's great masterpiece, an elephant,
The only harmless great thing; the giant
Of beasts; who thought, no more had gone, to make
    one wise
But to be just, and thankful, loath to offend,
385 (Yet nature hath given him no knees to bend)
Himself he up-props, on himself relies,
And foe to none, suspects no enemies,
Still sleeping stood; vex'd not his fantasy
Black dreams; like an unbent bow, carelessly
390     His sinewy proboscis did remissly lie:

## XL.

In which as in a gallery this mouse
Walk'd, and survey'd the rooms of this vast house,
And to the brain, the soul's bedchamber, went,
And gnaw'd the life cords there; like a whole town
Clean undermin'd, the slain beast tumbled down;          *395*
With him the murtherer dies, whom envy sent
To kill, not scape, (for, only he that meant
To die, did ever kill a man of better room,)
And thus he made his foe, his prey, and tomb:
   Who cares not to turn back, may any whither
     come.                                               *400*

## XLI.

Next, hous'd this soul a wolf's yet unborn whelp,
Till the best midwife, Nature, gave it help,
To issue. It could kill, as soon as go.
Abel, as white, and mild as his sheep were,
(Who, in that trade, of Church, and kingdoms, there     *405*
Was the first type) was still infested so
With this wolf, that it bred his loss and woe;
And yet his bitch, his sentinel, attends
The flock so near, so well warns and defends,
   That the wolf, (hopeless else) to corrupt her, in-
     tends.                                              *410*

## XLII.

He took a course, which since, successfully,
Great men have often taken, to espy
The counsels, or to break the plots of foes.
To Abel's tent he stealeth in the dark,
On whose skirts the bitch slept; ere she could bark,    *415*
Attach'd her with strait gripes, yet he call'd those,
Embracements of love; to love's work he goes,
Where deeds move more than words; nor doth she
   show,
Nor much resist, nor needs he straiten so

His prey, for, were she loose, she would nor bark,
420        nor go.

### XLIII.

He hath engag'd her; his, she wholly bides;
Who not her own, none other's secrets hides.
If to the flock he come, and Abel there,
She feigns hoarse barkings, but she biteth not,
425 Her faith is quite, but not her love forgot.
At last a trap, of which some everywhere
Abel had plac'd, ends all his loss, and fear,
By the wolf's death; and now just time it was
That a quick soul should give life to that mass
430    Of blood in Abel's bitch, and thither this did pass.

### XLIV.

Some have their wives, their sisters some begot,
But in the lives of Emperors you shall not
Read of a lust the which may equal this;
This wolf begot himself, and finishèd
435 What he began alive, when he was dead;
Son to himself, and father too, he is
A riddling lust, for which Schoolmen would miss
A proper name. The whelp of both these lay
In Abel's tent, and with soft Moaba,
440    His sister, being young, it us'd to sport and play.

### XLV.

He soon for her too harsh, and churlish grew,
And Abel (the dam dead) would use this new
For the field. Being of two kinds thus made,
He, as his dam, from sheep drove wolves away,
445 And as his sire, he made them his own prey.
Five years he liv'd, and cozen'd with his trade,
Then hopeless that his faults were hid, betray'd
Himself by flight, and by all followèd,
From dogs, a wolf; from wolves, a dog he fled;
450    And, like a spy to both sides false, he perishèd.

## XLVI.

It quicken'd next a toyful ape, and so
Gamesome it was, that it might freely go
From tent to tent, and with the children play.
His organs now so like theirs he doth find,
That why he cannot laugh, and speak his mind, 455
He wonders. Much with all, most he doth stay
With Adam's fifth daughter Siphatecia,
Doth gaze on her, and, where she passeth, pass,
Gathers her fruits, and tumbles on the grass,
    And wisest of that kind, the first true lover was. 460

## XLVII.

He was the first that more desir'd to have
One than another; first that e'er did crave
Love by mute signs, and had no power to speak;
First that could make love faces, or could do
The vaulter's somersaults, or us'd to woo 465
With hoiting° gambols, his own bones to break
To make his mistress merry; or to wreak
Her anger on himself. Sins against kind
They easily do, that can let feed their mind
    With outward beauty; beauty they in boys and
      beasts do find. 470

## XLVIII.

By this misled, too low things men have prov'd,
And too high; beasts and angels have been lov'd.
This ape, though else through-vain, in this was wise,
He reach'd at things too high, but open way
There was, and he knew not she would say nay; 475
His toys prevail not, likelier means he tries,
He gazeth on her face with tear-shot eyes,
And uplifts subtly with his russet paw
Her kidskin apron without fear or awe
    Of nature; nature hath no gaol, though she hath
      law. 480

466 **hoiting** romping.

### XLIX.

First she was silly and knew not what he meant.
That virtue, by his touches, chaf'd and spent,
Succeeds an itchy warmth, that melts her quite;
She knew not first, now cares not what he doth,
485 And willing half and more, more than half loath,
She neither pulls nor pushes, but outright
Now cries, and now repents; when Tethlemite
Her brother, enter'd, and a great stone threw
After the ape, who, thus prevented, flew.
    This house thus batter'd down, the soul possess'd
490     a new.

### L.

And whether by this change she lose or win,
She comes out next, where the ape would have gone
    in.
Adam and Eve had mingled bloods, and now
Like chemic's equal fires, her temperate womb
495 Had stew'd and form'd it: and part did become
A spongy liver, that did richly allow,
Like a free conduit, on a high hill's brow,
Life-keeping moisture unto every part;
Part harden'd itself to a thicker heart,
500     Whose busy furnaces life's spirits do impart.

### LI.

Another part became the well of sense,
The tender well-arm'd feeling brain, from whence,
Those sinewy strings which do our bodies tie,
Are ravel'd out; and fast there by one end,
505 Did this soul limbs, these limbs a soul attend;
And now they join'd: keeping some quality
Of every past shape, she knew treachery,
Rapine, deceit, and lust, and ills enow
To be a woman. Themech she is now,
510     Sister and wife to Cain, Cain that first did plow.

## LII.

Whoe'er thou beest that read'st this sullen writ,
Which just so much courts thee as thou dost it,
Let me arrest thy thoughts; wonder with me,
Why plowing, building, ruling and the rest,
Or most of those arts, whence our lives are bless'd,  515
By cursèd Cain's race invented be,
And bless'd Seth vex'd us with astronomy.
There's nothing simply good, nor ill alone,
Of every quality comparison
   The only measure is, and judge, opinion.  520

# DIVINE POEMS

## TO E. OF D. WITH SIX HOLY SONNETS

See, Sir,° how as the sun's hot masculine flame
  Begets strange creatures on Nile's dirty slime,°
  In me, your fatherly yet lusty rhyme
(For, these songs are their fruits) have wrought the
  same;
But though the engend'ring force from whence they
5     came
  Be strong enough, and nature do admit
  Seven to be born at once,° I send as yet
But six; they say, the seventh hath still some maim.
  I choose your judgment, which the same degree
10    Doth with her sister, your invention, hold,
As fire these drossy rhymes to purify,
  Or as elixir, to change them to gold;
You are that alchemist which always had
Wit, whose one spark could make good things of bad.

---

1 **Sir** According to Grierson this sonnet is addressed to the third
Earl of Dorset.    2 **Begets . . . slime** In his *Natural History* Pliny relates that the sun breeds living creatures in Nile mud.    7 **Seven . . .
once** Fecundity was supposedly promoted by the drinking of Nile
water.

## TO THE LADY MAGDALEN HERBERT

### *Of St. Mary Magdalen*

Her of your name, whose fair inheritance
    Bethina was, and jointure Magdalo:°
An active faith so highly did advance,
    That she once knew, more than the Church did
        know,
The Resurrection; so much good there is                    5
    Deliver'd of her, that some Fathers be
Loath to believe one woman could do this;
    But, think these Magdalens were two or three.
Increase their number, Lady, and their fame:
    To their devotion, add your innocence;                10
Take so much of the example, as of the name;
    The latter half; and in some recompense
That they did harbor Christ himself, a guest,
    Harbor these hymns, to his dear name address'd.

## HOLY SONNETS

### *La Corona*

1. *Deign at my hands this crown of prayer and praise,*
Weav'd in my low devout melancholy,
Thou which of good, hast, yea, art treasury,
All changing unchang'd Ancient of days;
But do not, with a vile crown of frail bays,                5
Reward my Muse's white sincerity,
But what thy thorny crown gain'd, that give me,

1–2 **Her . . . Magdalo** Donne identifies Mary Magdalene, who came
from Magdala, with Mary of Bethany, the sister of Lazarus and
Martha.

A crown of Glory, which doth flower always;
The ends crown our works, but thou crown'st our
    ends,
10  For, at our end begins our endless rest;
The first last end, now zealously possess'd,
With a strong sober thirst, my soul attends.°
'Tis time that heart and voice be lifted high,
*Salvation to all that will is nigh.*

## ANNUNCIATION

2. *Salvation to all that will is nigh;*
That All, which always is All everywhere,
Which cannot sin, and yet all sins must bear,
Which cannot die, yet cannot choose but die,
5   Lo, faithful Virgin, yields Himself to lie
In prison, in thy womb; and though he there
Can take no sin, nor thou give, yet he will wear
Taken from thence, flesh, which death's force may
    try.
Ere by the spheres time was created, thou
10  Wast in his mind, who is thy son, and brother;
Whom thou conceiv'st, conceiv'd; yea thou art now
Thy Maker's maker, and thy Father's mother;
Thou hast light in dark; and shutt'st in little room,
*Immensity cloister'd in thy dear womb.*

## NATIVITY

3. *Immensity cloister'd in thy dear womb,*
Now leaves his well-belov'd imprisonment,
There he hath made himself to his intent
Weak enough, now into our world to come;
5   But Oh, for thee, for Him, hath the inn no room?
Yet lay him in this stall, and from the Orient,
Stars, and wisemen will travel to prevent°

---

5–12 **But do not . . . attends** The imagery of these lines is drawn from
Isaiah XXVIII 3–5.  7 **prevent** anticipate. As Helen Gardner has
pointed out, since the Massacre of the Innocents, which was the
effect of Herod's doom, was not prevented, the word is used in its
earlier sense.

The effect of Herod's jealous general doom.
Seest thou, my soul, with thy faith's eyes, how He
Which fills all place, yet none holds Him doth lie?          10
Was not His pity towards thee wondrous high,
That would have need to be pitièd by thee?
Kiss Him, and with Him into Egypt go,
*With His kind mother, who partakes thy woe.*

## TEMPLE

4. *With His kind mother who partakes thy woe,*
Joseph, turn back; see where your child doth sit,
Blowing, yea blowing out those sparks of wit,
Which Himself on the Doctors did bestow;
The Word but lately could not speak, and lo,               5
It suddenly speaks wonders; whence comes it,
That all which was, and all which should be writ,
A shallow seeming child, should deeply know?
His Godhead was not soul to His manhood,°
Nor had time mellowed Him to this ripeness,                10
But as for one which hath a long task, 'tis good,
With the Sun to begin his business,
He in His age's morning thus began
*By miracles exceeding power of man.*

## CRUCIFYING

5. *By miracles exceeding power of man,*
He faith in some, envy in some begat,
For, what weak spirits admire, ambitious, hate;
In both affections many to Him ran,
But oh! the worst are most, they will and can,             5
Alas, and do, unto the immaculate,
Whose creature Fate is, now prescribe a Fate,
Measuring self-life's infinity to a span,
Nay to an inch. Lo, where condemnèd He
Bears his own cross, with pain, yet by and by              10
When it bears Him, He must bear more and die.
Now Thou are lifted up, draw me to Thee,

9 **His . . . manhood** Christ as perfect man possessed a human soul
distinct from his Godhead.

And at Thy death giving such liberal dole,
*Moist, with one drop of Thy blood, my dry soul.*

### RESURRECTION

6. *Moist with one drop of Thy blood, my dry soul*
Shall (though she now be in extreme degree
Too stony hard, and yet too fleshly be
Freed by that drop, from being starv'd, hard, or foul,
5   And life, by this death abled,° shall control
Death, whom Thy death slew; nor shall to me
Fear of first or last death,° bring misery,
If in Thy little book° my name thou enroll,
Flesh in that long sleep is not putrefied,°
10   But made that there, of which, and for which 'twas;
Nor can by other means be glorified.
May then sin's sleep, and death's, soon from me pass,
That wak'd from both, I again risen may
*Salute the last, and everlasting day.*

### ASCENSION

7. *Salute the last and everlasting day,*
Joy at the uprising of this Sun, and Son,
Ye whose just tears, or tribulation
Have purely wash'd, or burnt your drossy clay;
5   Behold the Highest, parting hence away,
Lightens the dark clouds, which He treads upon,
Nor doth He by ascending, show alone,
But first He, and He first enters the way.°
O strong Ram, which hast batter'd heaven for me,

---

5 **abled** strengthened, renewed.    7 **last death** Revelation II, 11: "He that overcometh shall not be hurt of the second death."    8 **little book** This may be a reference to Revelation XX, 12: "And I saw the dead, small and great, stand before God; and the books were opened: and another book was opened, which is the book of life and the dead were judged out of those things which were written in the books, according to their works."    9 **Flesh . . . putrefied** The body is ultimately resurrected.    7–8 **Nor doth . . . the way** According to Colossians II, 13–15, Christ led the host of the saved into Heaven, He being the leader (first) of that army as well as the first ever to have gone that way.

Mild Lamb, which with Thy blood, hast mark'd the
    path;                                                        10
Bright Torch, which shin'st, that I the way may see,
Oh, with Thy own blood quench Thy own just wrath,
And if Thy holy Spirit, my Muse did raise,
*Deign, at my hands this crown of prayer and praise.*


# HOLY SONNETS°

### *I. Thou hast made me*

Thou hast made me, and shall Thy work decay?
Repair me now, for now mine end doth haste,
I run to death, and death meets me as fast,
And all my pleasures are like yesterday;
I dare not move my dim eyes any way,            5
Despair behind, and death before doth cast
Such terror, and my feeble flesh doth waste
By sin in it, which it towards hell doth weigh;
Only Thou art above, and when towards Thee
By Thy leave I can look, I rise again;          10
But our old subtle foe so tempteth me
That not one hour myself I can sustain;
Thy Grace may wing me to prevent his art,
And Thou like adamant draw mine iron heart.


0 **Holy Sonnets** In his edition of Donne, Grierson wrote of this
group of sonnets: "I cannot find a definite significance in any
order. . . . Each sonnet is a separate meditation or ejaculation."
Consequently he printed the sonnets in the order in which they had
appeared in the editions of 1635 to 1669, though not in the edition
of 1633. This is the traditional order of the sequence and is followed
here. However, Helen Gardner, in her edition of *The Divine Poems,*
believes the sonnets, with the exception of the last three, which are
independent, are intended to form a true sequence in the formal
tradition of religious meditation. She prints the sonnets in the following order: II, IV, VI, VII, IX, X, XI, XII, XIII, XIV, XV, XVI,
I, V, III, VIII.

### II. *As due by many titles*

As due by many titles I resign
Myself to Thee, O God, first I was made
By Thee, and for Thee, and when I was decay'd
Thy blood bought that, the which before was Thine;
5  I am Thy son, made with Thyself to shine,
Thy servant, whose pains thou hast still repaid,
Thy sheep, Thine image, and, till I betray'd
Myself, a temple of Thy Spirit divine;
Why doth the devil then usurp on me?
10  Why doth he steal, nay ravish that's Thy right?
Except Thou rise and for Thine own work fight,
Oh I shall soon despair, when I do see
That Thou lov'st mankind well, yet wilt not choose me.
And Satan hates me, yet is loath to lose me.

### III. *Oh might those sighs*

Oh might those sighs and tears return again
Into my breast and eyes, which I have spent,
That I might in this holy discontent
Mourn with some fruit, as I have mourn'd in vain;
5  In mine idolatry what showers of rain
Mine eyes did waste? what griefs my heart did rent?
That sufferance was my sin; now I repent;
'Cause I did suffer I must suffer pain.
The hydroptic drunkard,° and night-scouting thief,
10  The itchy lecher, and self-tickling proud
Have the remembrance of past joys, for relief
Of coming ills. To poor me is allow'd
No ease; for long yet vehement grief hath been
The effect and cause, the punishment and sin.

### IV. *Oh my black soul!*

Oh my black soul! now thou art summonèd
By sickness, death's herald, and champion;

---

9 **hydroptic drunkard** Dropsy is characterized by an insatiable thirst.

Thou art like a pilgrim, which abroad hath done
Treason, and durst not turn to whence he is fled,
Or like a thief, which till death's doom be read,              5
Wisheth himself deliverèd from prison;
But damn'd and hal'd to execution,
Wisheth that still he might be imprisonèd.
Yet grace, if thou repent, thou canst not lack;
But who shall give thee that grace to begin?                   10
Oh make thyself with holy mourning black,
And red with blushing, as thou art with sin;
Or wash thee in Christ's blood, which hath this might
That being red, it dyes red souls to white.

### V. I am a little world

I am a little world made cunningly
Of elements, and an angelic sprite,
But black sin hath betray'd to endless night
My world's both parts, and, oh, both parts must die.
You which beyond that heaven which was most high          5
Have found new spheres, and of new lands can
    write,°
Pour new seas in mine eyes, that so I might
Drown my world with my weeping earnestly,
Or wash it, if it must be drown'd no more:
But oh it must be burnt! alas the fire                         10
Of lust and envy have burnt it heretofore,
And made it fouler; let their flames retire,
And burn me O Lord, with a fiery zeal
Of Thee and Thy house, which doth in eating heal.

---

5–6 You . . . write In her edition of *The Divine Poems* Helen Gardner says of these lines: "The original outermost heaven was the
eighth sphere, the sphere of the fixed stars. Ptolemy had added a
ninth, the Primum Mobile, to account for the two motions of the
eighth sphere, and Alphonsus of Castile had added a tenth, to account for a third motion. Copernicus observed a 'fourth motion';
and those who rejected his hypothesis of a heliocentric universe ex-
plained this fourth motion by postulating an eleventh sphere."

### VI. *This is my play's last scene*

This is my play's last scene, here heavens appoint
My pilgrimage's last mile; and my race
Idly, yet quickly run, hath this last pace,
My span's last inch, my minute's latest point,
5  And gluttonous death, will instantly unjoint
My body and soul, and I shall sleep a space,
But my ever-waking part shall see that face,
Whose fear already shakes my every joint:
Then, as my soul, to heaven, her first seat, takes flight,
10  And earth-born body, in the earth shall dwell,
So, fall my sins, that all may have their right,
To where they are bred, and would press me, to hell.
Impute me righteous, thus purg'd of evil,
For thus I leave the world, the flesh, the devil.

### VII. *At the round earth's*

At the round earth's imagin'd corners,° blow
Your trumpets, Angels, and arise, arise
From death, you numberless infinities
Of souls, and to your scatter'd bodies go,
5  All whom the flood did, and fire shall o'erthrow,
All whom war, dearth, age, agues, tyrannies,
Despair, law, chance, hath slain, and you whose eyes,
Shall behold God, and never taste death's woe.
But let them sleep, Lord, and me mourn a space,
10  For, if above all these, my sins abound,
'Tis late to ask abundance of Thy grace,
When we are there; here on this lowly ground,
Teach me how to repent; for that's as good
As if Thou hadst seal'd my pardon with Thy blood.

### VIII. *If faithful souls*

If faithful souls be alike glorified
As Angels, then my father's soul doth see,

1 At . . . corners Revelation VII, 1: "I saw four angels standing on
the four corners of the earth . . ."

And adds this even to full felicity,
That valiantly I hell's wide mouth o'erstride:
But if our minds to these souls be descried            5
By circumstances, and by signs that be
Apparent in us, not immediately,
How shall my mind's white truth by them be tried?
They see idolatrous lovers weep and mourn,
And vile blasphemous conjurers to call                 10
On Jesus' name, and pharisaical
Dissemblers feign devotion. Then turn,
O pensive soul, to God, for He knows best
Thy true grief, for He put it in my breast.

## IX. *If poisonous minerals*

If poisonous minerals, and if that tree,
Whose fruit threw death on else immortal us,
If lecherous goats, if serpents envious
Cannot be damn'd; alas, why should I be?
Why should intent or reason, born in me,               5
Make sins, else equal, in me more heinous?
And mercy being easy, and glorious
To God, in His stern wrath, why threatens He?
But who am I, that dare dispute with Thee
O God? oh! of Thine only worthy blood,                 10
And my tears, make a heavenly Lethean flood,
And drown in it my sins' black memory;
That Thou remember them, some claim as debt,
I think it mercy, if Thou wilt forget.

## X. *Death be not proud*

Death be not proud, though some have callèd thee
Mighty and dreadful, for thou art not so;
For those whom thou think'st thou dost overthrow
Die not, poor death, nor yet canst thou kill me.
From rest and sleep, which but thy pictures be,        5
Much pleasure, then from thee much more must flow,
And soonest our best men with thee do go,
Rest of their bones, and soul's delivery.

Thou art slave to Fate, chance, kings, and desperate
    men,
10  And dost with poison, war, and sickness dwell,
And poppy, or charms can make us sleep as well,
And better than thy stroke; why swell'st thou then?
One short sleep past, we wake eternally,
And death shall be no more; death, thou shalt die.

### XI. Spit in my face

Spit in my face you Jews, and pierce my side,
Buffet, and scoff, scourge, and crucify me,
For I have sinn'd, and sinn'd, and only He,
Who could do no iniquity, hath died:
5  But by my death cannot be satisfied
My sins, which pass the Jews' impiety:
They kill'd once an inglorious man, but I
Crucify him daily, being now glorified.
Oh let me then His strange love still admire:
10  Kings pardon, but He bore our punishment.
And Jacob came cloth'd in vile harsh attire
But to supplant, and with gainful intent:
God cloth'd Himself in vile man's flesh, that so
He might be weak enough to suffer woe.

### XII. Why are we by all

Why are we by all creatures waited on?
Why do the prodigal elements supply
Life and food to me, being more pure than I,
Simple, and further from corruption?
5  Why brook'st thou, ignorant horse, subjection?
Why dost thou, bull and boar, so sillily
Dissemble weakness, and by one man's stroke die,
Whose whole kind you might swallow and feed upon?
Weaker I am, woe is me, and worse than you,
10  You have not sinn'd, nor need be timorous.
But wonder at a greater wonder, for to us
Created nature doth these things subdue,
But their Creator, whom sin, nor nature tied,
For us, His creatures, and His foes, hath died.

### XIII. *What if this present were*

What if this present were the world's last night?
Mark in my heart, O soul, where thou dost dwell,
The picture of Christ crucified, and tell
Whether that countenance can thee affright,
Tears in His eyes quench the amazing° light,                    5
Blood fills His frowns, which from His pierc'd head fell.
And can that tongue adjudge thee unto hell,
Which pray'd forgiveness for His foes' fierce spite?
No, no; but as in my idolatry
I said to all my profane mistresses,                           10
Beauty, of pity, foulness only is
A sign of rigor: so I say to thee,
To wicked spirits are horrid shapes assign'd,
This beauteous form assures a piteous mind.

### XIV. *Batter my heart*

Batter my heart, three-person'd God; for You
As yet but knock, breathe, shine, and seek to mend;
That I may rise, and stand, o'erthrow me, and bend
Your force, to break, blow, burn and make me new.
I, like an usurp'd town, to another due,                       5
Labor to admit You, but Oh, to no end!
Reason, Your viceroy in me, me should defend,
But is captiv'd, and proves weak or untrue.
Yet dearly I love You, and would be lovèd fain,
But am betroth'd unto Your enemy:                              10
Divorce me, untie, or break that knot again,
Take me to You, imprison me, for I
Except You enthrall me, never shall be free,
Nor ever chaste, except You ravish me.

### XV. *Wilt thou love God*

Wilt thou love God, as He thee! then digest,
My soul, this wholesome meditation,
How God the Spirit, by Angels waited on

5 **amazing** terrifying.

In heaven, doth make His temple in thy breast.
5   The Father having begot a Son most bless'd,
And still begetting (for He ne'er begun)
Hath deign'd to choose thee by adoption,
Coheir to his glory, and Sabbath's endless rest.
And as a robb'd man, which by search doth find
10  His stol'n stuff sold, must lose or buy it again:
The Son of glory came down, and was slain,
Us whom He had made, and Satan stol'n, to unbind.
'Twas much, that man was made like God before,
But that God should be made like man, much more.

### XVI. Father, part of

Father, part of His double interest
Unto Thy kingdom, Thy Son gives to me;
His jointure° in the knotty Trinity
He keeps, and gives to me His death's conquest.
This Lamb, whose death, with life the world hath
5       bless'd,
Was from the world's beginning slain, and He
Hath made two wills,° which with the legacy
Of His and Thy kingdom, do Thy sons invest.
Yet such are Thy laws, that men argue yet
10  Whether a man those statutes can fulfill;
None doth; but all-healing grace and spirit
Revive again what law and letter kill.
Thy law's abridgment, and Thy last command
Is all but love; oh let this last will stand!

### XVII. Since she whom I lov'd

Since she whom I lov'd hath paid her last debt°
To nature, and to hers, and my good is dead,
And her soul early into heaven ravishèd,
Wholly on heavenly things my mind is set.
5   Here the admiring her my mind did whet
To seek Thee, God; so streams do show their head;

3 **jointure** "the holding of an estate by two or more persons in joint-tenancy" (*O.E.D.*).  7 **two wills** Old and New testaments.
1 **Since . . . debt** Donne's wife died on August 15, 1617.

But though I have found Thee, and Thou my thirst hast
    fed,
A holy thirsty dropsy melts me yet.
But why should I beg more love, when as Thou
Dost woo my soul for hers; off'ring all Thine:          10
And dost not only fear lest I allow
My love to Saints and Angels, things divine,
But in Thy tender jealousy dost doubt
Lest the World, Flesh, yea Devil put Thee out.

### XVIII. *Show me, dear Christ*

Show me, dear Christ, Thy spouse, so bright and clear.
What! is it She, which on the other shore
Goes richly painted? or which robb'd and tore
Laments and mourns in Germany and here?
Sleeps she a thousand, then peeps up one year?          5
Is she self truth and errs? now new, now outwore?
Doth she, and did she, and shall she evermore
On one, on seven, or on no hill appear?°
Dwells she with us, or like adventuring knights
First travel we to seek and then make love?          10
Betray kind husband Thy spouse to our sights,
And let mine amorous soul court Thy mild dove,
Who is most true, and pleasing to Thee, then
When she is embrac'd and open to most men.

### XIX. *Oh, to vex me*

Oh, to vex me, contraries meet in one:
Inconstancy unnaturally hath begot
A constant habit; that when I would not
I change in vows, and in devotion.
As humorous is my contrition          5
As my profane love, and as soon forgot:
As riddlingly distemper'd, cold and hot,
As praying, as mute; as infinite, as none.
I durst not view heaven yesterday; and today

8 **On . . . appear?** The Temple of Solomon was built on Mount
Moriah, Rome on seven hills, and Geneva, the center of Calvinism,
on no hill.

10  In prayers, and flattering speeches I court God:<br>
Tomorrow I quake with true fear of his rod.<br>
So my devout fits come and go away<br>
Like a fantastic ague: save that here<br>
Those are my best days, when I shake with fear.

## THE CROSS

Since Christ embrac'd the Cross itself, dare I<br>
His image, the image of his Cross deny?<br>
Would I have profit by the sacrifice,<br>
And dare the chosen altar to despise?<br>
5  It bore all other sins, but is it fit<br>
That it should bear the sin of scorning it?<br>
Who from the picture would avert his eye,<br>
How would he fly his pains, who there did die?<br>
From me, no pulpit, nor misgrounded law,<br>
10  Nor scandal taken, shall this Cross withdraw,<br>
It shall not, for it cannot; for, the loss<br>
Of this Cross, were to me another Cross;<br>
Better were worse, for, no affliction,<br>
No Cross is so extreme, as to have none.<br>
15  Who can blot out the Cross, which the instrument<br>
Of God, dew'd on me in the Sacrament?<br>
Who can deny me power, and liberty<br>
To stretch mine arms, and mine own Cross to be?<br>
Swim, and at every stroke, thou art thy Cross;<br>
20  The mast and yard make one, where seas do toss;<br>
Look down, thou spiest out Crosses in small things;<br>
Look up, thou seest birds rais'd on crossèd wings;<br>
All the globe's frame, and spheres, is nothing else<br>
But the meridians crossing parallels.<br>
25  Material Crosses then, good physic be,<br>
But yet spiritual have chief dignity.

These for extracted chemic medicine serve,
And cure much better, and as well preserve;
Then are you your own physic, or need none,
When still'd, or purg'd by tribulation.                    *30*
For when that Cross ungrudg'd, unto you sticks,
Then are you to yourself a Crucifix.
As perchance, carvers do not faces make,
But that away, which hid them there, do take;
Let Crosses, so, take what hid Christ in thee,              *35*
And be His image, or not His, but He.
But, as oft alchemists do coiners prove,
So may a self-despising, get self-love,
And then as worst surfeits of best meats be,
So is pride, issued from humility,                         *40*
For 'tis no child, but monster; therefore Cross
Your joy in crosses, else, 'tis double loss.
And cross thy senses, else, both they, and thou
Must perish soon, and to destruction bow.
For if the eye seek good objects, and will take            *45*
No cross from bad, we cannot scape a snake.
So with harsh, hard, sour, stinking, cross the rest,
Make them indifferent all; call nothing best.
But most the eye needs crossing, that can roam,
And move; to the others the objects must come home.        *50*
And cross thy heart: for that in man alone
Points downwards, and hath palpitation.
Cross those dejections, when it downward tends,
And when it to forbidden heights pretends.
And as thy brain through bony walls doth vent              *55*
By sutures, which a cross's form present,
So when thy brain works, ere thou utter it,
Cross and correct concupiscence of wit.
Be covetous of crosses, let none fall.
Cross no man else, but cross thyself in all.               *60*
Then doth the Cross of Christ work fruitfully
Within our hearts, when we love harmlessly
That Cross's pictures much, and with more care
That Cross's children, which our crosses are.

## RESURRECTION, IMPERFECT

Sleep, sleep, old Sun, thou canst not have repast°
As yet, the wound thou took'st on Friday last;
Sleep then, and rest; the world may bear thy stay,
A better Sun rose before thee today,
5   Who, not content to enlighten all that dwell
On the earth's face, as thou, enlighten'd hell,
And made the dark fires languish in that vale,
As, at thy presence here, our fires grow pale.
Whose body having walk'd on earth, and now
10  Hasting to Heaven, would that He might allow
Himself unto all stations, and fill all,
For these three days become a mineral;
He was all gold when He lay down, but rose
All tincture, and doth not alone dispose
15  Leaden and iron wills to good, but is
Of power to make even sinful flesh like His.
Had one of those, whose credulous piety
Thought that a soul one might discern and see
Go from a body, at this sepulcher been,
20  And, issuing from the sheet, this body seen,
He would have justly thought this body a soul,
If not of any man, yet of the whole.

                  *Desunt cætera.*

---

1 **repast** recovered from.

## UPON THE ANNUNCIATION AND PASSION FALLING UPON ONE DAY, 1608

Tamely, frail body, abstain today; today
My soul eats twice, Christ hither and away.
She sees Him man, so like God made in this,
That of them both a circle emblem is,
Whose first and last concur; this doubtful day      5
Of feast or fast, Christ came, and went away.
She sees Him nothing twice at once, Who is all;
She sees a Cedar° plant itself, and fall,
Her Maker put to making,° and the head
Of life, at once, not yet alive, yet dead.      10
She sees at once the virgin mother stay
Reclus'd at home, public at Golgotha;
Sad and rejoic'd she's seen at once, and seen
At almost fifty, and at scarce fifteen.
At once a son is promis'd her, and gone;      15
Gabriel gives Christ to her, He her to John;
Not fully a mother, she's in orbity,°
At once receiver and the legacy.
All this, and all between, this day hath shown,
The abridgment of Christ's story, which makes one      20
(As in plain maps, the furthest west is east)
Of the Angels *Ave,* and *Consummatum est.*
How well the Church, God's court of faculties
Deals in some times and seldom joining these!
As by the self-fix'd Pole we never do      25
Direct our course, but the next star thereto,
Which shows where the other is, and which we say
(Because it strays not far) doth never stray;
So God by His Church, nearest to Him, we know,
And stand firm, if we by her motion go;      30
His Spirit, as His fiery pillar doth
Lead, and His Church, as cloud, to one end both.

8 **cedar** symbol of the Godhead.    9 **Her . . . making** The Creator is subjected to creation.    17 **orbity** childless.

This Church, by letting these days join, hath shown
Death and conception in mankind is one;
35 Or 'twas in Him the same humility,
That He would be a man, and leave to be:
Or as creation He had made, as God,
With the last judgment, but one period,
His imitating Spouse would join in one
40 Manhood's extremes: He shall come, He is gone:
Or as though one blood drop, which thence did fall,
Accepted, would have serv'd, He yet shed all;
So though the least of His pains, deeds, or words,
Would busy a life, she all this day affords;
45 This treasure then, in gross, my soul uplay,
And in my life retail it every day.

## GOOD FRIDAY, 1613. RIDING WESTWARD

Let man's soul be a sphere, and then, in this,
The intelligence that moves, devotion is,
And as the other spheres, by being grown
Subject to foreign motions, lose their own,
5 And being by others hurried every day,
Scarce in a year their natural form obey:
Pleasure or business, so our souls admit
For their first mover, and are whirl'd by it.
Hence is it that I am carried towards the West
10 This day, when my soul's form bends toward the East.
There I should see a Sun, by rising, set,
And by that setting endless day beget;
But that Christ on this Cross, did rise and fall,
Sin had eternally benighted all.
15 Yet dare I almost be glad I do not see
That spectacle of too much weight for me.

Who sees God's face, that is self life, must die;°
What a death were it then to see God die?
It made his own lieutenant Nature shrink;
It made his footstool crack, and the sun wink.                    20
Could I behold those hands which span the poles,
And tune all spheres at once, pierc'd with those holes?
Could I behold that endless height which is
Zenith to us, and our antipodes,
Humbled below us? or that blood which is                          25
The seat of all our souls, if not of His,
Made dirt of dust, or that flesh which was worn
By God, for His apparel, ragg'd, and torn?
If on these things I durst not look, durst I
Upon His miserable mother cast mine eye,                          30
Who was God's partner here, and furnish'd thus
Half of that Sacrifice, which ransom'd us?
Though these things, as I ride, be from mine eye,
They are present yet unto my memory,
For that looks towards them; and Thou look'st to-
    wards me,                                                     35
O Saviour, as Thou hang'st upon the tree;
I turn my back to Thee, but to receive
Corrections, till Thy mercies bid Thee leave.
O think me worth Thine anger, punish me,
Burn off my rusts, and my deformity,                              40
Restore Thine Image, so much, by Thy grace,
That Thou mayst know me, and I'll turn my face.

---

17 **Who . . . die** Exodus XXXIII, 20: "And he said, Thou canst not
see my face: for there shall no man see me, and live."

## TO MR. TILMAN°

Thou, whose diviner soul hath caus'd thee now
To put thy hand unto the holy plow,
Making lay-scornings of the ministry
Not an impediment, but victory;
5   What bring'st thou home with thee; how is thy mind
Affected since the vintage? Dost thou find
New thoughts and stirrings in thee? and as steel
Touch'd with a loadstone, dost new motions feel?
Or, as a ship after much pain and care,
10   For iron and cloth brings home rich Indian ware,
Hast thou thus traffick'd, but with far more gain
Of noble goods, and with less time and pain?
Thou art the same materials, as before,
Only the stamp is changèd; but no more.
15   And as new crownèd Kings alter the face,
But not the money's substance; so hath grace
Chang'd only God's old image by creation,
To Christ's new stamp, at this thy coronation;
Or, as we paint Angels with wings, because
20   They bear God's message, and proclaim His laws,
Since thou must do the like, and so must move,
Art thou new feather'd with celestial love?
Dear, tell me where thy purchase lies, and show
What thy advantage is above, below.
25   But if thy gainings do surmount expression,
Why doth the foolish world scorn that profession,
Whose joys pass speech? Why do they think unfit
That gentry should join families with it?

0 **Mr. Tilman** Edward Tilman was a Cambridge man who was ordained an Anglican priest in 1619, after long hesitation. The little that is known of him is gathered together in Appendix D of Helen Gardner's edition of *The Divine Poems*. Apparently he was an exemplary priest despite his initial reluctance to take orders. Grierson remarks, "The poem is a strange comment on the seventeenth century's estimate of the clergy," and Miss Gardner believes it throws light on Donne's "own reluctance to enter the ministry."

As if their day were only to be spent
In dressing, mistressing and compliment;                    30
Alas poor joys, but poorer men, whose trust
Seems richly placèd in sublimèd dust;
(For, such are clothes and beauty, which though gay,
Are, at the best, but of sublimèd clay.)
Let then the world thy calling disrespect,                    35
But go thou on, and pity their neglect.
What function is so noble, as to be
Ambassador to God and destiny?
To open life, to give kingdoms to more
Than Kings give dignities; to keep heaven's door?                    40
Mary's prerogative was to bear Christ, so
'Tis preachers' to convey him, for they do
As Angels out of clouds, from pulpits speak;
And bless the poor beneath, the lame, the weak.
If then the astronomers, whereas they spy                    45
A new-found star, their optics magnify,
How brave are those who with their engines can
Bring man to heaven, and heaven again to man?
These are thy titles and pre-eminences,
In whom must meet God's graces, men's offenses,                    50
And so the heavens which beget all things here,
And the earth our mother, which these things doth
    bear,
Both these in thee, are in thy calling knit,
And make thee now a bless'd hermaphrodite.

# A HYMN TO CHRIST, AT THE AUTHOR'S LAST GOING INTO GERMANY°

In what torn ship soever I embark,
That ship shall be my emblem of Thy Ark;
What sea soever swallow me, that flood
Shall be to me an emblem of Thy blood;
5    Though Thou with clouds of anger do disguise
Thy face; yet through that mask I know those eyes,
    Which, though they turn away sometimes,
        They never will despise.

I sacrifice this island unto Thee,
10   And all whom I lov'd there, and who lov'd me;
When I have put our seas 'twixt them and me,
Put thou Thy sea betwixt my sins and Thee.
As the tree's sap doth seek the root below
In winter, in my winter now I go,
15       Where none but Thee, the eternal root
        Of true love I may know.

Nor Thou nor Thy religion dost control
The amorousness of an harmonious soul,
But Thou wouldst have that love Thyself: as Thou
20   Art jealous, Lord, so I am jealous now,
Thou lov'st not, till from loving more, Thou free
My soul: whoever gives, takes liberty:
    O, if Thou car'st not whom I love,
        Alas, thou lov'st not me.

25   Seal then this bill of my divorce to all,
On whom those fainter beams of love did fall;
Marry those loves, which in youth scatter'd be

0 In 1619 King James sent Viscount Doncaster on an important
diplomatic mission to Germany. Donne, who was already suffering
from intimations of the cancer from which he was to die, was appointed to the mission, but was given the lightest duties. At this
time Donne appears to have been in a depressed state because of
his "infirm and valetudinary body."

On Fame, Wit, Hopes (false mistresses) to Thee.
Churches are best for prayer that have least light:
To see God only, I go out of sight:                          *30*
    And to scape stormy days, I choose
      An everlasting night.


## HYMN TO GOD MY GOD, IN MY SICKNESS

Since I am coming to that holy room
    Where, with Thy Choir of Saints for evermore,
I shall be made Thy music, as I come
    I tune the instrument here at the door,
    And what I must do then, think here before.          *5*

Whilst my physicians by their love are grown
    Cosmographers, and I their map, who lie
Flat on this bed, that by them may be shown
    That this is my Southwest discovery
    *Per fretum febris,*° by these straits to die,      *10*

I joy, that in these straits, I see my West;
    For, though their currents yield return to none,
What shall my West hurt me? As West and East
    In all flat maps (and I am one) are one,
    So death doth touch the Resurrection.                *15*

Is the Pacific Sea my home? Or are
    The Eastern riches? Is *Jerusalem?*
*Anyan,* and *Magellan,* and *Gibraltar,*°
    All straits, and none but straits, are ways to them,
    Whether where *Japhet* dwelt, or *Cham,* or *Sem.*°  *20*

We think that *Paradise* and *Calvary,*
    *Christ's* Cross, and *Adam's* tree, stood in one place;

10 **Per . . . febris** Since *fretum* may mean either heat or a strait,
Donne is punning here. The fever that will bring about Donne's
death is a strait that leads him to Eternity (his West).    18 **Anyan
. . . Gibraltar** Donne names three straits here. Anyan is Bering Strait.
20 **Whether . . . Sem** The sons of Noah, who divided the world
among them.

Look Lord, and find both *Adams* met in me;
   As the first *Adam's* sweat surrounds my face,
25    May the last *Adam's* blood my soul embrace.

So, in His purple wrapp'd receive me, Lord,
   By these His thorns give me His other crown;
And as to others' souls I preach'd Thy word,
   Be this my text, my sermon to mine own,
30    Therefore that He may raise the Lord throws down.


## A HYMN TO GOD THE FATHER

### I.

Wilt Thou forgive that sin where I begun,
   Which was my sin, though it were done before?
Wilt Thou forgive that sin through which I run,
   And do run still: though still I do deplore?
5     When Thou hast done, Thou hast not done,
      For I have more.

### II.

Wilt Thou forgive that sin by which I won
   Others to sin? and, made my sin their door?
Wilt Thou forgive that sin which I did shun
10   A year or two: but wallow'd in a score?
    When Thou hast done, Thou hast not done,
      For I have more.

### III.

I have a sin of fear, that when I have spun
   My last thread, I shall perish on the shore;
15 But swear by Thyself that at my death Thy Son
   Shall shine as He shines now, and heretofore;
    And, having done that, Thou hast done,
      I fear no more.

# An Elegie upon the Death of the Dean of Paul's, Dr. John Donne

## By Thomas Carew

Can we not force from widowed Poetry,
Now thou art dead (Great DONNE) one Elegie
To crown thy hearse? Why yet dare we not trust
Though with unkneaded dough-bak'd prose thy dust,
Such as the unscissor'd Churchman from the flower     *5*
Of fading rhetoric, short liv'd as his hour,
Dry as the sand that measures it, should lay
Upon thy ashes, on the funeral day?
Have we no voice, no tune? Didst thou dispense
Through all our language, both the words and sense?     *10*
'Tis a sad truth; the pulpit may her plain,
And sober Christian precepts still retain,
Doctrines it may, and wholesome uses frame,
Grave homilies, and lectures, but the flame
Of thy brave soul, that shot such heat and light,     *15*
As burnt our earth, and made our darkness bright,

Committed holy rapes upon our will,
Did through the eye the melting heart distill;
And the deep knowledge of dark truths so teach,
20  As sense might judge, what phansie could not reach;
Must be desir'd forever. So the fire,
That fills with spirit and heat the Delphic choir,
Which kindled first by thy Promethean breath,
Glow'd here a while, lies quench'd now in thy death;
25  The Muses' garden with pedantic weeds
O'erspread, was purg'd by thee; the lazy seeds
Of servile imitation thrown away;
And fresh invention planted, thou didst pay
The debts of our penurious bankrupt age;
30  Licentious thefts, that make poetic rage
A mimic fury, when our souls must be
Possess'd, or with Anacreon's ecstasy,
Or Pindar's, not their own; the subtle cheat
Of sly exchanges, and the juggling feat
35  Of two-edg'd words, or whatsoever wrong
By ours was done the Greek, or Latin tongue,
Thou hast redeem'd, and open'd us a mine
Of rich and pregnant phansie, drawn a line
Of masculine expression, which had good
40  Old Orpheus seen, or all the ancient brood
Our superstitious fools admire, and hold
Their lead more precious, than thy burnish'd gold,
Thou hadst been their Exchequer, and no more
They each in other's dust, had rak'd for ore.
45  Thou shalt yield no precedence, but of time,
And the blind fate of language, whose tun'd chime
More charms the outward sense; yet thou mayst claim
From so great disadvantage greater fame,
Since to the awe of thy imperious wit
50  Our stubborn language bends, made only fit
With her tough-thick-ribb'd hoops to gird about
Thy giant phansie, which had prov'd too stout
For their soft melting phrases. As in time
They had the start, so did they cull the prime
55  Buds of invention many a hundred year,

And left the rifled fields, besides the fear
To touch their harvest, yet from those bare lands
Of what is purely thine, thy only hands
(And that thy smallest work) have gleanèd more
Than all those times, and tongues could reap before;    60
But thou art gone, and thy strict laws will be
Too hard for libertines in poetry.
They will repeal the goodly exil'd train
Of gods and goddesses, which in thy just reign
Were banish'd nobler poems, now, with these    65
The silenc'd tales of the Metamorphoses
Shall stuff their lines, and swell the windy page,
Till verse refin'd by thee, in this last age,
Turn ballad rhyme, or those old idols be
Ador'd again, with new apostasy;    70
Oh, pardon me, that break with untun'd verse
The reverend silence that attends thy hearse,
Whose awful solemn murmurs were to thee
More than these faint lines, a loud Elegie,
That did proclaim in a dumb eloquence    75
The death of all the Arts, whose influence
Grown feeble, in these panting numbers lies
Gasping short-winded accents, and so dies:
So doth the swiftly turning wheel not stand
In the instant we withdraw the moving hand,    80
But some small time maintain a faint weak course
By virtue of the first impulsive force:
And so whilst I cast on thy funeral pile
Thy crown of bays, Oh, let it crack a while,
And spit disdain, till the devouring flashes    85
Suck all the moisture up, then turn to ashes.
I will not draw the envy to engross
All thy perfections, or weep all our loss;
Those are too numerous for an Elegie,
And this too great, to be express'd by me.    90
Though every pen should share a distinct part,
Yet art thou theme enough to tire all art;
Let others carve the rest, it shall suffice
I on thy tomb this epitaph incise.

95      *Here lies a King, that rul'd as he thought fit*
        *The universal Monarchy of wit;*
        *Here lie two Flamens, and both those, the best,*
        *Apollo's first, at last, the true God's priest.*